THE
NIEKRO
FILES

THE NIEKRO FILES

The Uncensored Letters of Baseball's Most Notorious Brothers

Phil and Joe Niekro
WITH KEN PICKING

CB
CONTEMPORARY
BOOKS
CHICAGO · NEW YORK

Library of Congress Cataloging-in-Publication Data

Niekro, Phil, 1939–
    The Niekro files : the uncensored letters of baseball's most
notorious brothers / Phil and Joe Niekro, with Ken Picking.
      p.   cm.
   ISBN 0-8092-4601-5
    1. Niekro, Phil, 1939–   .   2. Niekro, Joe.   3. Baseball
players—United States—Biography.   4. Brothers—Unites States—
Correspondence.   I. Niekro, Joe.   II. Picking, Ken.   III. Title.
GV865.N5A3   1988
796.357′092′4—dc 19
[B]
                                                      88-6878
                                                         CIP

To our parents, wives, sister, and children, without whom
we would be nothing.

Contents

Acknowledgments

This postman must ring more than twice. The letters in *The Niekro Files* were delivered by more carriers than just this coauthor, and each deserves a toll. Phil and Joe were given their start by Mom and Dad, Philip and Ivy Niekro of Lansing, Ohio. Dad taught the boys the knuckleball in the backyard. My start came from loving Ohio parents, as well, Marshall and Ruby Picking of Ashland, Ohio. Mom typed the long-hand scratchings of the first games I covered on the kitchen table. They never gave me anything less than love and support in anything I attempted.

I'm also appreciative of non-Buckeye natives. My love and appreciation to wife January for her many contributions. Daughter Misti and son Lucas gave this postman the will to persevere through sleet, snow, and sometimes the silent treatment. For putting me on a most exciting mail route—major-league baseball—I thank *USA Today*. My personal postmaster and friend, Joe Safety, was chief negotiator and cheerleader, and his talents made the book a reality. "Safety First" is exactly that with me. Bruce Church, the Niekros' agent-advisor from Atlanta, consummated the deal with the class for which he is known. I am one of many, the Niekros included, who have received the kindness and caring of Claire Smith, the best woman baseball writer in the country. Claire's father, William H. Smith, blessed the Niekros and these pages with the marvelous lithograph that appears in this book. Much appreciation to many major-league media and public relations directors for their help, especially Harvey Greene and Lou D'Ermilio of the New York Yankees; Rick Minch of the Cleveland Indians; Tom Mee, Remzi Kiratli, and Laurel Prieb of the Minnesota Twins; and Bob DiBiasio and Jim Schultz of the Atlanta Braves. For giving this postman the warm climate and privacy of Florida for working conditions, thanks to Dan McDonald and Leroy Melsek. And thanks to Contemporary Books and Shari Lesser Wenk for publishing this postman's first book.

Ken Picking
December 1987
Alexandria, Virginia.

Introduction

By Ken Picking

Brothers are not known for writing letters to Mom and Dad, much less to one another.

As close as they can be biologically, mentally, or emotionally, once brothers turn from teenagers running from reality into men chasing dreams, keeping in touch usually means an infrequent backyard football game and long-distance telephone calls.

The brothers Niekro, Phil and Joe, never were accomplished letter writers, as their mother and wives will attest. In fact, they had never written to each other until they made a commitment to preserve the baseball season of 1987, a year they anticipated would be like no other.

Ever since they stopped sharing the same double bed in an upstairs bedroom of Philip and Ivy Niekro's home in Lansing, Ohio, in 1959, Phil and Joe have traveled in different directions to pursue their passion, baseball. It's not as if they didn't see each other; there were family reunions, visits to Lansing, and the brothers would get together for a fun night out whenever their teams met during the season.

But the daily brotherly contact was gone; the familiarity and understanding of each other's emotions and personal preferences became more past than present tense. And it bothered them.

When they toasted each other at midnight in the first moments of 1987, Phil and Joe knew it would not be the last time they tasted champagne together that year. Baseball's sibling knuckle-ball—sometimes knucklehead—pitchers had been imagining the taste and tingle of the magnum they planned to pop after they passed the Perrys, Jim and Gaylord, as the winningest brothers in baseball history. Phil and Joe saw the magic number 530, one victory more than the Perrys achieved, as the Niekro family's baseball legacy. Phil and Joe figured it was a lock; they entered the 1987 season needing six wins.

The Niekro brothers reported to spring training—Joe, 42, to Fort Lauderdale, Florida, with the New York Yankees, and Phil, at 47 the oldest player in the game, to Tucson, Arizona, with the Cleveland Indians—dreaming also of dousing themselves in bub-bly in an October clubhouse celebration, since their teams were expected to compete for the American League East division cham-pionship. Phil was the wise, wily old-timer, climaxing a Hall of Fame career with the young Indians, baseball's new springtime darlings and *Sports Illustrated* cover boys. Joe was in limbo with the unpredictable Yankees, a potential powerhouse if the walls don't come tumbling down.

Would this finally be the year a Niekro played in a World Series after a combined 45 seasons?

Would this be the last year Phil and Joe were active players together?

This was a baseball season to be shared and remembered, the Niekro brothers agreed, even if that required committing them-selves to correspondence for the first time in their lives. They wanted to catch up and then keep up with each other before they fell too far behind.

Inspired by the prospect of achieving 530 victories early in the season, they figured an exchange of letters once, sometimes twice a week would help them learn the new and remember the old about each other. They actually worried about whether they could come up with enough to talk about.

For Phil and Joe the 1987 baseball season—which, indeed, turned out to be their last together as active players—said a mouthful. It was nine months of thrills and spills, pain and pleasure.

- They pursue the Perrys and establish a record the Niekros say will stand forever.
- Joe considers retirement when the Yankees trade him to the Minnesota Twins, who ultimately take him where no Niekros had been before.
- Joe's trusty emery board gets him a starring role in sports blooper films, a date on "Late Night with David Letterman," and a 10-day suspension from the American League.
- Phil gets one last shot at pitching in a World Series when the Indians trade him to the Toronto Blue Jays, who release the old knuckleballer 22 days later.
- Proving you can go home again, Phil pitches his farewell game as he always dreamed, wearing an Atlanta Braves uniform.
- The Twins win the World Series and Joe, with Phil almost missing it after losing his ticket, pitches two innings to break Walter Johnson's record for longest service before participating in a World Series.

Joe skipped the Twins' visit to the White House, and one week after the World Series was over he was preparing his waterfront condominium in Chokoluskee, Florida, on the edge of the Everglades, for the arrival of seven serious fishermen—including old "Orlando Wilson" himself, Phil.

When Phil and Joe fished together in the same boat, as they recall doing as boys with Dad, they talked little. There was no urgency. For the first time in a long time they knew what the other had been up to, and the bond between them never felt stronger.

February: "Nothing Like Last Spring"

February 23. Tuesday. Fort Lauderdale, Florida

Phil:

Don't faint, Knucksie.

I told you when we were home with Mom and Dad I was going to write. Maybe it took me 42 years, but I don't recall you wearing out the postman. I also told you this wouldn't be my last letter either.

Let me catch you up. This is the first time in 20 years I walked in late to spring training. I wasn't in the clubhouse 20 seconds before Dave Righetti was ragging on me. "Nice you could make it." You remember the Yankee clubhouse; those guys never let up on the old-timers.

I wanted to be on time Saturday, but your old buddy George Steinbrenner wanted me to see a chiropractor in Tampa for my back and stay up there for a couple of days of examinations.

I tried to fight it—like I had a prayer against George, right?— because I figured I could see a chiropractor here and double up on treatment from the Yankees' trainer, Gene Monahan.

Anyway, I'm here, I've arrived, and as first days of nine-month seasons go, it's nice to know things probably will get better.

Last time I saw you, we were back home with Mom and Dad

in Lansing, listening to that movie producer and writer talk to us about making a film about our family. That's pretty unbelievable. It's a tribute Mom and Dad sure deserve: raising three children on a coal miner's salary and overcoming their own illnesses.

I finally figured out who I want playing me: Jon Voigt. Remember the movies *Coming Home* and *The Champ*? He looks like me. We're both around 6'1", 200 pounds. Maybe he has more hair, but we're both blond. Your niece, my dearest Natalie, says Don Johnson should play me. My daughter knows a handsome face when she sees one, right?

Everybody insists it's got to be Kirk Douglas to play you; people have said for years you look like him.

I drove my black jeep Cherokee down from home in Lakeland, moved into my condo, and it hit me when I walked through the door: I'll be without you this spring. In our hearts we probably knew last spring those precious days together as Yankee teammates shouldn't be taken for granted, even though we didn't know then that you'd be released in late March.

I remember opening the sliding glass doors to the condo last year and seeing you fishing in the back pond. I'm further up the road this year, so no back lakes this time. Maybe it's good they won't be so close to tempt me because fishing just won't be the same, Knucks, with you out in Arizona training with the Cleveland ball club.

I've tried to prepare myself for a lonely spring. I finally got over your release late last season, so at least my mind is focused on the job now. I'll miss those good steamed vegetables we'd cook up and eat so often together last year as roommates. And all those fish we caught and broiled.

The drive down here went fast because I had a lot on my mind. I'm letting what's past be past. Ever since you sat me down in the bullpen last September and aired me out about letting your release mess my mind up so, I've realized how happy you are with the Indians, and I'm determined to have a good frame of mind this season. We're both big boys who know how to survive on our own.

Actually, the questions I have about myself right now are

physical. The arm bothered me the second half of last season, and it was diagnosed as a frayed rotator cuff. The Yankees told me not to throw all winter, so I'm coming to camp not having thrown a ball in about five months. My back—get this, at home I was bending down to pick up a log, and halfway I felt something pop. I had been swimming a mile and running three miles each day before my back went out; I haven't been able to do anything the last month.

It's still sore, but they wouldn't let me do anything during today's first workouts. The guys kept asking me if drinking Geritol makes an old-timer late for spring training; you know how they'll bust a 40-year-old's chops any chance they get. It didn't matter that I was only doing what George told me to do; maybe that's why they were dumping on me.

Monahan—you know what a terrific trainer he is—had me in his office all day sprawled out on his table. He had heat packs on me, and muscle stimulators and ultrasound machines hooked up to me. The way he's treating me, I'd say it's going to be awhile before they let me throw. He talked like they want to make sure I'm 100 percent before I go out on the field. I can understand that. We'll see if I'm so understanding in a few days.

Righetti—Rags—is my new locker mate, and Army—Mike Armstrong—is on the other side, so you know I won't have a quiet or dull spring. They won't let up on me about being late. Bob Shirley, of course, is as crazy as ever. Tim Stoddard's in our locker line, so I know where I can get a smoke when I'm out.

What's odd is no Ron Guidry—Gator. Strange not seeing him walking around and talking in his Louisiana accent. George and Gator were $25,000 apart and missed the free-agent deadline, so Gator can't re-sign with us until May 1. Everybody expects him back. We're going to miss Gator, not just in the clubhouse but on the mound—the man can still pitch. He was 9–12 last year, but I think eight or nine losses were by one run. I'm surprised George let this happen for what's pocket change to him.

I showered and was almost out the clubhouse door when the New York press caught up to me. What was that Jack Nicholson

line in *Terms of Endearment?* "Almost a clean getaway . . ." You
know how they can pin you in, about seven or eight of them in a
semicircle, sort of a rugby scrum.

Right away they wanted to know why I was late, like there
might be something brewing there. I told them it was all George's
idea, and then right away I tried to turn everything positive: "My
mental approach will be better this year. I know I've got to prove
myself to George and Lou Piniella." I promised to be a happy and
healthy Yankee this year, and that I think the ball club needs me to
have a good season.

"With our hitters and a reliever like Rags, if I can win 15 or
more games, I think I can help us go all the way." I was a helluva
good interview, Knucks.

That ended the day on an upbeat note, so, of course, it put me
in the mood to go fishing. I know some days after practice I'll
whip up to George Lott's marina in West Palm Beach and fish for
snook under the bridge like we did last year. Remember, you
caught a 14-pounder there?

Thinking back to all we did last spring makes me realize how
much of each other's lives we've missed. Except for a few months
as teammates with the Braves and Yankees, we've been headed in
different directions since you left home in 1959 to play for the
Milwaukee Braves' Class D team in Wellsville, New York. I was 13
and you were 19.

That's why I want us to keep up with what we're doing, what
we're thinking and feeling this season. The phone's not really like
being there—I don't care what the TV commercials say—and it's
too damn expensive for conversations of any meaningful length. I
want to know more about what's going on with you than: "Hi.
Wish we could go fishing. Bye."

We'll be shooting for the Perrys' record for most wins by
brothers—we only need six to break it—and playing for teams that
should be going head-to-head for the pennant. This might be our
last season as active players together; I don't want this year to slip
away from us like so many in the past. I talked it over with Nancy
and she thinks it's a good idea. I'll be in touch if you keep in touch,

big brother. I doubt we'll be passing this way again.
—Joe

February 25. Wednesday. Tucson, Arizona

Joe:

It's cold, cold, cold here, barely 40 degrees. Believe it or not, they're predicting snow. Can you imagine snow for spring training?

I've heard of hurricanes and thunderstorms for the opening of spring training. I've heard of players' kids making sand castles at the beach, but never snowmen behind the hotel.

I like your idea—about time you had one, Knucklehead. I've never been much of a letter writer either; maybe once in a while to Mom, Dad, or Nancy, mostly notes scribbled on postcards, though. My handwriting has gotten awful; maybe practice will improve it.

I'll miss the fun we had together last spring. Fishing. Going to the Polish-American Club in Lake Worth, Florida, for polka dancing. Drinking moon shooters, my special shot of Bailey's and Midori. I'm going to want to know what I'm missing out on back there, so you better keep the letters coming.

Flew in Monday, so I really couldn't see much of Tucson because of the dark. The next morning, though, I walked out of the hotel about 10:30, and what a feeling it is to be surrounded by mountains. I'm used to the palm trees and the uninterrupted blue skies of Florida from training there every spring since 1961. I felt a little lost and disoriented carrying my duffel bag to the car to drive to the clubhouse at Hi Corbett Field; mountains make me feel so tiny.

As you know, the first day of spring training is always the most exciting. Saying hello, shaking hands, bullshitting, getting ready to spend more time with a group of guys than with your wife and children for the next eight months. That first day in the clubhouse has a Moose Lodge atmosphere about it.

Nobody threw much the first two days because it was so windy and cold. I don't mind a little breeze, especially for the knuckleball, but this was heavy-jacket weather. I've been throwing back home in Atlanta, so I've felt pretty loose.

As soon as I got back to the hotel, about 3:30, the first thing I thought about was going fishing. That's going to be a problem, I can see that already. Ernie Camacho, our reliever and a guy who loves to fish, told me where I could get a license and some gear, a spinning rod, lures, and a tackle box. Ernie says there are a couple of two- and three-acre suburban lakes stocked with trout, bass, and catfish. Trouble is, since there are so few places to go, the lakes look like bathtubs jammed with toy boats on the weekends. Staying at the hotel by myself for six weeks, I know I'm going to have to go out and throw in a line a few times or I'll go berserk.

I brought my golf clubs but haven't been out. My golf clubs appreciate that, I know.

—Phil

February 28. Saturday. Tucson, Arizona

Dear Joe:

Since this letter idea was yours, I wanted to show you I'm with you all the way, so here's my second in a week. When you can't go fishing you have plenty of time to sit on the balcony and push a pen. That's probably exactly how it is: I'm writing, and you're fishing.

It snowed the other day. Not right here, but the mountains are covered and it's beautiful. I hear some places up there got as much as eight feet. Still cold as hell, which has prevented us from doing a whole lot. Basic stretching, calisthenics, infield drills, light throwing. Being in the American League, with the designated hitter, they won't let the pitchers even pick up a bat. I don't even own a batting glove anymore.

Our manager, Pat Corrales, and his coaches like everybody running. You walk out of the clubhouse, and even before you do your calisthenics, you run a mile and a half. Come back and do calisthenics and then run another 10 minutes. I get tired just watching those guys run their laps.

As you know, I don't run, and I told Pat that before spring training started. My back quit bothering me six years ago when I stopped running, so basically Pat has let me be on my own program. He knows I know how to get myself ready; all I ask from him is enough innings to get comfortable with my knuckleball.

I'm still amazed at being at spring training, and seeing all the snow on the mountains. I keep waiting to hear yodeling.

Wish the weather would cooperate so we could get something accomplished. The rest of the club is going to be coming in soon and I want to get this old right arm cranked up so I can throw some BP early. Actually, I've been ready to throw BP for about a month. I started watching what I eat for a change; you ought to try that.

Been eating only one or two meals a day. I even got into aerobics. When everybody would leave the house I'd put on a sweat suit, get out those Jimmy Sturr albums, and do about 45 minutes of exercise to some good, lively polka music. I left home weighing 188 pounds; I haven't been that light in 10 years. I wanted to see how much weight I could lose before spring training because I heard you don't sweat down here like you do in Florida.

It won't be easy to keep the weight down. Corrales says this is the place for outstanding Mexican food, and you know how I like tacos and tostadas. I'm trying to see how long I can go before breaking down and having some.

How's that back of yours doing, anyway? I'm sure the Big Boss, George, is getting it taken care of for you. As much as you run in the off-season, plus staying in that hot sun in Lakeland all the time, I'm sure you're in good shape. I hope you guys have had a better start to spring training, weatherwise, than we have.

Anyway, take care of your back and let's get the most out of these next five weeks. We've got six wins to get early in April so we can celebrate 530.

Don't catch every bass in Florida, OK?

—Phil

March: "They Can't Stop Me from Doing the Polka"

March 2. Monday. Fort Lauderdale, Florida

Knucks:

Well, big brother, remember how I wanted this to be a fun upbeat spring for me and the Yankees? That lasted about a week. I'm ticked off, as I think you would be, too. I don't know what's going on. God, why does it have to be like this with this team all the time?

I feel good and they still won't let me do anything. I threw 15 minutes, but they didn't want me to throw any knuckleballs. I did anyway. I really haven't thrown in almost two months. I was thinking about breaking off a few curves and sliders, but mainly I just wanted to throw some fastballs and get the feeling back for the knuckleball again. As you know, you can lose that feeling in your fingertips. I'm going to throw as many knuckleballs as I can get away with so I can get that feeling back in time to take on the hitters in batting practice.

After I throw, it's back to see Monahan again. He's waiting for me every day with my private table in the corner. That man's got to be tired of looking at my butt because he's rubbing it down every day. He's anxious for me to get out of the training room, too, because I'm driving him crazy.

I want to get back in the program with the other guys so they'll get off my back. Rags, Shirley, Stoddard, Rick Rhoden walk into the clubhouse after throwing and I'm sitting there on my stool sipping a cup of soup or biting a piece of cantaloupe. They're sweaty, breathing heavy, looking like they just walked 72 hours in the Everglades, and I look like I'm waiting for the luau to begin.

"Will you be joining us anytime soon?" Rags teases me. I don't have an answer, of course. I can handle the razzing; my frame of mind is still reasonably good. But I've got to talk to somebody soon and get some answers or I'm going to go bananas. George is supposed to come down in a few days, so maybe I can talk to him or Piniella.

At least they were letting me ride the bike until last Thursday. I was in the trainer's room early in the morning and Monahan got a telephone call from George. He wanted to know if I was riding the bike. Gene told him I was and that I was feeling great.

Suddenly, Monahan almost drops the phone receiver; I thought he got an electrical shock. He straightens up, listens, and hangs up.

Gene walks over to me and says: "The surgeon general from New York told me you can't ride the bike anymore."

I don't know why; Gene doesn't know why. I think George contacted the doctor he knows from Tampa, and *he* said he didn't want me to ride the bike when he examined me last month. I'm seeing a chiropractor down here and he says I *can* ride the bike. Then there's Dr. Kanell in New York. I'm getting four different opinions. I don't know what the hell's going on.

Wish you were here, Knucks, to advise me on what to ask them. They're saying they don't want my back to blow out again. Who can guarantee that Don Mattingly's back isn't going to blow out in workouts tomorrow? Who knows, maybe Rhoden comes up with a sore arm. You can't predict what will or won't happen on the field. I just hope they don't have anything in mind for me like they had for Tommy John last spring; leave me in Fort Lauderdale to be their one-man taxi squad if something happens up in New York.

I have no pain in my arm, shoulder, or back, and I feel 100 percent, I keep telling them. But they won't turn me loose and I don't know why. I need to be more involved with the team; the isolation and teasing are getting to me. I know I'm singing the "Training Room Blues," but the Yankees move in such mysterious ways.

Nancy and Lance have been here. Natalie couldn't come because of her modeling classes. Nancy came down because she couldn't miss Jimmy Sturr playing up in Lake Worth. She and I have been dancing our butts off up there. Jimmy played the "Hey Niekro Polka" and dedicated it to you, of course, Phil.

We took Jimmy a bottle of Dom Perignon for winning the Grammy, and he got a kick out of that. I told him how I about went through the ceiling when I saw him wearing a tuxedo with a red tie and red cummerbund for the Grammy show. He looked like a first class Polack that night. It was Jimmy's first bottle of Dom, so I told him to save it since he's used to drinking cheap whiskey.

I came out of that Polish-American Club soaking wet. We had a couple pops for you, but our Polish parties just aren't the same without you. Everybody asks about you, Knucks, and hopes you can find some polka music in Arizona.

All I know is, if I can polka like that for a couple hours, I'm sure I can go jog a few laps around the field.

Later.

—Joe

March 8. Sunday. Tucson, Arizona

Joe:

First outing of the spring, a B game against San Francisco, and I got my butt kicked royally.

Had to get up at 6:30 in the morning to make the 7 o'clock bus for the two-hour drive up to Scottsdale, where the Giants train. I should have known I was going to have problems when I didn't have time for my usual 10 cups of coffee in the morning.

Warming up, I wasn't getting a good grip or feel for the knuckleball, and sure enough I couldn't get it over the plate. The first inning was a nightmare: three or four base hits, I walked a guy, three runs. Not exactly an "A" performance, although the callus from the blister on my finger finally fell off.

It's tough throwing a knuckleball out here, Joe. You can't sweat because there's no humidity. Your hands feel like they're covered with baby powder. You know you have to have a good grip, or the knuckleball is going to slip and do nothing, except maybe get hit 400 feet. I haven't had a good knuckleball since I got down here. I'm a little concerned that I'm going to come out of spring training still searching for my knuckleball, and that's not the frame of mind I want to start the season with. Tom Candiotti, my knuckleball buddy with the Indians, said he had the same trouble getting started last spring and ended up winning 16 games. So I'm trying not to panic.

The old screwball, a pitch that's been good to me, is working; I'm throwing it for strikes. My slow curve is OK, and I'm experimenting with a little slider. Do you think it's too late for me to become a power pitcher?

I know I can't pitch that way, so I'll just have to keep bearing down on my knuckleball. I've got to figure out how to get a good grip, that's all. Scuffing doesn't work for me, but a little moisture from somewhere might be the ticket.

Called Mom and Dad tonight. I asked Dad how he was doing and he said, "No good, I'm on a diet." You know how Mom watches everything he eats. It was about 75 degrees up there today so Uncle Frank took Dad out on the front porch. I'm glad he's getting some fresh air and not cooped up in the house all the time. Mom took a shot in her knee and it was still bothering her, but they sounded good. I know they'd appreciate a call from you, Joe.

Can you believe our sister Phyllis's oldest boy is in pro baseball, too—? PT reports to the Indians' minor-league camp next week, so it will be great to have some family out here. I told Phyllis I'd feed him every now and then and keep an eye out for him. He's a good-looking young left-handed pitcher who might make a Double A club this year.

I've finally been getting in some serious fishing. I've been up to Candida Lake twice in the last week. First time, using a little white jig for a lure, I caught two trout about 12 to 13 inches and a bass around three-quarters of a pound. Next time I went up was the most fun away from the hotel I've had. Caught six nice trout; I released two because of the limit. Caught three bass, too, one about 10½ pounds.

I feel like I'm starting to know the lake a little bit. Camacho, who's not the luckiest guy in the world anyway, can't believe I'm catching fish up here. He says he's been going up to Candida for a couple of years and hasn't caught anything. Camacho calls me Orlando Wilson, the TV fisherman. Ernie thinks I can catch fish in a bathtub.

Saw on ESPN that Roger Clemens walked out of the Boston Red Sox camp over his contract. Sure is nice to know we're signed, isn't it? Imagine where a couple of old-timers like you and me would be negotiating a contract if a young superstar like Clemens can't get the contract he wants.

I don't know what I'd do if I was Clemens. He's coming off an incredible year, one almost impossible to duplicate. He's at the top of his profession. I agree that you've got to show two or three good years to get a huge raise, but I don't think Roger is asking too much for what he can do for the Red Sox. He made $350,000 in 1986; he wants more than $1 million this season. To me, if Roger doubles his salary, that's a fair-size raise.

On the other hand, Joe, with our teams being in the same division with Boston, maybe we ought to send Roger a letter encouraging him to stick to his guns and not take a cent under $1 million.

Except for this damn hacking cough, I feel great. The doctor gave me my physical and said I came to camp in good shape, which was nice to hear. Doc said my arm is just like last year; my range of motion is good. All the X rays checked out. When you turn 48 in less than a month, and you take those physicals, you are silently praying that they won't find something wrong you have no idea about.

Even if I say so myself, this is probably the best I've looked in a baseball uniform in a long time. I'm like you, if I put on two or three pounds it feels like 10, so I'm always trying to keep an eye on the scale. When I get up to 192 I start panicking. I'd like to stay under 190 this year, but I know sometime, somewhere, I'm going to break down and pig out on a tableful of fattening food.

I keep looking in the newspaper for your name to see how my old Yankee team is doing. I see you guys are 3–0 already in exhibition games. I hope George decides you can help them win and starts giving you some innings. I know you're like me, you need all six weeks of spring training to get the feel for the knuckleball again.

Claire Smith of the *Hartford-Courant* called me and said they're playing around with you, still keeping you out of action. I don't know what they're trying to do, but hang in there, partner. If you get knocked down, you've got two choices: stay down or get back up, and I know you're the type to get up fighting. Don't give them a clue they're getting to you. Just be smarter and stronger than they are. That's about all the brotherly advice I can give you on this one.

When it's building up inside you and you feel like you're going to explode all over somebody, drive down to the Everglades and go fishing or get up to Lake Worth and listen to some good Jimmy Sturr polka music. That'll get you through it.

Hang tough, brother.

—Phil

March 10. Tuesday. Fort Lauderdale, Florida

Phil:

I'm packing suitcases already. This has to be a first: an eight-day road trip in spring training. I've never heard of such a thing, but as I keep forgetting, this is the Yankees.

Fortunately for me—and I'm sure this trip wasn't planned for my benefit—we're going to be based in Tampa. That's close enough to Lakeland that I can stay home with the family and commute to the games. What a bonus: fishing off the dock at night with Lance. Thank you, Yankees.

The team is staying at George's hotel, the Bay Harbor in Tampa. The strange thing is we play eight games and not one in the Tampa area. Cincinnati, Philadelphia, St. Louis, and the New York Mets all are in the Tampa–St. Petersburg area, and we don't play any of them. Figure that one, Knucks.

The closest to Tampa we play is in Dunedin, where the Toronto Blue Jays train, and it's at least 40 minutes from the hotel. The rest of the games are an hour to 90 minutes away. We play twice in Orlando, once in Winter Haven, once in Lakeland, twice in Sarasota. And then we end the adventures of "George's Traveling All-Stars and Motor Kings" with a three-hour bus ride up to Gainesville for a game against the University of Florida—you know what a Gator booster the Boss is. At least the university is flying us back on its plane.

To me, it's amazing. You're supposed to be getting a team ready for the season, and you know you've got a World Series–caliber team. But you go across state to Tampa, stay eight nights in a hotel, set up a half-assed trainer's room in a hotel room—it's something I've never heard of before. Spring training is turning into the "Yankees Spring Showcase," the way we're being trotted around like zebra-striped show ponies.

But there's no mystery why we're here: George is cracking the whip. He's big in this area and wants to have his boys around so his good old buddies can see real, live Yankees with their own eyes. I can hear it now: "Shit damn, George, that Winfield'd make some bitchuva thoroughbred."

You wouldn't believe yesterday, Knucks. We play Baltimore in a 1:30 game and at 9 o'clock in the morning it's pouring down rain. You remember those Florida downpours; they hit like a tidal wave. There's no way I thought we'd play.

I get to the clubhouse around 9:45 and the game's called off. I'm having a cup of coffee and, evidently, the groundskeeper told George the weather was going to clear around 11. So, a half hour after they called the game off, it's back on.

So George goes into his working man's routine. He brings in the helicopters to put on a show drying the field. Then he walks to the outfield, takes his shoes and socks off, and rolls his pants legs up around the knees. The Boss is stomping through the water and he's got one of those long-handle squeegies. The owner of the Yankees, proving no job is too small or dirty for him, is going to help the humble grounds crew get the water off the field.

Let me tell you, George Steinbrenner might be a master shipbuilder, but he's a horseshit groundskeeper. You're supposed to push the water away from you with the squeegie. Big George was pulling the water into him and it's slopping all over his pants.

You know George. He's going to do it his way, even if it does make him look like a big dummy. He strolled into the clubhouse the other day wearing a baseball hat that said: "Top Gun." It should have read "Machine Gun," the way he shoots people down.

I've cooled down about not being turned loose, mostly because the first day they let me run a little, I felt a twinge in my back. I've eased up, just riding the bike and throwing on the side. I still feel like I'm going to be their one-man taxi squad, like Tommy John last year. I'm going to try to pitch better than they expect when I get the chance and mess up their plans as much as possible. I get ornery when someone's pissing on me the way the Yankees are right now.

There was a story in *USA Today*. A writer asked me how I felt and I told him I felt ready to pitch, but they won't let me. The story said I was getting impatient and ticked off at the Yankees. Just the truth.

But you know how those New York newshounds are: first thing in the morning they're sniffing around me for some controversy. All I told them was that if George read the *USA Today* story, then I'm sure he's upset with me again. I told them: "Joe Niekro is ready to go. If they don't turn me loose pretty soon I'm not going to be ready when the season starts. That would give them the perfect excuse for keeping me back in Fort Lauderdale so I'm their Tommy John insurance policy for 1987."

I heard something about Piniella saying he's not going to get me into a game until two weeks into the exhibition season. I wish they'd come ask me how I feel instead of deciding for themselves.

Everybody's got an opinion on how my back feels, but I'm the one who knows best, and I know I'm ready to begin a pitching routine. I'm not going to take any stupid risks.

We had our annual Players Association meeting with Don Fehr and Mark Belanger and they are painting a dark picture, Knucks. They're confident about the players' collusion case against the owners, but today's free-agent market is all but out of business. I wonder if the young guys will ever have free agency the way we did. The owners are out to kill it, or at least that's how you have to feel when nobody is getting offers. When a player like Tim Raines can't bring about competitive bidding between teams, there's an agreement been made somewhere.

The free agents after the 1987 season—Mike Schmidt, Cal Ripken, Dale Murphy, superstars like that—when they look back at this past winter and see what happened to Raines, Lance Parrish, Bob Horner, Jack Morris, top talent like that, and see nobody signed for more than their old team offered, I can't believe you're going to see superstars changing teams. The owners will have killed free agency for superstars and drastically reduced the salary structure for middle-level free agents.

Anyway, all the people in Chokuluskee—I managed to drive down after practice one day for some snook fishing—send their best; they all hope one of us can finally get to the World Series. After 43 seasons between us, I think the odds are with us.
—Joe

March 16. Monday. Tucson, Arizona

Joe:

Saw your name in the newspaper this morning—they let you pitch an inning. That's good, man. Of course, you're going to need more than one inning, but it's a start. You broke the ice. Hope you felt all right.

We've got work to do. Let's get 530 as soon as possible and then start pitching for the pennant. I'm pitching tomorrow, about three innings against the Giants, and I hope I can get my knuckleball over the plate more this time.

It was good to talk to you on the phone a few days ago, but you didn't sound very good mentally. I just don't understand why they're messing with you so. You're ready to pitch, Monahan says you're ready to pitch, the doctors have given you the OK to pitch, Mark Connor knows you're ready to pitch, Lou knows you need innings to get ready for the season, but they're moving so slow on you.

If it's a week before you pitch again, you've got to go in and talk to somebody. Get eyeball-to-eyeball with Lou, Connor, Monahan, even the Big Boss if he'll face you. Find out why they're jerking you around. What have you done to them? You've got two years left on your contract, at almost $800,000 a year, and they're going to let you sit and rot? They can't do that.

George ought to just let you out of there if he has no use for you. If he had any feelings for human beings, he ought to know what you're going through and let you out of there.

Come over to the Tribe. We'll take you in a minute. Corrales and Goryl both said they'd like to have you over here. Knowing the Yankees, though, as soon as someone showed interest they'd want Lake Erie and part ownership in the Cleveland Browns to trade you.

It just doesn't make sense, Joe. It's not like they're flying high with pitchers over there. Guidry isn't even back on the staff yet. Rhoden will win. But Dennis Rasmussen was the only starter with double figures in wins last year.

I can understand them wanting to be protective of you, but damn, you've hardly worked out. You don't need to be somebody's insurance policy; too many teams can use you. You'll be a basket case if this keeps up.

When I left the Yankees I thought it was the end of my career. But I can't tell you how happy I am to be with the Indians. What a difference. There's no pressure; they just let you play. I think Corrales's spring training is a lot tougher than the Yankees'.

Corrales and the pitching coach, Jack Aker, know I've been a winner and they let me go about my business. They know I'll be ready when the season starts, and they also know I have to pitch in spring training to be ready.

It seems the Yankees are the damn opposite. I know what's going to happen. At the end of training camp they are going to say, "Oh, we can't put Joe in the rotation because he ain't pitched 10 innings here." I bet that's what's coming. Just so they have an excuse. George is protecting himself, not you.

I'm pretty mild-mannered, but the more I think about what you're going through—after the way they kicked me out the door—the madder I get. I know what the hell we'd do if I was over there with you. We'd have that whole organization in an uproar. They'd have to kick us both out the door.

I've been through the ringer you're in. But when we're working for somebody, I guess we have to go by their rules. We ain't got a lot of say-so. We can bark as much as we want, but we can't bite back. Do what you've got to do. Things have always worked out for the Niekros. We've been released, traded, stepped on here and there, and we keep getting back up. Get knocked down, get back up. Accept your losses and setbacks without being defeated.

When you go in and talk to them, let me know. I'll keep my ears open and throw a few bugs around.

Speaking of bugs, I still can't get this fuzzy critter out of my throat. I've been taking your recommended daily dosage of three shots of Jose Cuervo tequila. I still got the cough, but I don't mind it as much.

Corrales called in everybody to be weighed and I tipped the scales at a greyhoundlike 187 pounds. That's outstanding for me. I can't remember weighing in under 190. I guess staying away from the Mexican food has paid off.

I'm still struggling on the mound, though. Against Seattle I gave up nine hits and five runs in three innings. I threw about 70 pitches and they must have hit 65 of them solidly. My knuckleball moved more, so at least I feel that's on its way to coming around. What I need is more work, that's all.

I'm not the only pitcher getting crushed. Everybody on the staff is giving up runs. I sure hope it's not an indication of what's ahead for us. All of a sudden there are more than one or two pitching spots open, especially in the bullpen to set up Camacho.

Anybody can get a job with a couple of strong outings.

Candiotti looks like he's getting close with five perfect innings the other day. His knuckleball was moving, a pleasure to watch. Reminded me of myself at 26.

Before Candiotti pitched, Corrales called a team meeting and chewed on our asses pretty good, which we deserved. It got us concentrating a little more, and we went out and played good baseball behind Candiotti to win our second game.

Our nephew PT arrived at the Indians' minor-league camp. Took him out to dinner at a place called Pinnacle Pete's. PT got one of those two-pound T-bones, salad and everything. You were right, Joe, the boy can eat like a buffalo. He threw down that two-pound steak like it was a burger before everybody else was half done. I know he could have eaten another one, but he held back, trying to be polite.

I hope PT can have a good spring; he says he's lost 12 to 14 pounds. He could be up with the Indians in a year or two. I wonder, since PT is a blood relation, if his major-league wins could go on our family total? Probably not, but we could make PT feel like we're adding his wins to ours.

For the next couple weeks I'm going to keep my eye on him. I'll take him out for some food and fishing. He's staying in a little motel outside of town. The team provides transportation and they give them free-eats tickets at the Ramada Inn. I think they give him four dollars a week—could you get by on 57 cents a day, Joe?—spending money, so you know he won't be out having too much fun.

It's going to be nice to have some family around here to be concerned about.

Anyway, the highlight of my week was seeing your name in the box score. Just be ready and get the ball over the plate when they give it to you.

Oh, yes, I did bring my polka tapes, but it's no fun dancing by yourself in the hotel room. Wish I could fly out for one of your parties; I miss them.

—Phil

March 22. Sunday. Fort Lauderdale, Florida

Knucks:

Strike up the polka band. I finally got into a game today and pitched pretty darn well, says this humble reporter.

I was supposed to pitch three innings, six through eight. But Dennis Rasmussen started and got into trouble in the fifth. I came in with runners at first and third and Eddie Murray looking at me and loosening up that monster left-handed swing of his. I got ahead of him one ball, two strikes and threw him a knuckleball. He hit it off the end of his bat and into a double play.

Pitched three more innings and gave up three hits and one run. My knuckleball came alive for the first time, and God, I felt a sense of relief. You know what I mean: you know it's there, you're looking for it, you're telling yourself not to panic, you keep believing it will not leave you forever, and then one day, your bread-and-butter is back. Glory hallelujah. You haven't lost it.

Jim Dwyer went down and got a good 0-and-2 knuckleball and golfed it for a home run. Murray got back at me, leading off the eighth with a double. Then, Knucks, the best part: I closed the inning out like Goose Gossage, sort of. Three straight strikeouts— Ray Knight, Ken Gerhart, and Floyd Rayford. I showed the Yankees I'm healthy and capable of pitching more than a couple of innings.

If, as they say, you're only as good as your last game with the Yankees, then today things are looking up for me. I hope I've convinced them I should be in the starting rotation. We've got six starters: Rhoden, Tommy John, Rasmussen, Bob Tewksbury, Charlie Hudson, and myself. Surely, they'll only keep five, but who knows who will get the ax? I've got a two-year guaranteed contract, so they've got to pay me no matter what. But I don't want to be on the team that way. I'd rather get out. I want to pitch for the Yankees, and right now I feel like I can help this club win a pennant.

After the game, Lou and Connor both came over and said, "Nice going." Mark told me that was the best I've thrown since early 1986.

I told him I thought it was because my arm felt good. I got my arm up, kept the elbow back, and my shoulder felt strong. My ball was moving quite well.

This Baltimore outing, I think, is a continuation of the last few weeks for me. Since we took the eight-day bus trip to Tampa, and I was able to operate out of home with the family, things have been happening for me.

Our first workout at Redsland, the Cincinnati ball club's minor-league complex, March 11, I threw batting practice and felt great. Connor liked how I threw. I told him my arm felt great, my back felt better. My sinker, slider, and knuckleball looked Opening Day ready. I was about to tell Connor I was ready to pitch in a game when he says to me: "I've got some news for you. You can't pitch for two weeks."

What? I thought Rags and Shirley had put him up to busting my chops some more. Hello, Mark? April Fools isn't for a couple of weeks. His face told me he was not joking. He tells me Dr. Kanell says I can't pitch for two weeks.

Three days after being told I couldn't pitch for two weeks, they gave me one inning, my first game action in about six months. It was extra enjoyable for me because it was against Detroit in Lakeland and I had a lot of friends out there. I didn't walk anybody, got ahead of hitters, and the knuckleball felt pretty good, even if it wasn't moving much.

When I was told I would be pitching a couple innings up in Gainesville against the University of Florida, I wasn't sure how to feel. You know those types of games: you're expected to pitch well. If you do, it doesn't mean anything because it was against college kids. But if you get your butt lit up, George is down on you bigtime: you can't pitch anymore; you're back to fighting to stay on the staff.

We got on the bus at 7:30 in the morning for a three-hour bus ride from Tampa to Gainesville and put a 14–2 job on the Gators. The guys were hitting the hell out of the ball. I pitched two innings and felt all right. But I was still searching for the knuckleball; the wind was behind me and, as you know, the ball gets pushed and doesn't move that well.

The flight back from Gainesville to Fort Lauderdale will not soon be forgotten. I thought it was great. We were on the University of Florida plane, a little two-engine job that held only 31 people and put our butts right on the runway. Knucks, you wouldn't have flown in this thing without a parachute strapped to your back.

I was sitting next to Joel Skinner, and Rick Cerone was on the other side of the aisle. Rick was sweating bullets; he's not a flier and this was a roller coaster with wings. He got the barf bag out, and I thought he was going to give it all up a couple of times. It was hotter than hell in that plane, but Rick made it back all right.

Remember Dominic Scala, the Yankees' bullpen catcher when you were here? He had a jewelry business in New York and sold big Yankee rings with "Pride" and "Tradition" on the sides, rings that could be used as paperweights. Well, last Christmas Dom sent one to George to say thanks for giving him permission to sell Yankee items. I don't know exactly what happened, maybe George forgot he gave Dom permission, or never gave Dom permission in the first place, but shortly after George got the ring, Dom was fired.

King George drops his ax on another head.

The kid who took Dom's place as bullpen catcher is Mike Fennell. He was warming me up for the first time and I had a little breeze in my face, just the way we like it. I threw knuckleballs for 20 minutes and, I tell you Knucks, I beat the shit out of that poor kid. I felt really sorry for him. I must have hit him six times and he didn't lay a glove on one. Got to give him credit, he took me on and put up a fight.

I called Mom and Dad, so you can rest easy. Dad sounds great. Getting his leg amputated took that poison out of his system, and it really helped. He said he's getting around in the wheelchair and gaining weight. Mom says she's going to put him on a diet because he's gaining too much weight.

It's really wonderful to have him feeling good again after all the pain and suffering he went through the last few years. Let's hope he can live the rest of his life comfortably, with no pain. If I could have one wish, it would be to turn back the clock and take away all the pain Dad has had to endure.

Having been home with the kids for a while, when the team was based in Tampa, makes me miss them all the more. Lance is already a ballplayer. He could have played one more year in t-ball, but the kid is such a good athlete, so advanced for eight years old, I figured he was going to hurt one of those little kids in t-ball. So we moved him up to the older kids.

I went to see his first practice game and the kid was awesome: 3 for 3 with a triple, stolen base, three RBI, a couple of runs scored. Lance pitched the last inning and punched out the three batters he faced on 12 pitches. A dad could not have been more proud than I was.

Natalie has matured so much the last seven months, it scares her old man. She's been going to modeling school in Winter Haven, and the lady who runs it is really high on Nat. She's getting a portfolio together and entering a few magazine contests to become a cover girl. The lady at the modeling school wanted her to begin with *Seventeen* magazine even though Nat's only 13. I'll send you a picture; you won't believe your niece. She looks 21 when she's all made up. I guess it's time to dust off the old double barrel shotgun.

I know I'm prejudiced and I don't care; Natalie is a beauty. Nancy has done such a wonderful job with her and Lance. She takes Natalie to modeling classes twice a week, carts Lance around to baseball practice and games. As you know, Knucks, a baseball wife has to be both mother and father, and I really thank her for the way she has raised our kids.

I ordered your gift for your 48th birthday on April 1. Sorry I won't be there to present it, but you'll know what to do with it. I wanted to give it to you last year, but you got released before I could give it to you.

You deserve all the best, big brother.

—Joe

March 31. Tuesday. Tucson, Arizona

Joe:

Yesterday was my last start of spring training in Arizona; went five innings for the third straight time, but I don't like the pattern I see developing.

It was up in Tempe against Seattle. I wasn't good, but I wasn't bad. I wanted to kick myself in the butt for not covering first base on one play. I don't know why I didn't, I've only done it—what?—10,000 times. It was the kind of mental mistake that burns me up.

I was supposed to pitch five innings or 100 pitches, whichever came first. I threw 82 pitches in five innings and I was gone. It pissed me off because I was feeling good and I wanted to end spring training by going as long as I could. I just hope Corrales doesn't think that when the season starts I'm going to be strictly a five- and six-inning pitcher. Right now, that's all he wants.

If we're ahead or I'm pitching all right, I want to go eight or nine innings just like the younger guys. I'm supposed to start an exhibition game in Buffalo, where the Indians' Triple A team plays, before we open the season at Toronto. I hope Corrales lets me go seven or eight innings, so when the season starts, I've been that far and know how I'll feel.

My knuckleball really has been coming around the last week. I threw five good innings at Palm Springs, California, against the Angels. It was pretty much the same when I pitched five at Chandler, Arizona, against the Brewers.

Believe it or not, I stayed away from the Mexican food all spring until Nancy came down on the 27th. I was a good boy, though. I only had three tacos, beans, and rice. This has been a great spring physically for me. I feel I'll be starting the season in the best condition in years. My mind's fine now that my knuckleball is back. I'd probably feel better if I knew you were feeling as good as I am.

I heard you pitched well the last week, and that's good news. I've been worried about you this spring, Joe. Sometimes I don't think it's fair that I'm here in Arizona feeling so comfortable and you're back in Florida going through hell not knowing what to expect tomorrow.

I'm sure Big Boss Steinbrenner has everything in that part of the country running his way, whether it makes sense or not. He's got to run everything, and Lord help anybody or anything that gets in the way. Again, all I can says is, I've been through it, too. I still get pissed off when I hear through the grapevine what they're doing to you.

Just keep your head up, and when you get your opportunity, grab the bull by the horns and go for it. I've always said no one person in any one organization is going to keep me from doing what I want to do. We may get knocked off the road for a while, but the Niekros get back up and go forward. When the season starts they'll realize they need you, and all of this spring training madness will be forgotten.

Joe, you won't believe what happened to me two nights before Nancy got here. This is an all-timer. You've heard of living in shit? Well, that was your big brother's residence for about 10 hours.

I was in my hotel room watching television when I heard something running in the bathroom. I took a peek in there and heard water running, but I couldn't see anything so I went back to watching television.

I tried to ignore the sound, but I kept hearing the water. I went back to the bathroom and noticed that under the commode the floor was a little wet. I figured it was a small leak somewhere so I didn't pay much attention to it and flopped back on the bed to watch TV.

The water kept running and the sound got more distracting. I went back in and this time the water was about a half-inch deep all over the floor; it was almost seeping out into the room. I figured I'd better do something, so I piled a bunch of towels in front of the door to block and soak up the water. I called the front desk and asked them for a maintenance man. They said he quit at six o'clock, but I told them they had better get someone to fix this leak or my room was going to be flooded and their carpet would be ruined.

The desk clerk said they'd get someone over to my room in about 20 minutes. As you might figure, the water seemed to slow down in that time. When a maintenance man arrived he spotted a bolt under the commode that had popped open. He said he'd have to take the whole commode off to fix it, but that there wasn't any place open at that hour to take it. Water was still seeping in, so we threw more towels down and I called the front desk to see if I could switch rooms.

Of course, the hotel was packed and no more rooms were available at 10 o'clock. I told them I could rough it for the night. The maintenance man said he'd be back at eight in the morning to fix the commode. I got more towels to use later and went back to watching television.

It wasn't 15 minutes before I heard the bubbling and gurgling of water again. I felt like checking out of the hotel right then, but knew what a hassle it would be. I knew damn well if I opened the bathroom door again what I'd find: more water and no way to stop it. I got up, and sure enough the water had leaked out onto the carpet. I moved some of the furniture back, set up a barricade of towels, turned the volume up on the TV, pulled the covers over my head, and concentrated on getting to sleep.

Joe, I'm telling you. It must have been three or four in the morning. I rolled over and woke up long enough to hear water running that sounded like one of those country creeks we've fished in. I sat up in bed and put one foot down and it was like stepping into a damn swamp. The entire room was soaked. I squished my way to the bathroom door, took a deep breath, and opened the door.

Joe, I've never seen anything like what was in that bathroom. I don't know how big Tucson is or how many people live there and I have no idea what the size of the Tucson city waste department is, but that sucker had to be dry because it all was in my bathroom.

I'm talking about in the commode, over the commode, in the shower stall, up on the sink. It must have been over a foot deep. I'm talking about toilet paper, whole turds, cigarette butts, tampons, sanitary napkins—anything that was headed for the Tucson cesspool department was in my hotel room. As you can imagine, the smell was beyond description. The only thing I can compare it to is a portable john after its been used all day. I don't know what was worse, the smell or the sight.

At four in the morning, what are you going to do? I couldn't go anywhere, there were no rooms available. I closed the bathroom door, opened up the windows, and somehow got back to sleep.

The next morning I squished my way to the bathroom and there was twice as much shit in there. Back home I've seen people clean out their cesspool tanks, but I couldn't imagine where all this stuff had come from. I've never seen such a stinking mess.

When I got back to the hotel from the ballpark, the room was cleaned up and the commode was off for repairs. I changed rooms. I checked with the maintenance man about what the hell happened. Seems the sewer line had broken, not exactly a big surprise. And since I was at the end of a wing of about 30 rooms, every time someone flushed the toilet or took a shower, the sewage kept backing up for two or three days. As soon as the pipe broke, all that stuff dropped into my bathroom.

I started thinking this was the ultimate April Fools' joke, but then I realized it was a few days early. Never have I had an experience like that, so I thought I'd tell you about it, for whatever it's worth.

—Phil

April: "Ants and Size 17 Shoes"

Phil:

Happy birthday, Knucksie. Another year older, number 48, and you're still in baseball. That's amazing. I'm really proud to be your little brother.

Hope you enjoyed the birthday present I sent you, that old-timer's tricycle with the wire basket and orange warning flag. I had a lot of fun coming up with that for you. I can just see you riding that trike, keeping up with the other pitchers who have to run. Like I said in my card, five years after you retire you can pedal that bike up to the Hall of Fame and maybe I can ride along in the basket.

I'm finally feeling better about my situation because I've finished spring training pretty strong. I don't see how I can't be the Yankees' fifth starter. Right now I see our rotation as Rhoden—he's number one—Tommy John, Rasmussen, Tewksbury, and then either myself or Charlie Hudson as number five. They know I'd rather not pitch out of the bullpen, and I don't think they want a knuckleball pitcher in that role.

My last start against Texas I was pleased. God, it was hot that day. I almost was exhausted before I was finished warming up in the bullpen, but hot weather is what us old-timers like, right Knucks?

32

I went out and pitched five innings. I gave up one run on a real good sinker. Rick Cerone caught me and I really like pitching to him. He's a veteran and knows how to work hitters. We started a lot of guys off with fastballs, sinkers, and sliders, and then came with the knuckleball, the pitch they're always looking for when you or me are out there on the hill. When I got behind a couple of left-handed hitters, Rick called for the backdoor slider and I got a couple of strikeouts on it. I don't know why I didn't throw that pitch more last year; maybe we'll remember to use it this season.

I hope I'm starting to change some minds around here with the way I've finished up spring training. When I first came down here, I think the Yankees definitely had me diagnosed for the disabled list because of my arm and back. But I've come along a lot faster than they thought.

Bobby Valentine, the Rangers' manager, came up to me and said, "You're not starting for this ball club?" I told Bobby it was still up in the air. "With your track record, and the way I saw you throw the ball today, I can't believe you're not a starter," Bobby told me.

As you can imagine, rare words of praise like that put a smile on my face.

I was about ready to tell Valentine that if he wanted another knuckleball pitcher to go with Charlie Hough, come get me, because I'd like to pitch for him. But after the way I've been throwing, I feel like I'm going to be all right with the Yankees, so I figured I better not stir it up.

My heart goes out to Righetti; Rags is really struggling. We played Boston and had one of those usual sellout crowds at Fort Lauderdale Stadium. Rags came in with a two-run lead in the ninth and ended up giving up a grand slam to Jim Rice.

Afterward, Rags was as down as I've ever seen him. I tried to console him a little like I did last year in Toronto when George Bell hit a slam off him. I gave him the speech you've given me before: one good game can turn things around, stay positive, keep your head up, believe in yourself. Rags is a little depressed because George is on his case, making him watch films every day and having him work on stuff.

George probably thinks Rags has to save 46 games every year like he did last year. George probably doesn't know that nobody ever saved that many games in a season before and it's going to be tough for even Rags to duplicate that. Rags is still in his prime and he still has great stuff, so if he can get a win or a save, he'll be back on track.

Tommy John astounds me. TJ throws that sinker like a machine. Against Atlanta he gave up 12 hits in four innings—10 of them were ground balls through the infield. If he stays healthy, he can win until he's 50. As you know, Phil, when a pitcher gets into his forties, people don't want to believe anymore the guy can still win. But as you have been preaching for almost a decade, if the guy goes out and gets the job done, why should it matter if he's 25, 35, or 45?

Maybe guys like TJ, you, and maybe even I can shatter the myth about age.

Age is not Rod Scurry's problem, but it seems like everyone and everything's against him making the pitching staff. To me, Rod has one of the best—maybe the best—left-hand curveballs I've ever seen. He's just not getting a chance to show what he can do. I don't think he's pitched in nine days. I don't know if they had something in the back of their mind about him or not, but he's not getting a fair shot. Rod came over from Pittsburgh last year, overcame his drug problem, and battled back. If the Yankees pass him up, a team would be foolish not to give Rod a look, because the man can get people out.

Nancy and Lance came down to Fort Lauderdale a few days ago, and here's another beauty of a Steinbrenner story for you.

I took Lance to the ballpark and asked Lou if he could sit in the dugout during the game with me—you know how much Lance loves that. Lou said it was no problem, but I guess I should have known that, with the Yankees, something that simple would blow up somehow.

Big Ken Kaiser was umpiring and evidently he forgot the brush he uses to sweep off home plate. Kaiser started yelling at one of the batboys, who was about eight years old and didn't understand what Kaiser wanted. Kaiser, I think, went overboard and started screaming at the kid.

George was sitting up in his box and noticed the commotion on the field, so, of course, he comes down to the dugout to stick his nose in. George sees two batboys, one 14 or 15 years old and then this little eight-year-old. I'm sitting there on the bench with Lance on my lap, so he doesn't get into any trouble.

George walks over to Lou and says, "Where'd that batboy come from?" Lou says he didn't know. So George calls the little kid over to him and asks, "Son, who told you that you could be batboy?"

The little kid, who is more than a little nervous by now, says softly: "Mr. Winfield."

As you can imagine, the word "Winfield" gets George all steamed. He tells the kid to sit beside me and Lance the rest of the game so he won't get hurt. Then George tells Lou there's only one person with the authority to delegate batboys, and that's Marsh Samuel, the Yankees' spring training coordinator who wears those wild-looking slacks.

George tells Lou to tell Winfield he wants to see him in his office after the game. I don't know what happened in there, but later a notice was pinned on the bulletin board: "No children will be permitted in the clubhouse. Only boys designated as batboys will be allowed in. Children of players can only come in after the game."

That's our George: he exercises his power whenever he can. The man's a mindblower.

Natalie couldn't come down with Nancy and Lance because she's on a class trip to New York. My girl's really been traveling a lot and I'm happy for her. I know when we were young we didn't have the opportunity or financial support to go to places like New York and California. I hope the travel will help her out down the line because the more you can see and get out when you're young, the more it's going to help you later in life.

Lance is following in our footsteps: baseball and fishing— that's all he wants to do. Sound familiar?

When Lance first came down he showed up carrying his bat, glove, and ball. The first thing he wanted to do when we got back to the Bonaventure Resort, where I've been staying, is play catch. We didn't hit any, because there wasn't enough room, so I let him pitch in game conditions. I was calling the balls and strikes, setting up situations for him. Gosh, Knucks, I'm amazed at the kid's talent for being only eight.

By the way, if you see PT, tell him Lance and I send our best. He's got a great shot at the major leagues if he can work on his control. When he was at Florida Southern he had trouble getting his fastball over and would fall behind hitters. But PT throws in the high 80s and he's got a pretty good curve and change-up. Being left-handed, he's got a future with the Indians if they let him develop at his own pace.

Well, Knucks, I want you to go out and have a birthday drink on me. Maybe a moon shooter? Sure wish I was there to have one with you, but we'll make up for it, I'm sure.

—Joe

April 3. Friday. Buffalo, New York

Joe:

Just got in from Arizona. I'm supposed to pitch in an exhibition game tomorrow, but I don't think I will because it's snowing outside right now and I'm told it's been raining pretty steady up here for a couple of days.

The way our rotation is set up, I'll follow Tom Candiotti and Greg Swindell and start, weather permitting, Thursday in Toronto. This season, my 24th in the major leagues, and I still feel the butterflies like a rookie this time of the year.

We ended spring training in Tucson with a loss to Milwaukee. Joe, the Brewers are a team to keep your eye on. They are being picked pretty much for last, but they've got talent and I think they're going to surprise people.

Oh, yes, thanks for the birthday present. It was quite a surprise and the Indians really put on a nice party for me.

Joe Carter called a team meeting and you know something is up, when it's both April Fools' Day *and* your birthday. So I walked into the clubhouse a little cautiously because I didn't know what might happen.

They brought in a birthday cake and sang to me and gave me a blue denim jacket I can wear when I go fishing. Then I heard somebody yell, "Cut the cake, cut the cake!"

Someone handed me a kitchen knife, and just as I was ready to cut it Tony Bernazard pushed his way through and said: "Wait, the cake's sour, it's bad."

Like a dummy, I put my head down to smell it, and as soon as I did, I felt a hand on the back of my head—Ernie Camacho's hand. He was supposed to push my face into the cake, but he didn't shove hard enough and I came up with just a little icing on the tip of my nose. Everybody got on Ernie for not doing the job.

Then Carter gave me your card and brought out the tricycle you got me. I liked the license plate with "PHIL" on it. It really got to me, Joe. I thought you might send me a card, but I wasn't expecting anything like that. You really shouldn't have.

I jumped on the bike and rode during the morning session. The guys were throwing in the outfield and I was out there pedaling my three-wheeler. I think I got as tired from riding the bike as the other pitchers did from running. There wasn't much air in the tires, and with all the high grass out there, by the time I got through I was worn out.

Corrales made me take it off the field; he was ticked off at Mel Hall for not doing some sort of exercise, so Pat really wasn't in the mood for me to be clowning around.

The bike's going back to Cleveland with me. I might ride it from the hotel to the ballpark on a nice day if the traffic's not too bad.

How about that Bobby Knight? I don't know why I didn't pick Indiana to win the NCAA tournament when I know the coach like I do. Bobby sure knows how to get the most out of what he's got. To me, that's what managing's all about.

I remember meeting Bobby through our old neighborhood

marbles champion, and a pretty good basketball player, John Havlicek, when John and Bobby played together at Ohio State. I've been watching Bobby's career ever since and the man knows how to get the job done on the basketball court.

That's it for now. Let's get ready for a big season because I know exciting things are going to happen to both of us.

—Phil

April 6. Monday. Fort Lauderdale, Florida

Phil:

It was Opening Day today for the Yankees in Detroit and I felt a little strange still being in Florida. I missed all the excitement, but at least I'm in the rotation, the fifth starter. They wanted me to pitch one more time down here before I join the team. I'm not so stubborn I can't understand that reasoning. It looks like my first start of the season is April 12 in Kansas City.

We've got a one-game lead on you guys since we beat Detroit and Jack Morris 2-1. Rasmussen pitched seven strong innings for us; the only run he gave up was a monster home run to Larry Herndon. It's 440 feet to center in Tiger Stadium, and I heard Herndon hit it to dead center off the facing of the upper deck. He either has his bat corked or the ball's livelier. Herndon doesn't usually have power like that to that part of a ballpark.

Righetti came in and pitched three good innings to close it out. Like I told you earlier, Rags had a rough spring, but an outing like today's can really take care of any doubts. We all knew he was a better pitcher than he showed this spring and that he'd be back to his usual self when the bell rang.

Boston got Clemens back; he ended his 29-day walkout in time to start the season, and I hear he's going to get $2 million for two years if he gets all the incentives. The Red Sox knew they didn't have a chance of defending their American League East title without Clemens.

We beat Baltimore in our last spring training game, and Danny Pasqua hit a bomb off Ken Dixon over the right-field fence.

The wind was blowing out, but Danny still got it all; it measured at 540 feet. I've never seen a ball hit that far. God, is this kid strong. If he can be a little more disciplined as a hitter, laying off the breaking balls and change-ups and just picking out his pitch, I swear Danny's got 40 home runs in him.

Just as I suspected, George wasn't too pleased with my last outing of the spring. I gave up five runs against Minnesota; the 10 hits were all singles, and four of them didn't get out of the infield. I thought I threw pretty well, actually, and Mark Connor thought so, too. Lou didn't say anything to me.

The way I judge my knuckleball is by what the batters are doing with it. If they are hitting line drives over the shortstop or hitting the ball out, it's pretty obvious it's not moving. Like I said, there were maybe three line drives and the rest were worm-beaters that either did or didn't get out of the infield. That's when I know my knuckleball is moving, and it has been my last couple of times out.

The next day, as soon as I arrived at the ballpark, Stan Williams, the Yankees' assistant pitching coach and "eye in the sky" for ball games, told me to be in the film room at 9:30. I watched myself on a split screen: one half was my good game against Texas and the other half was the game against Minnesota. I didn't see much difference. I had a good knuckleball in both games and there was no change in my delivery.

Funny thing was, when we were watching the films, Stan asked me if my arm or back were bothering me. I wanted to know what made him ask that. Stan said, "The man upstairs"—You know who that is—said I got under a couple of knuckleballs and he thought my arm was hurting.

I told Stan to tell the "man upstairs" my arm and back are fine and I'm ready to start the season.

Statements and insinuations like that make me feel like they're looking for an excuse, or waiting for me to mess up, to dump me. I felt all along that if I didn't have this two-year guaranteed contract that I wouldn't even have been invited to spring training. I don't know why they don't want me to feel wanted. I realize they have a lot of good arms and promising kids they want to look at, but I don't think the Yankees are in a position to turn away pitchers with proven track records.

I know what I'm up against. I can't have a bad week, a bad game, a bad inning, or a bad batter, or I'll be packing my bags. That's not too much pressure is it, Knucks? Can it be like this anywhere else?

At least they haven't sent me down to Columbus, which is what happened to Army, Mike Armstrong. They did it to him in a pretty rotten way, too, if you ask me. I walked into the clubhouse the other morning and from the look on Army's face, you knew something happened. He was severely pissed; I mean smoke seemed to be pouring out of his ears.

Here's what happened: Army was having breakfast and reading the Fort Lauderdale newspaper. He was reading the baseball roundup and got to a paragraph that said: "Right-hander Mike Armstrong was optioned to Columbus of the International League."

Nobody had told him. That's a pretty tough way to find out you're going to Triple A.

I heard that they had been looking for him the day before to tell him, but they couldn't find him. I'm sure. Army said he stayed around the clubhouse a long time after that last game because it was the day before another payday of meal money. Usually that's when they send guys down. Army said he purposely waited around long enough so that if they were sending him down he could find out and stop all the wondering. When he went home, Army thought he'd dodged another bullet—until he picked up the morning newspaper.

Army said he wanted to have a meeting with Piniella and somebody from the front office about it. I'd love to be a fly in that room.

Since I'm writing about sad stories, how about Dwight Gooden? What a tragedy.

Here's a kid who had New York right where he wanted it, making a ton of money, the star pitcher for the world champion

New York Mets, and he gets picked up. Well, not exactly picked up—he admitted himself to a drug rehabilitation center. I hope this is not another "Superstar turns Druggie" story.

Living in Lakeland I've been reading about Dwight's problems with the Tampa police, and you just hoped drugs were not behind it. It's a sad day for baseball, a sad day for kids. I hope the rehab center can get him straightened out, because with what he has accomplished in such a short time, he was working on a potential Hall of Fame career. Now he had this black mark to overcome.

A couple more years, Nolan Ryan, Tom Seaver, Steve Carlton, Mike Schmidt, Pete Rose, Reggie Jackson, the Niekros, we'll all be out of the game. Baseball needs talent like Dwight Gooden's to keep the game strong and popular.

I know Dwight Gooden is not a bad kid—maybe weak when it came to drugs and resisting temptation from his running mates—but not a bad individual. I remember the first time I pitched against him in New York in 1985—my last season with the Astros before getting traded to the Yankees; Dwight beat me 2–1. I think I had him 1–0 going into the eighth when the Mets scored twice.

Joe Sambito, my old buddy with the Astros, was with the Mets then and I went over to their clubhouse to get him before going out to dinner. Dwight came up to me from behind and said, "Mr. Niekro, it was a pleasure pitching against you." Knucks, you know that doesn't happen very often, especially coming from a kid who's got the world on a string.

That really impressed me about Dwight, and even after this drug incident, that's the impression I still have of him. I just hope he can put the problem behind him, pick himself up, and do what he's capable of doing in this game.

On a brighter note, I got your T-shirts the other day. We're starting the season with 524 combined wins, that's five shy of Jim and Gaylord Perry's record for victories by brothers. I love the idea of starting the season wearing the T-shirt that says "Six more," then after one of us wins, we switch to the T-shirt that says "Five more," and on down the line.

I have just one problem. You've got the record-breaking shirt reading "531"; our record will be 530. We're going to have to get that last shirt changed to "530." You must have messed up counting somewhere.

Whatever, I know I'll wear my T-shirts with pride, and maybe we can put on "530" within the month. You know, if we can get four combined wins right off the bat, the record-tying victory and maybe even the record breaker could happen in that Yankee-Indian series in Cleveland, April 23–26.

Now that would be theater: the Niekros back in their home state, going for the Perrys' record, maybe even going head-to-head. I know Mom and Dad would be mighty proud, but awful nervous.

Let's get it done.

—Joe

April 9. Thursday. Toronto.

Dear Joe:

Well, the Indians finally won a game. Your big brother was on the mound and we made history. Not bad for an April afternoon.

I'm writing this while we fly back to Cleveland with a 1–2 record; tomorrow's our home opener against Baltimore and we're coming home one excited ball club.

It wasn't exactly an impressive start: I was in a bases-loaded jam in the first. I threw Ernie Whitt a sinker and he hit it to Bernazard at second to get out of it. I felt good. It was one of those days when I was on the mound at the right time; I left after five innings leading 7–3, and we ended up winning 14–3. Our hitters were all over Blue Jay starter Joe Johnson, a former Brave.

Why Corrales took me out, I don't know. The fifth was my best inning: 1–2–3. I came in and Pat told me that was it. It ticked me off, but I kept it to myself. It looks like spring training all over again—five innings and hit the showers. I just hope that's not his plan for me all season. If he thinks I'm just a four- or five-inning pitcher, he ought to move me to long relief and put somebody out there to start he believes can pitch a complete game. I don't think they should look at me as strictly a five-inning pitcher, especially when I'm feeling and throwing as well as I am.

Lefty, Steve Carlton, came in and shut out the Blue Jays for the last four innings. It was the first time two 300-game winners pitched for the same team in the same game. It was neat knowing Lefty and I made some history together. I hope we can do it again, but I'd rather have it be me going seven or eight and then have Carlton finish up the last one or two. I've known for many years, though, you can't always have it your way.

Besides making me 1–0 and giving me career victory number 312, that's 525 for us, little brother. Five more and the Perrys are in our rear-view mirror. You pitch Sunday in Kansas City; go get 526.

They are expecting over 60,000 for our home opener in big old Cleveland's Municipal Stadium. It's supposed to be around 65 degrees, so it should be a fun day. Northern Ohio is really pumped up about the Tribe, especially after all that upbeat preseason publicity. I hope all the prognosticators picking us to win the AL East aren't setting us up for a big fall. We've got great offensive talent with Joe Carter, Cory Snyder, Pat Tabler, Julio Franco, Brook Jacoby, Brett Butler, Mel Hall, and Andy Thornton. I just hope our defense gives the pitching a chance to hold the other team down. We can't score 14 runs every day.

Opening day is usually an exciting event for me, but up in Toronto, it was cold and rainy, and Jimmy Key, quite frankly, stuck the bats up our ass. If he keeps throwing like that, Key's got a chance to win the Cy Young Award. The Blue Jays look just like I thought they would: tough. They've got good starting pitchers, a great bullpen, and with that outfield of George Bell, Lloyd Moseby, and Jesse Barfield, you know they are going to hurt some pitching staffs. The one player they probably can't afford to lose, though, is shortstop Tony Fernandez, who's probably second only to Ozzie Smith.

I said before spring training that you guys and the Blue Jays had to be favored in our division. We feel like we can compete with you guys, but we're long shots at best because our pitching is basically unproven and I'm still not sure about our defense.

This will come as no surprise: after one game I went to the Kon Tiki at the Westin for some of that good Polynesian food. I can eat that sweet stuff all night. I pulled away from the table before I blew my spring training diet in one night.

I thought about getting Camacho and going fishing up here on our off day, but I shipped my gear from Tucson directly to Cleveland and I didn't feel like buying any new stuff.

Give those Royals hell Sunday, will you?

—Phil

P.S.: You're right, I did mess up counting somewhere on those T-shirts. I'm glad they didn't count on me to keep track of our victories.

April 16. Thursday. New York.

Philip Henry:

Believe it or not, we had a real, honest-to-goodness day off today, and George didn't even have us work out. I guess he must like our 6–3 start after we swept you and the Indians three games at Yankee Stadium.

You guys are really struggling right now, but you can tell you have a better ball club than 1–8. If it goes down to the wire and I'm still on this team—and I have my doubts—I want it to be a two-team race between the Yankees and Indians. May the best team win.

Knucks, you had a good knuckleball against us Tuesday night—you just couldn't get it over the plate. I was rooting for the Tribe to get you off the hook and they did, so you weren't stuck with that 10–6 loss.

My situation right now can best be described as murky, uncertain. I'm in the bullpen and working with Hoyt Wilhelm, the old knuckleball master, at George's insistence. Nobody's saying too much to me right now; Lou did ask me if I've been working with Hoyt.

I guess I've been in the doghouse since my start in Kansas City. The box score didn't look too good—$4\frac{1}{3}$ innings, seven hits, five earned runs, and we lost 8–2—but I thought I threw better than that. I don't want to name anybody, but I thought a couple of plays could have been made that might have helped me out.

Naturally, I got killed in the New York newspapers, far worse than I deserved. The headlines shouted: "Royals rip Niekro."

That's when George brought in Hoyt. They said I'm not getting the spin off the ball on my knuckler. If I'd have had a good game, I don't know if I'd have heard any of that or seen Hoyt or not. Anyway, I'm dealing with it and hoping to learn something from Hoyt so I can get another start and make George look like a genius.

Is it too much to want to pitch for a ball club that won't shove you aside after one bad ball game? It's times like this I think a change of scenery for me might not be a bad idea. Listen to me, one start in April and already I'm talking about getting out. See what the Crankees can do to you?

As if things aren't going badly enough for me, I got kicked in the teeth at the Yankees' annual "Welcome Home" banquet.

You remember what it's like. Everybody sits at a long head table and gets introduced. Art Rust, a New York radio broadcaster, was the emcee, and I felt like he really did a number on me. He's introducing this guy and that guy, saying he can do this or he will do that. Then Rust gets to me.

"Well, this next guy has had nothing but trouble since he joined the Yankees. Hopefully, he can do better. Joe Niekro."

Nice intro. I wondered how long he prepared for it. It really ticked me off and the guys knew it. I could have walked over and decked Rust right there. I mean, what was the guy trying to do? It's like he wanted to say, "Hey, this guy's got a bad rap and we're going to keep getting on him until we run him out of town."

Then there was this piece in the *New York Post* by Steve Wilder, a guy I thought I was fairly friendly with. Bob Tewksbury got sent down to Columbus. I didn't think he deserved it, but guys who don't deserve crap have to take it around here all the time. Wilder writes about Tewk's demotion and he ends the article with something like, "And for all you Bob Tewksbury fans out there, if you were wondering why it wasn't Joe Niekro to go, Niekro has a two-year guaranteed contract. That's why the Yankees didn't let Niekro go."

Maybe that was the truth, but there's no reason for a writer to put that in the newspaper without direct quotes from someone in the front office—unless the writer is trying to do a hatchet job on the player. It certainly ticked me off. I realize most of the people in the organization are down on me right now, and now some of the press guys are kicking me like a dog.

What did I do? I've had one start, it didn't go well, but I don't think I stunk the place out. I had a decent enough spring to earn a spot in the rotation. It's like they *want* me to pitch badly so they can get my butt out of here; that's sounding better and better all the time.

They've got the "Gator Watch" in the newspapers every day, anticipating Ron Guidry's return in May. Gator's a helluva pitcher and there's no doubt he'll get into the rotation once he returns. But why there is this campaign to make me the fall guy, I have no idea.

Bob Shirley and I kid each other about which one of us is going to drop through the trapdoor. Right now, I feel like I've got one foot dangling.

That's enough about me and my dark cloud. The club's playing well. This probably is the most talent I've ever been around. Don Mattingly is regarded as the best player in the game. Dave Winfield has been a perennial All-Star in both leagues. There's no better leadoff hitter in the game than Rickey Henderson. We have Willie Randolph at second, Rags coming out of the pen to close games out.

A guy who's a lot better ballplayer than I thought is Gary Ward. He's a quiet, Don Baylor type of leader. When Donnie was here he was the leader and everybody looked up to him. Wardo's got that quality, too. He's a guy who's been around for quite a while with Minnesota and Texas and never been with a winner. He can see the same thing about this ball club I do. He's really excited about having a chance to win it all. You'd like his intensity, Knucks.

Wasn't that something about Al Campanis? What a shame he had to resign as general manager of the Los Angeles Dodgers because of the unbelievable racial comments he made on the ABC "Nightline" show.

I was watching something else that night, but I saw some film clips of Ted Koppel's interview. It was amazing. I don't think Campanis realized what he was saying, which is no excuse, but it makes it all the more incredible. After the Dwight Gooden stuff, baseball sure didn't need more bad publicity like that.

As far as I'm concerned, blacks certainly have the "necessities" to manage and I would have no trouble playing for one. I've seen some white guys who probably didn't have the necessities to manage, but it didn't stop the ball club from hiring them. Nobody can tell me a Don Baylor or a Joe Morgan, maybe even Bill Madlock, couldn't manage.

I don't think the public realizes how well white and black and Latin players get along in the clubhouse. We're all ballplayers—that's the bottom line. It's when you get the white-collar executives or the redneck old-timers involved that the racism comes into play. Players are together for seven months of the year. We travel together, eat together, shower together. I've never seen a problem with players mixing.

I feel sorry for Campanis; he's been a great man for baseball and the Dodgers' organization. It's just too bad a man with his background, his knowledge of the game, and his accomplishments has to go out on such a sorry note. I'm sure if he could do it all over again, he'd have made his remarks in a different way. I think he meant well, but he just got a couple of sentences mixed up in his mind. I don't think he's a racist, but, unfortunately, in many people's minds he's branded as one now.

Belated congratulations, big boy, on your getting number 525 a few days ago in Toronto. Tell your guys to save some of those runs; they don't need to waste 14 in one game for you. I know you like to pitch more than five innings, but as they say, "Five and fly." That's the bit about pitching: you have to go five innings to get a win, but you can throw one bad pitch to the first batter in the first inning and you can get the loss. When I feel like ragging on a hitter, I always ask him, "Can you take an 0 for 4 on one at-bat?" They can't say a whole lot to that one.

And old Lefty Carlton finished up for you; the old-timers took it to the Blue Jays. I love it. Tell Steve thanks for saving number 525. This very minute I'm wearing my "Five more" T-shirt under my dress shirt.

It's amazing to me how close we are to this record and there are still a lot of people in baseball who don't even know it. I mean this is an all-time record. We sure aren't getting the hoopla Pete Rose got when he was chasing Ty Cobb's hit record. Maybe we're not flashy like Pete. I remember when he was within 100 hits of Cobb, most every newspaper had a countdown to the record. With only five wins to go, I don't think it would be too much for us to get a countdown, too.

It's not that we're begging for publicity, but when you think you're about to accomplish something special in baseball, you want it to be recognized. Here we are, both in our 40s, still pitching, and about to set a record I don't think will ever be broken. I can't imagine two brothers playing 20-plus years each and staying healthy enough to win even 500 games again.

What the hell, we'll know we did it, and I know two people back in Lansing, Ohio—not to mention a group at the Sportsmen's Club there—who will feel mighty proud.

By the way, I talked to Mom and Dad the other night and they sound terrific. I know Dad can't travel anymore, but if we happen to go for the record later this month in Cleveland, I'll pray to God he could somehow get to Cleveland Stadium for it. To see him and Mom together the moment the record is broken would be a highlight of my life, and I'm sure it would be for you, too.

Good luck on your next start.

—Joseph Franklin

April 18. Saturday. Baltimore.

Brother:

We're down, Joe. Really down.

After reading and hearing all that great stuff about ourselves all winter and spring, nobody can believe this team is 1–10. That's the worst start the Indians have had since they were 1–15 in 1962.

Heads are hanging, asses are dragging. And the scariest thing about it is we've still got 151 games to go. If we keep playing like this, we're going to finish 50 games out. We'll make the 1962 Mets seem like the 1927 Yankees when it's all over.

The only people who look worse than the Cleveland Indians are the people who picked the Cleveland Indians to win the pennant. You've heard about the danger of reading your own press clippings? This team is living that. *Sports Illustrated*, *The Sporting News*, *The New York Times*, a lot of well-respected writers picked us to beat you guys and Toronto this year.

So many people jumped on the bandwagon, the axle broke and the wheels fell off.

We couldn't play any worse if we were throwing the games. The pitching has been atrocious, and that includes me, I'm afraid. We're giving up home runs, walking guys after being ahead in the count, and everybody's stealing bases on us. Our team ERA has to be at least my age. We've got to be leading the league in getting our asses kicked and in red faces. It's embarrassing for all of us.

We know our pitching's not great, but we think it's good enough in this division, no insult intended to you guys. We're going to score runs, there's no doubt about that with the sticks we've got.

What we've got to do is catch the ball better, throw to the right bases, hit the cutoff man, turn the double play. Teams that are picked to win the pennant are supposed to do those things. We're really sloppy.

We can't keep thinking we can win by outhitting people every day. As far as I can tell, one of the worst things the Indians' management has done is take the team's .282 batting average in

1986, the best in the major leagues, too seriously. Bobby Bonds, our hitting coach—and you know what a fantastic player he was for the Giants—told me in spring training he thought we could hit .290 as a team this season.

That shows how offensive-minded the Indians are. We have talent to deal for pitching—teams were lining up for Brett Butler, Brook Jacoby, and Julio Franco—but we stood pat with our pitching staff.

On Opening Day in Cleveland, with 65,000 fans foaming at the mouth for us to win, we got beat 12–11 by Baltimore. We scored 11 runs and lost. When we look back, that one game, the first of 162, may say it all about this team this season.

It looks like Cal Ripken Sr. has turned the Baltimore ball club around. Ray Knight, an old National League opponent of ours from Georgia, looked great at third base and killed us with the bat.

It was great getting back to New York, even though you guys handed us our asses three straight. That crowd of 50,000 on Opening Day at Yankee Stadium brought back some special memories. I heard fans in the stands yelling, "Wish you were back!" Some said, "George was nuts to let you go."

If the people back there really knew what happened—hell, if I knew what happened. Somebody tell me. But I guess George doesn't have to explain releasing me to anybody. The thing I keep thinking, and what all the New York sportswriters keep telling me, is that if I had stayed on the ball club in 1986, the Yankees would've won the American League East, not the Boston Red Sox.

The Yankees had one pitcher who won in double figures that season: Rasmussen went 18–6. I was 11–11 for Cleveland and lost seven games out of the bullpen after the seventh inning. You figure with the kind of year Righetti had last year, saving a record 46 games, if he saves five of my bullpen losses that puts me at 16 wins for the third consecutive season. You guys finished five games behind the Red Sox. And don't forget I beat the Yankees one game.

I'll tell you what bothers me, Joe. Everybody asks me the questions: "What happened? Why did they release you?" I've got no damn answers for them. I know what George's lieutenants,

Clyde King and Woody Woodward, told me, and then they said they'd deny it to anyone outside the room we were in. They had the balls to release me, but they haven't got the balls to explain to the New York press or the New York fans why they did it.

It never, ever will make sense to me. You go up there and win 32 games in two years, as many as anybody else on the ball club, wear the Yankee pin stripes with as much pride and dignity as you can, and then the grateful Boss kicks your ass out the door without the courtesy of an honest explanation.

All I can come up with is age, pure and simple. George may say it's not, and I know Clyde and Woody will deny it to their deathbeds, but Clyde and Woody told me, "Between the three of us," that, yes, age was a factor in my release. I was about to turn 47. I talked to two lawyers about filing an age discrimination suit but didn't follow through.

Considering you're 42, Joe, if they end up dumping you this year, I'll bet age plays a role in that decision, too.

George always makes a big deal about what an "inspiration" older athletes like myself, George Blanda, Gordie Howe, Kareem Abdul-Jabbar are. All I know is that Big George cut *this* inspiration when I was 47 years old and coming off a 16–12 season.

I can see why nobody wants to play for George again after they leave. As much as I enjoyed the Yankees—the fans, the ballpark, the coaches, Mattingly, Guidry, Righetti, Winfield, Randolph, Nick Priore in the clubhouse, Vapor Man, Lou, Billy Martin—I would never be an employee of George Steinbrenner again. I was looking forward to pitching for Lou. We spent a lot of time together in the dugout, talking about strategy and situations, and I thought we had something good going. Evidently not.

I'm not bullshitting one bit; I don't care how much money Steinbrenner's got, he doesn't have enough to get me to put the Yankees uniform back on as long as he is commander in chief. Money is not important, not that kind of money from that kind of man. It's just a feeling deep in my heart; no way in the world would I ever play again for Steinbrenner, not in this or any other lifetime. Not as long as George sits up there in his eagle's nest, putting his players in his sights and shooting them down like they're his personal clay pigeons.

Even with our terrible record, I feel great with the Indians. I could not be happier. It's a family over here; everybody cares about what happens to everybody else. The front office just lets you play. Pitch your way in or out of the rotation; hit yourself in or out of the lineup—the way it's supposed to be. There's no big hand hovering over the ball club, ready to drop a finger on this guy, then this guy, choking the whole team with pressure.

If you pitch a good ball game for George, he pretends to like you. But if you lose a game, make an error, or go 0 for 4, he crushes you like you're an ant and he's a size-17 shoe. George thinks athletes respond to pressure, but he's never had to produce under it.

I just wish people would go to George, not me, with their questions about why I'm no longer a Yankee. He's the only one with the answer, but maybe he feels he screwed up so badly he doesn't want to say anything and bring more attention to his mistake. George is smart in devious ways like that—yet so dumb in common sense.

Being in New York also made me think about what you were saying, Joe, about Dwight Gooden; what a tragic tale if he can't come back to his original form. All I know about cocaine is that it's a drug that has done its damage to baseball. I've never seen it; I'd like to think that's because nobody I know uses it. But it could be they know how I stand on it and they respect me enough not to bring it out in front of me.

The last few years I was with the Braves they had some problems with marijuana, and they weeded those players out fast. One road trip I was invited into a hotel room, and it didn't take long to smell what they were smoking. Same thing happened to me when I went to a party in Cincinnati. I did the same thing in both situations: left without even good-bye to the hosts. I figured if they were going to let that go on, I didn't have to worry about a formal farewell.

To me, drugs are like doctoring baseballs; I'd be too afraid I'd get caught. You never know who's waiting to turn you in. The

Pittsburgh drug trials put a scare in every teams' clubhouse, and I think the game's been cleaned up considerably the last three years.

Joe, we're not winning, so you've got to get the next one toward the Perrys' record; it will be just like me winning, as far as I'm concerned. Let's get this thing rockin' and rollin'. Getting 530 is going to be so special I can't wait.

All the best.

—Phil

April 29. Wednesday. Arlington, Texas

Phil:

We lost a tough one tonight. How tough was it? It was so tough I even got a call in the bullpen. Can you believe that? I thought Piniella forgot I was out there. It's been seven days since I pitched.

Charlie Hudson, who's had a good April, got in trouble against Texas in the first inning and the call came for Bullet Bob Shirley and Joe "Nowhere Man" Niekro to warm up. Charlie pitched out of it and did pretty well after that. Once we got past the third inning, I knew I could take off my uniform and sit in the bullpen in my underwear for the rest of the game, because they weren't going to call me.

Afterward, I got cornered by the press: Claire Smith, Tommy Pedulla, and Mike Martinez. They were asking the pitchers' for their thoughts now that the Gator Watch is down to a couple of days. As I told them, "I've been playing long enough to know that my thoughts don't mean a damn thing, especially on this club." I keep calling myself a right-handed Bob Shirley. This organization is going to do whatever it wants, and I'm sure they've got the gameplan set in their minds already.

Maybe there's a trade in the works. I want to pitch; my arm and back are fine. Until I get back out there, there's nothing I can do about my situation. If they trade me, that's fine with me; if they release me, I hope somebody picks me up. I know I can still do the job, and I'd like to think there are some people in baseball who think I can, too. It's down to two days on the Gator Watch and people are getting itchy, including me. If I'm the odd man out, that's the way the old ball bounces. At this point, I won't be heartbroken.

After our day-off workout here Monday, I rented a car and drove down to Houston to see old friends. I hadn't been back to the Astrodome since I was traded to the Yankees. It took me three hours to get down there, but it was worth it.

I walked around the Astrodome and it brought back fond memories: back-to-back 20-win seasons, my 100th and 200th career victories, pitching 10 shutout innings against Philadelphia in the 1980 playoffs. My 11 years in Houston definitely were the prime of my career, and I'll admit I miss pitching for the Astros quite a bit.

Like you do with the Braves, I always check the box scores to see how my old teammates are going: my old knuckleball catcher Alan Ashby, Denny Walling, Billy Doran, Craig Reynolds, Nolan Ryan, Terry Puhl, Dave Smith. Old teammates are like family, you're always concerned about them.

We've really been playing well—9-0 at home, which should make the Boss happy. In 1986 we struggled at home, only two games over .500, and I think that's the main reason we didn't win the division. Even though Milwaukee got off to that record-tying 13-0 start, we're still only 3½ games back, which has to be a little disheartening to the Brewers.

Our pitching has been much better than people thought. All the preseason publications said the Yankees' strength was supposed to be offense, and the pitching was supposed to be terrible. So far, our pitching and right-handed hitters—Winfield, Ward, Randolph, and Henderson—have carried us. Our left-handed hitters—Mattingly, Mike Pagliarulo, and Pasqua—haven't gotten it going yet.

I really don't know why I'm not pitching, because the saying around here is that you're only as good as your last game, and my last one was good. I took a no-hitter into the seventh against Detroit April 21st before John Grubb's line drive hit me on the wrist and they took me out. We won 3-1—it made me 1-1 for the season, number 214 for my career and 526 for us. I put on my "Four more" T-shirt for the interviews that night.

It's amazing how your feelings swing with this club. If you pitch badly, they start pressuring you, and all you can think about is getting the hell out. But when you win, there's nothing like being on top in New York. Trouble is, you can be on the bottom in a day or two. It's such a fragile existence and such a furious descent.

My win against Detroit was also a positive reflection on Hoyt and the work he's been doing with me, which I am pleased about. He's really helped me, Knucks. He's got me throwing my knuckleball higher in the strike zone. Hoyt noticed in Florida that my knuckleball was moving good, but a lot of times it would break out of the strike zone. I was throwing them too low. So I've been throwing them higher and a little easier, too, and I've been around the plate more.

I call Hoyt my guru, my roommate in the clubhouse. After learning the knuckleball from Dad, and getting advice from the two greatest knuckleball pitchers of all time—you and Hoyt—I feel like I've been taught by the best. I hope I can pass what I've learned along to Lance, or any kid who really has an interest in throwing our strange pitch.

Of course, I missed another Easter with the family. By the way, big brother, happy Easter to you. Did you color any eggs? I called Mom and Dad and wished them a happy Easter. I called home and Natalie was in Orlando for a modeling convention. I hate having our family so spread out for holidays—those are the times we're supposed to be together. Maybe when our baseball careers are over, it will change.

All that's on everybody's mind right now is the last couple of days of the Gator Watch and whose head will roll when Guidry returns.

Keep your fingers crossed for me, big brother.

—Joe

May: "Racing in Different Directions"

May 1. Friday. Kansas City.

Joe:

No. 527 is history, little brother.

Rich Yett and I shut out Kansas City 2–0. God, I felt good; went $7\frac{1}{3}$ innings this time, allowing six hits. After the fifth, even with a shutout going, I looked over at Corrales to see if his hook was reaching out for me. Pat gave me until the tying run came to the plate before bringing in Yett, who wasted no time recording the final five outs.

Took my shower and put on the T-shirt, "Three more," for the postgame interviews.

Not only are we closing in on the Perrys' record for brothers, this win puts me at 313, one back of Gaylord Perry for 11th on the all-time list. When I sit and think that with two more victories, the only pitchers in the history of baseball with more wins than me will be Cy Young, Walter Johnson, Christy Mathewson, Grover Cleveland Alexander, Warren Spahn, Kid Nichols, Pud Galvin, Tim Keefe, John Clarkson, and my teammate Lefty Carlton, it almost takes my breath away.

I know I've got to win more than two, though, if I want to stay 11th. Don Sutton, our old adversary from the National League going back to 1966, is in the California Angels' rotation again, and he came into this season only one win behind me.

This was our third win in a row, first time we've won three straight this season. It brought us to five games under .500, 9–14, but with those red-hot Brewers at 19–3 and playing out of their minds, we're still 10 games out.

We're playing much better, Joe. We're up to major-league caliber now. For a while, we played barely Double A ball.

All three wins have been by one run. After we shut out the Royals, a team that has a chance to go to the World Series every year, the clubhouse was more alive than it's been since spring training. Everybody hopes this is the start of a hot streak and that our dog days are already behind us.

Maybe the reason I feel like the Indians are a tightly knit ball club is because our clubhouse is so small, everybody can't help but get to know each other well. If the guy two lockers down doesn't use deodorant, you know it. If a guy goes to the toilet and takes a dump and doesn't flush it, everybody knows it. Our quarters are that close.

Are all trainers great guys? Seems so. Ours sure are—Jim Warfield and Paul Spicuzza. In their room there's a whirlpool with "U.S.S. Thunder" on it. "Thunder" is the nickname for Andy Thornton, the team captain. If Andy's not sitting in it, I usually am, so there's a running dialog between us about who's going to captain the ship first that day.

I've been having so much fun I even bought a baseball cap and had "U.S.S. Thunder" sewn on the front, and now I wear it whenever I'm sitting in the whirlpool. I love ragging on Andy about it. I tell him that if he's not sitting in the whirlpool, I call up to Joe Klein in the front office and ask if I have permission to board the U.S.S. Thunder.

That's pretty much the tone of our clubhouse. Lots of laughs, lots of football talk and agitating. The equipment manager, Cy Buynak, and his boys create a family atmosphere. Even with the long faces after losses, this is probably the most pure fun I've had in a clubhouse, anywhere, as far as good fellowship and happiness.

How about Corrales checking Tommy John's glove for sand-paper when you guys played in Cleveland last week? TJ was pitching great, but Pat thought the old left-hander was doing some-thing abnormal with the ball in his glove. When Pat went out to have Tommy checked, Pat swears he saw Tommy drop something off the back of the mound. The umpires, of course, didn't find anything because by that time the Yankee infielders had closed in around the mound and probably covered it or got rid of it somehow.

The umpires didn't do anything because they didn't find any-thing on him. But a little hole the size of a quarter in the pocket of TJ's glove sure was suspicious.

TJ is playing this "Does he or doesn't he scuff?" stuff like Gaylord Perry used to. Tommy loves people thinking he's a doctor on the mound. After the game, Tommy told the press about Cor-rales, "I'd like to thank him" for putting the thought in all the hitters' minds.

But TJ pitched seven one-hit innings. The man's about to turn 44 and he ties the hitters up like that—and they say the old men can't pitch. Horseshit.

What's the inside scoop over there, little brother? Tell your big brother the truth about old TJ. Does he or doesn't he? I'd like to know. If you're having trouble, maybe TJ can teach you something.

Get back to me on that, will you? I haven't heard any good baseball gossip in a while.

Lefty Carlton and I are getting to be something of a quiniela. He has relieved me in four of my five starts, and the team has won three of them. Imagine: 325 wins coming in to relieve 313 wins. I get a kick out of that.

I'd heard a lot about Lefty—mostly how he doesn't talk to the press—but never knew him before he came to the Indians. The thing that has impressed me about Steve is his dedication at age 42 once he gets to the ballpark.

Sometimes guys get lost for a half hour or an hour after they get to the ballpark. You might not see Steve for a while, but it's because he's so involved with his physical routine he doesn't want to do it where anybody can watch him. He's one of the best competitors I've been around—no wonder he's the 10th winningest pitcher of all time.

I wonder sometimes why Carlton doesn't talk to reporters. I realize there are reporters who can blow things out of proportion or quote things wrong, or take a hatchet to you, but you just have to write off those individuals. The majority still give you a fair shake if you are fair and honest with them.

Everybody knows what a connoisseur of wine Lefty is. He collects wines, knows about the growers, the vineyards of France, the good years, the exceptional harvests. Dempsey and I went out to dinner with Lefty and he insisted on buying the wine. It was a good thing because Rick wouldn't know good toilet water from bad, and I'm not much better.

Anyway, now it's your turn to put another win on our pile. Three more to 530, Joe-Joe. Do it, little brother.

—Phil

May 5. Tuesday. Chicago.

Phil:

I think I threw a wrench in the Yankees' plans today. I pitched a two-hitter and lost 2–0 to a kid named Bill Long with the White Sox. What can I say? I was good, but he was better. Our hitters couldn't do anything with him—we had just two hits, too.

Since I hadn't pitched in two weeks, I really was pleased. I had an outstanding knuckleball, and Piniella and Connor had to see that. Working with Hoyt Wilhelm has helped. I had my doubts when he first told me to throw the knuckleball higher in the strike zone. As you know, you don't want to put anything up in the hitter's eyes. But it seems to be moving more up there and I'm happy with the results.

I hope I can pitch this well and win next time, and really make it tough for them to dump me when Guidry comes back. Gator's pitching in Class A, so I think he'll join us on our West Coast trip the middle of the month.

It's my guess that whoever's pitching the worst will be the one out of the rotation when they put Gator back on the roster. Trouble is, everybody's pitching well right now. I have no idea who might get the ax.

Pitching like I did for Chicago was exactly what I needed. I'd gotten some bad press the other day that I thought might not only hurt me when Gator comes back, but also should I happen to get released.

USA Today had a free-agent watch for guys like Guidry, Tim Raines, Rich Gedman coming back this month. The headline said: "May Day arrives; free agents go home at last." There was a graphic and story about the free agents and the guys they'd be replacing. Evidently, at least in this article, Guidry is replacing Joe Niekro. It was by a guy named Mel Antonen. His opinion, but it ticked me off.

They took Guidry's April statistics from 1986 and compared them to my stats of this April. It's amazing how writers can set things up anyway they want to make a story. The conditions of Guidry's and my Aprils were different; there are factors that go beyond the numbers and can't be computed. I thought it was horseshit.

The article went on about me being the likely man out of the rotation because I've missed two starts with a sore back. Here's a guy who writes an article that goes all over the country, that everybody in baseball reads, and he doesn't know what the hell he's talking about. My back's not bothering me. Antonen never even talked to me; he did no research at all.

The reason I missed two starts was because we had two days off and I'm the fifth starter, so they passed me up to keep the other guys on their normal four days rest. How tough would that have been to check out? Things like that can kill a ballplayer hanging by a thread, which is just about my situation. Baseball people read that my back's giving me trouble again, which is not true, and how many do you think will take a look at me if the Yankees decide to drop me?

I thought *USA Today* owed me an apology; the Yankees' public relations director Harvey Greene thought so, too, and he gave Antonen a call. It wasn't long before I got a call back. Antonen apologized and said the material in the article was not all his, that some of it was added after he turned in the story. That's all a writer has to say—that somebody added it to his story after he went home—to get out of admitting he screwed up. I asked Antonen what kind of operation puts stuff in a story after the writer goes home? He just said that's the way *USA Today* sometimes operates.

I accepted his apology because that's how Mom and Dad brought us up, to forgive and forget. But that was after I told him the article was 100 percent pure horseshit. I gave him grief for his research and for publicizing something nationwide that was not true and could have an effect on my future—if I have one. He said he anticipated that I was the guy who would be out of the rotation once Guidry came back. I asked him if he called the Yankees. He said no. I wanted to know where he heard his information. He said he got it from a couple of reporters, to which I replied, "So, I guess a couple of reporters are running the ball club, huh?"

I know I made him feel terrible, which I wanted to do so he'll never screw a ballplayer from coast to coast like that again. By the end I was feeling sorry for him because he sounded like a good guy. It's just that writers don't realize how one sentence, one wrong fact, can be damaging.

Anyway, I think I got my point across.

Outstanding game you pitched against Kansas City for number 527. Looks like in a couple of weeks we'll be drinking Dom Perignon—at least I hope so.

I'd sure like to get 530 and be in a pennant race wearing these Yankee pinstripes. We've got a helluva club that's only going to get better, and Milwaukee is already coming back to earth; we're just $4\frac{1}{2}$ out. I still feel the team we've got to watch out for is Toronto.

Give 'em hell, old-timer.

—Joe

May 11. Monday. Cleveland.

Joe:

It rained here today, but not soon enough to save my butt. I was losing 6–3 to Texas when I got taken out in the fourth. Frank Wills pitched the fifth, and I'll be damned if we didn't finish five innings before the skies opened up and washed out the rest of the game. That's my second straight loss, and makes me 2–2.

Remember my last letter? We had just won three straight and the guys were starting to get pumped up?

My loss today was our seventh defeat in the last eight games since then. We're 11 games under .500, 11 games out of first, and asses are dragging again.

I don't know what it is about the Rangers, but I can't get guys like Larry Parrish and Pete O'Brien out; Oddibe McDowell gives me fits, too. How do you throw those guys, Joe? Any tips?

Yesterday was Mother's Day, as you know, but it was also a mother of a day for Ernie Camacho, who got sent down to Triple A. He was supposed to be our stopper; he's got a great arm. But the fans and writers were down on him, and with Ernie being so emotional, the pressure kept building up and eventually crushed him.

Ernie's got a decent curveball, but it would get him in trouble sometimes. Some games he'd fall in love with it and throw it in situations when Corrales and Jack Aker wanted his 92-mile-per-hour heater. I think Ernie lost confidence because he couldn't pitch the way he wanted to.

Even though Corrales got into some tense sessions with Ernie, I don't think Pat was *that* down on him. But the way we're going—or rather the way we're not going—he had to make a move of some kind with the pitching staff to keep the fans interested.

And who do we get to replace Camacho? Our old buddy Army, Mike Armstrong. I still think Mike can pitch if he gets the ball over the plate. He'll feel much more at ease over here than with the Yankees. He's flying high; I hope it works out for him.

Joe, this Greg Swindell, a left-hander from Texas, is looking sharp for us. Yesterday he struck out 15—the most strikeouts by an Indians pitcher since another pretty good left-hander named Sudden Sam McDowell struck out 15 Washington Senators in 1970—in beating Kansas City 4–2. It looks like he caught on to pitching, not just throwing, in a hurry. He's not afraid to throw his change-up and off-speed stuff, and the kid's real calm out there. If he stays healthy the Indians have a helluva good-looking pitcher for quite a while.

Tell Nancy happy Mother's Day from me, will you? Our wives have done so much for us, Joe.

We still have three more to go to get to 530. Go get 'em.
—Phil

May 13. Wednesday. New York.

Phil:

Knucks, I was thinking about this the other day. Isn't it kind of ironic that Joe Niekro, lover of the Everglades, the natural habitat for alligators, would be waiting around for a Gator to determine the direction of his Yankee career?

I'm talking about Gator Guidry; what will happen when he returns to the team next week has been the hot topic for days. The latest word is that he'll join us in Anaheim and that he may be in the bullpen for a while. You know Gator will eventually start because the Yankees won't pass up a sellout crowd. But right now it's not easy to pick which starter should be dropped.

There were some quotes in the newspaper saying that Tommy John and I aren't in jeopardy; I don't know if that means as starters or as members of the pitching staff. Knucks, you and I both have been around the barn enough times to know that could be a smokescreen for a swift kick out the door. Who knows?

Surely they're not going to take Chuckin' Charlie Hudson out of the rotation the way he's going. Charlie's been outstanding; he's 5–0 with a shutout and, I guess, the hottest thing to hit New York since Dwight Gooden. Hudson is a completely different pitcher than when he was in the National League with Philadelphia. Lately

I've been thinking about what a change of scenery can sometimes do for a player, and Charlie is living proof it can turn a guy's fortunes completely around.

At this time in 1986 I was 4–0 and felt like the Big Apple was in the palm of my hand. Then after I hurt my arm I went 5–10 the rest of the way and nearly got booed out of town. New York can turn on you in a hurry, and I think Charlie knows that after what he experienced in Philadelphia.

Rhoden has won his last two starts and looks like he's finding himself. You know how good Rick is from his days with the Los Angeles Dodgers and Pittsburgh Pirates. It's a shame the American League has the designated hitter; Rick's a helluva hitter. The DH also keeps another heavy hitter out of action—me. You'll never forget that home run I hit off you in Atlanta, big brother, because I won't let you.

Rasmussen pitches pretty consistently, but gets no respect from the Yankees. How can they not be sold on a left-hander who won 18 games for them last year? All Ras needs is confidence, and you get it from people believing in you. As you know, Knucks, that's the kind of support that's lacking around this ball club. I think Ras is one of the better left-handers in the league; he's mixing in that good slow curve. He just needs to get rid of the negative feelings he has about himself, but that's what the Yankees do to you. When are they going to learn that it would be more productive for them to be pumping a guy up instead of kicking a guy's pride all the time?

It has to be me or TJ who goes if they want Gator in the rotation. TJ's had two fairly shaky games in a row, while I've been making the decision tough for them with two straight good games. I almost had number 528 for us against the White Sox. I left in the seventh leading 3–1, but Gary Redus hit Righetti's third pitch for a two-run home run to take me out of the win; we ended up winning 5–4 in 13 innings, so I was glad my start ended in victory.

I've been thinking ahead to our West Coast trip; it looks like I'll get a start in Anaheim against the Angels. What do you know about Doug DeCinces? The guy's been a thorn in my side since I came to the American League. I do pretty well with the rest of the

California ball club—Anaheim's where I had my one-hitter last year. But DeCinces seems to hit everything I throw up there.

I almost had every knuckleball pitcher's nightmare two days ago, Knucks; I damn near tore my fingernail off. I was running in the outfield and a ball came to me. Like a dummy I tried to stop it with my bare hand and tore back the fingernail on the index finger of my right hand—only the most important finger for my knuckleball.

Good old Gene Monahan fixed me up; he filed it down and put some of that "hard as nails" stuff on it. The nail was shorter than I liked, but I pitched all right with it against Chicago.

This I don't understand. We're 13–2 at home, we've run down Milwaukee and moved into a virtual tie for first place in our division, we're pulling games out in the bottom of the ninth. Yet all the headlines around here have been about Gooden pitching down in Tidewater in his comeback from drug rehab. It's amazing what people think is news. Here's a guy pitching a Triple A ball game and he gets more publicity than the Yankees, who could move into first place any day. It's sad to see a young guy like Gooden get swept up in drugs like he did, but I think the press goes overboard when these guys come back. I mean, they had pitch-by-pitch reports, and every TV station in New York interviewed him on the flight down.

There are so many guys who play for years and don't get the publicity over their entire careers that Gooden got for pitching one game in Triple A.

Knucks, you asked about Tommy John scuffing baseballs, and I forgot to respond. I honestly don't know. I've never actually seen him do anything from the dugout. I don't know about TJ any more than I know about Rhoden or Sutton or Mike Scott, and they've all been accused. The way TJ's sinker goes down, though, it wouldn't surprise me.

Paul Berry came down from Boston and brought me some "530" shirts; he's sending you some, too. Now that we've got the record-breaking shirts, we'd better concentrate on doing some record breaking.

—Joe

May 16. Saturday. Detroit.

Joe:

Detroit kicked me in the butt again, little brother. I couldn't get out of the first inning. I should have known better than to throw Lou Whitaker a fastball; he hit it for a leadoff home run and the Tigers led 4–0 when I came out. It was my third loss in a row.

Jack Morris struck out 11 and beat us 5–3. I'll tell you, people aren't giving the Tigers much respect right now. But when Kirk Gibson and Alan Trammell are 100 percent physically, and with a stopper like Morris starting every five days, Sparky Anderson will have this team in the pennant race, you can bet on that.

Detroit, like Texas, murders me. Basically, it's because of that short right-field fence. Sparky throws all those left-handed hitters at me: Whitaker, Gibson, Johnny Grubb, and this rookie Matt Nokes, who really has a smooth, powerful swing. I can't seem to get our good buddy Darrell Evans out anymore. I've been pitching to him for at least 15 years and by now it seems he owns me.

I pitch much better against the Tigers in Cleveland, where they don't have those double-deck right-field stands to shoot at. I think I won my first game at Tiger Stadium in 1984, when I was with the Yankees, and I don't think I've won here since. Joe, if you know anything about these Tigers that might help me, don't keep it to yourself.

It surprises me to hear that DeCinces gives you so much trouble. He's one guy I feel I'm going to get out every time he walks up to the plate. I just change speeds on my knuckleball with him, and vary my delivery from overhead to sidearm. I'll jam him with a fastball once in a while just to keep him guessing. It's to the point now where I'll get him swinging at bad balls out of the strike zone a lot of times. You should be able to frustrate him like that, too, Joe.

A writer talked to me today about pitchers over 40—me, you, Carlton, Sutton, Tommy John—for a magazine article he was doing. Like I told him, I don't look at us as being over 40. I see us as pitchers who have won more games than most.

Every fourth or fifth day, we are not just 40-year-old pitchers; we are the best pitchers our teams have to put on the mound that day. We can beat a team just as well as a guy in his early 20s throwing 95 miles per hour.

The thing that bothers me is that sportswriters bring up the 40 thing every time they talk to you, especially when you lose. We play the game the same as younger guys. Maybe our reaction time is not what it used to be, maybe we don't run as fast or throw as hard. But we compensate with experience, knowledge, finesse, competitiveness.

We all have to be a little lucky to pitch 15 or 20 years, but we have made a lot of breaks for ourselves. Most of us have pretty much kept our eyes and ears open and our mouths shut. We've always been eager to learn and improve.

That's about it for today, Joe.

Oh, yes, I heard this joke the other day: What's got three inches of powder and five inches of base? Tammy Bakker.

You heard one lately? Pick me up, brother. We need a win and some laughs.

—Phil

May 23. Saturday. Anaheim, California

Phil:

Hello, Jim and Gaylord. The Niekro brothers are shoulder-to-shoulder with the Perry brothers: 529 wins for each family.

Knucks, I put the record-tying game in the books tonight; we beat the Angels 3–0. Your baby brother was sharp, if I do say so myself. I allowed five hits in $7\frac{2}{3}$ innings to put me over .500, 3–2, for the season. If that doesn't show them this old knuckleballer can still pitch, I've got a lost cause on my hands.

As you can imagine, this was one time I really wanted to walk off with the ball in the end. In the eighth I had a runner at second with Wally Joyner up, and Lou came out to the mound. "I want to finish this baby," I told Lou. He said he knew that, but in this situation he had to bring in Righetti. I understood, I think. Rags smoked them for the last four outs and his 10th save. It would have been great to have "complete game" in the box score for number 529, but I'll take the win.

When we got into the clubhouse, Bob Shirley and Tim Stoddard broke out a few bottles of champagne they bought and poured them all over me for tying the Perrys' record. It was cold as hell and I thought I was going to have, as Fred Sanford used to say, "the Big One" right there.

When I was talking to you on the phone—and thanks for the call—they poured more over me. You couldn't tell, but Rags even took the receiver and poured some into it and said: "This is for you, too, Old Man." They all wish you good luck Wednesday in Boston when you go for the one we've been waiting for.

Wednesday I'll fly up to Boston—if the Yankees let me, and I can't see why they wouldn't—and watch you go get 530. I just wish Mom and Dad could be there, too, but you know they'll get the game tuned in on the radio.

People keep asking me what the 530 record means to us, and I keep telling them it's a Niekro record, not just Phil and Joe but the whole family. It's something the two of us accomplished, but not without the strength and support of the people behind us.

Our team is really rolling; we've been in first place for nine straight days and we're 12 games over .500. All the newspaper articles are about how the Yankees are getting along; they are calling us "Team Tranquil," which seems pretty amazing. Lou has really put a lid on the controversies the Yankees are notorious for and kept us focused on what's important: playing good ball every day.

Maybe the most valuable guy on the club is the littlest guy, Wayne Tolleson. He's played super shortstop. If he hits .250 it will be great, because he is so outstanding with the glove. If Tolly would get hurt, it really would set us back.

Gator's with us, but nobody's been taken off the roster, so we're still waiting to see. I know one guy they aren't taking off the roster and that's Mattingly. Donnie's getting hot and he's looking like the Mattingly of the last two years. He's hitting the outside pitch to left and pulling the ball. He hit his first grand slam; the man's on fire.

It seems like I'm in a good grove right now. The start before this, in Seattle, I also went $7\frac{2}{3}$ innings and gave up five hits and three runs. My knuckleball and slider are working for me. Cerone caught both wins and called a great game; we're on the same wavelength now. I know that for this team to win the division, I've got to contribute. They are starting to count on me for the first time this year, and it's a good feeling.

Knucks, wait until you see this kid Mark McGwire for Oakland; what a horse. A big, 6′3″, 220-pound redhead who looks like this year's Jose Canseco. I don't know if he's as strong as Canseco, the A's rookie of the year in 1986, but McGwire might be a little more disciplined at the plate. He hit three home runs against us in Oakland. We don't know how to pitch to him yet; we have to figure out a way to keep him out of the stands when he comes to New York next week.

As if big, strong kids like McGwire and Canseco are not enough trouble, you can make good pitches in these American League ballparks and still give up home runs. I can see why this is a breaking-ball league. Places like the Seattle Kingdome and the Metrodome in Minneapolis are so short down the lines and in the power alleys.

And I swear the baseballs are juiced like people are saying. I've seen a lot of home runs already this season, a lot of long home runs. You expect the big hitters—like Mattingly, Winfield, Eddie Murray, Jim Rice—to go deep like that, but little guys are hitting balls out the opposite way and to straightaway center. If they don't watch it, a pitcher is going to get seriously hurt the way line drives jump off the bats. I can't believe some of the balls being hit in batting practice. Canseco, who's strong as a bull anyway, crushed one over the wall and off the back concrete wall in Oakland. That's a cannon shot.

I might hate to pitch in the Kingdome, but Seattle is my kind of place, Knucks. I had a great view from my hotel window and I just stood admiring the beauty of the country. After I get out of baseball, I'm going to take a trip to Seattle for some salmon fishing.

Before we left on this West Coast trip I said good-bye to my guru, Hoyt Wilhelm. I really appreciate what he did for me; having him work with me was one of the Boss's better ideas. In spring training the Yankees were saying I was struggling—which I wasn't—but people can get to your mind after a while. Because of their lack of confidence in me, I was feeling a lack of confidence in myself. You can't pitch like that. Hoyt came to New York and convinced me I still have a good knuckleball, to just go out and throw it and have fun again.

I'll see you in Boston, and let's make it a celebration to remember.

—Joe

May 27. Wednesday. Boston.

Joe:

It's two in the morning and I'm out of beer. I just said good-bye to you and I'm still thinking about probably the best game I ever could have pitched.

Who knows? Maybe it will be the last great game I ever pitch—and I lost. Damn. Now I'm 2–5 and we're still stuck on 529.

I couldn't bag us 530, brother; you saw me beat 1–0 by the Red Sox and Roger Clemens, who looked every bit the MVP and Cy Young winner he was in 1986.

God, what a tough loss, and with so much on the line, too. I didn't find out until afterward that it was my 700th career start and that only Cy Young and Don Sutton have started more games. I probably was more into this game mentally and physically than any in a long time. You being there was a big boost. I felt the adrenaline flowing all day.

Sorry you had to split so quickly afterward, so we really didn't get time to rehash the game. After a beauty like that I can't imagine too many pitches you'd second-guess me on.

I had everything going for me against the Red Sox, but I couldn't get the job done. I had a lively knuckleball, a decent fastball, a good change of speed. I thought for sure I was going to get it tonight even though it was in Fenway Park with that Green Monster left-field wall for the hitters to shoot at.

But Clemens was fabulous. When Roger's hot he's as tough as anyone I've seen in my 24 years in the big leagues. When he's on, like he was against us, you can't do anything with him. When you're going head-to-head with Clemens you have to be prepared to pitch a shutout.

I had good stuff in my first shot at 530, last Friday in Milwaukee, but Bill Wegman outpitched me and won 4–2. I've felt the mental pressure build for each of these 530 starts because of how badly we want the win and how many people have their eyes on the game. Milwaukee seemed like a fitting setting for 530, too; I played my first big-league game there for the old Braves in 1964, and Jimmy in the visitor's clubhouse fed me some of that great kielbasa and sauerkraut, the Polish breakfast of champions, before I went out to pitch.

I know there's most of the season to go, but I just want to get this 530 over with and I wanted to do it on an effort like that. Shit. A one-run complete game. At age 48, to throw a four-hitter at Fenway Park and lose.

You've got the ball now, Joe. Put the hammerlock on whoever it is. We'll get it sometime.

I've got more to write about, but I'm in such a shit-ass mood right now I just want to go to sleep. Tell me a new joke, I need one about now.

G'night.

—Phil

May 30. Saturday. New York.

Brother Phil:

Destiny was written all over this day, Knucks.

I thought about it all morning before I went out to pitch against Oakland. I thought it was ironic: we're going after win number 530, and if I win today I would date the ball "5-30-87." Going for 530 on 5-30. That's destiny calling, I figured.

Well, big brother, destiny did not call us loudly enough, because the Athletics beat me 4–3.

I was respectable; I went 5⅔ innings with a 3–1 lead. But I made a bad 0–2 pitch in the sixth to Tony Phillips, a knuckleball down and in, and they ended up scoring three in the inning. We couldn't do anything against Oakland's bullpen. That's the way it goes sometimes.

Now it's your turn again, big boy. Of course, I'd like to have won 530 tonight, but I've said all along that you should be the one to win it since you have most of our wins. I sure appreciated you being in the stands and seeing you in the clubhouse afterward.

I don't know if I'll make it to Cleveland for your start against Detroit. Sometimes, most times, you get the feeling around here you're asking too much, so I don't know if they'll go for me taking off another day to see you pitch. Hey, you've won over 300 games without me, so I'm sure you can win another one. Maybe Mom can come up from Lansing to give you some family support. You know I'll be watching the scoreboard.

You making an appearance in our clubhouse made the guys remember how pissed they are at George for letting you go. They all miss you. Somebody reminds me every day, "If only Knucksie were still here . . ." I hope you realize how much you mean to so many people around here.

I had to leave so fast Wednesday after the game I didn't get to really tell you how proud I was of you in Boston, losing 1–0 to Clemens. To me, you outpitched him. Think of the ammunition Clemens brings to the mound, and then compare it to the guns you take out there. You're a master of your craft, Knucks. I can't tell you how proud I was to sit in Fenway Park and watch my brother pitch like that. I had sweaty palms the entire game.

The all-night trip home to Lakeland was exhausting, but what a wonderful time I had with the kids. Natalie looks more mature every time I see her; she's 5'8" and only 13. The modeling has been so good for her, she's becoming such a refined young lady. She got some exciting news: she and some friends are going to be on the TV show "Puttin' on the Hits." They're going to lip-sync "Didn't Mean to Turn You On" by Robert Palmer. You've heard that tune, haven't you, Knucks? It's no polka.

When you're away as much as ballplayers are, people don't realize how much you miss your family. It's lonely at times, and it's awful tough on your wife having to communicate by the telephone so much and carrying the burden of all the responsibilities at home.

But the game's been good to the Niekros, wouldn't you say, big brother?

Go tame those Tigers, will you? I know they give you trouble, especially those left-handed hitters. All I can tell you about them, and the Rangers you're having trouble with—Larry Parrish and Pete O'Brien—is knuckleballs, knuckleballs, knuckleballs. Then knock them back with an occasional fastball up and in.

I'm telling *you*? I only pitch the way I've learned from you.

I'll have my 530 baseball cap and 530 T-shirt with me when you pitch Tuesday. Go get it, Knucksie.

—Joe

June: "Brothers, Second to None"

June 2. Tuesday. Cleveland.

Dear Joe:

Can't go to sleep, Joe. Not that I really want to. It's 5:30 in the morning and I've been drinking champagne since about 11 o'clock. Right now I miss not being with you. We should have our arms around each other pouring Dom Perignon over our heads.

We got it, we did it, it's over. God bless America, let's polka. We, the Niekros, Phil and Joe, are the winningest brothers in baseball history.

God, I can't tell you how proud I am to be able to say that. It's absolutely the best feeling I've ever had since the day I signed my first professional contract in 1959.

Your big brother rang up number 530, one victory more than two pretty good pitchers from North Carolina, Jim and Gaylord Perry, and it was probably one of my worst games of the season. The team got me a 7–1 lead after three innings, and I needed every bit of it. I barely made it through five innings to be able to collect the victory.

Only about 8,000 people showed up at Cleveland Stadium—it looked like an invitation-only affair with more than 60,000 empty seats. Maybe the game didn't mean much to anybody else, but I

74

woke up this morning thinking about this being my home state, and how this game meant everything to me.

I had my doubts all along that I could beat Detroit because of the way the Tigers have treated me the last couple of years. I felt like I had to pitch a shutout after giving up only one run against Boston and losing.

Just the damn opposite. We won 9–6. Darrell Evans did it to me again; my old Atlanta teammate knocked me out with a bases-loaded triple in the sixth. Our bullpen did the job. Ed Vande Berg, Mark Huismann, and Scotty Bailes got the last four outs.

"I'm the answer to a Trivial Pursuit question: who saved Phil and Joe Niekro's 530th victory?" Scotty told me in the clubhouse.

I showered and sat in the clubhouse sweating out the last innings. When it was over I got called back out on the field. I stepped up out of the dugout and immediately got drenched with a bottle of champagne. And who was standing there: Mom.

I didn't know she was coming; I didn't see her in the stands. They hid her pretty good. Whenever I got close to where she was sitting, Mom held a newspaper up in front of her face. She rode up with a gang from Lansing; Dad, of course, had to stay home. I understood why you couldn't be here, Joe, so it was doubly nice that at least Mom was here. I gave her a bear hug from both of us.

Two brothers winning 530 games still amazes me. I can't imagine it ever being broken. Two brothers have to make the big leagues and then stay healthy enough to pitch more than 20 years apiece.

I keep wondering what Dad must be feeling, what he must be thinking, sitting there in his wheelchair. I hope he's thinking: "I am the man whose two sons won more big-league games than any brothers in baseball history." Sandy Koufax's dad can't say that; neither can Bob Gibson's or Tom Seaver's. Nobody but Philip Henry Niekro can say that.

We might not have been the best pitchers of all time, but our record says we are the best two pitchers ever to come from one set of parents. My God, how fortunate we are. But to me it's a reward for the sacrifices and hardships our parents have endured.

Back in 1964 I didn't know if I'd last two years in the major leagues, and you were a college student in West Virginia. If anybody would have asked me if we'd end up winning 530 games, I'd have bet everything I owned there was no way possible. But we did it. I guess we made some good decisions along the way. Special credit to Mom and Dad, our Nancys, and our families for what they have sacrificed and invested in our careers. They pushed us, held us, let us cry on them—everything. This record belongs to them, too.

I want this record to belong to Bridgeport High School, the Sportsman's Club, Lansing Grade School, St. Joseph's schools, all the coaches we played for, all our relatives, and the little town of Lansing. Ninety-nine percent of the people in Ohio don't know where Lansing is, and two brothers, sons of a coal miner and his loving wife, won 530 games in the big leagues. I hope our home area feels as good about this as we do. The Niekros always represented Lansing wherever we pitched.

I'm happy for everybody who's ever touched our lives. I'm even happy for the people who never thought we'd get this far or last this long, and there were a number of them. Back then I couldn't blame them. We weren't the best-looking prospects around.

What makes 530 special for me, though, is doing it with a brother like you, Joe. We tried to be together for this, but old 530, like an overdue baby, came when the time was right.

We've helped each other mentally and spiritually, as baseball players and brothers. I look back at all our years together: as kids learning the knuckleball in the backyard from Dad, pitching against each other nine times, batting against each other, playing together.

The number 530 has taken on new meaning for me today; it's our number, Joe. Whenever someone asks for the time, and the reply is "5:30," I'll think of our record.

I love you, Joe. Go get 531.

Phil

June 4. Thursday. Milwaukee.

Phil:

Something's coming. I can feel it, big brother.

My instincts tell me the mystery of who disappears when Gator returns to the starting rotation is about to be solved.

We lost 9–3 to the Brewers, but I didn't think I stunk out the joint. Rob Deer hit a couple of home runs off me, one on a knuckleball that jammed the heck out of him. I couldn't believe that ball went out of the park. I know Deer's big and strong, but the guy hit it four inches from his hands, and Rickey Henderson just stood there waiting for it. But it kept drifting and drifting and finally went out.

I gave up seven runs, four earned, and my record slipped to 3–4. We're trailing 2–0 going into the fifth. I strike out the first guy and walk a batter. The next guy hits one to Winfield, and Winny loses it in the lights for an error. Then the roof falls in. A guy hits a double to right. I'm not saying Winny should have had that ball, but the way he broke, it looked like he lost that one in the lights, too.

Molitor hits a hard ground ball to our shortstop, Bobby Meacham. You know how things are when they're going horseshit. Two more feet and Meacham starts a double play. But it kind of short-hops Meach and glances off his glove into short right field, and Molitor reaches second. It could have been an inning-ending double play; instead it turns the inning uglier still.

I make a bad pitch to Deer: threw him a fastball and he pulls it to left for his second home run off me. I'm sure Lou, Mark Connor, all the powers that be, are looking at it as a bad outing for me. And since you're only good as your last game around here, who knows? My fifth day would be Tuesday against Toronto at home, but I've got this feeling something's going to happen by then. George, as you know, is known to panic and do strange things before we play the Blue Jays. That's usually when George rips Winfield or the manager. There's no team George worries about more than Toronto.

I know they're itching to get Guidry back in the rotation, and I know they'll bring him back with a start at home, because the Gator's return to Yankee Stadium is a guaranteed sellout. I'd buy a ticket for that. If I didn't have two guaranteed years left on my contract, I'm sure I'd be gone by now. They just might be looking for a couple of bad games to shove me into the bullpen. If that happens, I'll be asking out.

I'm still answering questions about 530 and loving every second of it. I'm still passing out 530 T-shirts; gave some to the guys, the coaches, the clubhouse guys, the batboys. Gave Harvey Greene one, Claire Smith, Tommy Pedulla—people who have been nice to us over here. Harvey said it was the first time he got something from a player that didn't give him a rash. Some of the guys said they'd never wear them, that they wanted us to sign them and they'd put them in their trophy case.

You winning 530 was exactly how I hoped the Perrys' record would be broken; Mom's being there was a bonus. I got 529 to tie, and you got 530; it was perfect.

I still get chills when I think of 530 victories: more than the Perrys, more than Dizzy and Daffy Dean. When you beat the Tigers in Cleveland, I wanted to run through the streets of New York yelling, "We're number one! We're number one!"

Like we've said all along, it's a record that will stand for generations. The only way it might get broken is if Cy Young has a younger brother—and boy, he'd have to be a helluva lot younger—who comes out of nowhere and wins 30-odd games.

We were losing at home to California and I hardly took my eyes off the scoreboard. When you guys jumped out to a 7–1 lead, the guys on our bench kept coming by me saying, "This is the night. This is the night." Next thing I knew you guys were up only 7–6 and I started getting nervous. Rhoden told me not to worry, because he said you guys were going to score more runs, and damn it if you didn't.

I found out in the eighth inning of our game that you won, and everybody started coming over to congratulate me. When the inning was over they asked me to step out of the dugout and take a bow. George had it announced over the PA system—you can imagine how nice it sounded with Bob Sheppard's velvety voice—and they put our pictures with 530 up on the scoreboard screen.

I felt kind of dumb because it was the first time I ever got a standing ovation, and I wasn't even in the game. It felt good; I enjoyed it. I thought about the ovation the Cleveland fans, all 8,000 of them, must have given you.

When I got back to the dugout after the ovation, I saw Bob Boone, the Angels' catcher and another old National Leaguer, give me thumbs up from behind home plate. What a class move. De-Cinces, at third base, did it, too. I gave them double thumbs back. It's great to have your peers salute you like that during a game. I felt very proud to be a Niekro.

I wish I could have been there with you, but I didn't feel I was in the position to ask for another favor right now. I made a toast for both of us anyway. I put a second glass of champagne down beside the one I was drinking, like you were right there, and I drank both of them.

When we get together I'm going to give you a big hug and kiss, brother. You know how dearly I love and respect you.

—Joe

June 7. Sunday. New York.

Phil:

Speaking as one former Yankee to another, the Niekros got the boot out of New York again, big brother. Even though I had a feeling something was about to happen, as I told you, I still was shocked when Piniella told me yesterday I had been traded to Minnesota for catcher Mark Salas.

My first thought was to retire, hang it up, and go snook fishing. Getting sent packing at 42 makes you think that it's time to turn your spikes in for house slippers.

But then I talked to you, Nancy, Mom and Dad, and I've done a lot of thinking. Maybe it's time for me to get out of New York and try to help a good-looking, up-and-coming team like the Twins win the pennant.

The events of the last two days, though, keep rattling around in my head. The day before I was traded, Friday, was crazy and I should have been better prepared mentally for what came down Saturday.

Just after noon, Pat Clements and Bob Tewksbury, two pitchers from Columbus, show up in the hotel lobby. Nobody knew they were coming. Lou got steamed because a couple of reporters saw them. That's how the day started.

We get to the ballpark and Bob Shirley gets released. I guess I should have seen that coming with Clements, also a left-handed reliever, in town. I know everybody either retires or gets released, but when a buddy gets released, it hurts. Bob probably did what no other pitcher could do for this organization: he was a swing guy who could pitch five innings one night, four innings the next, then not pitch for a week. He was always ready and willing to do what they needed. He didn't cause any trouble, never shot off his mouth when they dumped on him, and—boom—they release him.

When baseball fans talk to me about a player's loyalty to his team, I'll tell them to go talk to Bob Shirley about a team's loyalty to a player.

After the game, Righetti, Cerone, Gator, Rich Bordi, and I gave Shirley a send-off. It was a sad night because Bobby and Rags, two crazy lefties, had become real close. A few tears were shed. I think Rags is going to be a little lost without Shirley; I hope it doesn't affect his pitching.

Of course, Bobby went out under some strange circumstances. The hot rumor was that Shirley was getting released because he and Mattingly got into something more serious than a wrestling match, and Mattingly hurt his back. I remember sitting in the clubhouse when Mattingly came in and said he hurt his back bending over for a ground ball. The next day the newspapers were filled with this supposed Shirley-Mattingly incident—good old-fashioned Yankee controversy as far as the papers were concerned—but as far as I know it was false.

Now to Tewks, and that's the funny part of this story.

Clements and Tewksbury are told to stay at the hotel. Nobody knows what's going on: they call up Tewks from Columbus, have him meet us in Milwaukee, and then tell him to stay at the hotel. I've seen strange organizations, but nothing like these pinstripers. It's like that time with Paul Zuvella in Seattle; they brought him in and for four days, all he did was take BP.

If that wasn't enough for one day, Rickey Henderson goes on the 15-day disabled list with a pulled hamstring, and Mattingly is sent back to New York because of back spasms.

The next day I walk into the clubhouse and—zap—I'm traded to the Twins. Phil, I can't tell you how that caught me off guard, and I'd been waiting for something to happen for a couple of days. I must have had it in the back of my mind that it would be someone else, that they were going to stick with me this time.

I certainly don't think the Yankees' pitching staff is that sound for them to be trading a starting pitcher and not getting one in return. Hudson and Rasmussen have been struggling. TJ's been good, but you never know about injuries with him.

Knucks, I don't know what the Niekro name means to the Yankees, but evidently after your release and my trade, we're not well respected by some people in the organization. I suspect it's George, but something tells me it might be someone else, too. Clyde King or Woody Woodward or maybe Billy Martin. Who knows?

Overall, I've pitched well for the Yankees. I had the second-best ERA, 3.55, in our starting rotation. But you know I've felt all along they were looking for any excuse to get rid of me.

My reservations about the trade were not because of Minnesota. They've got a good ball club, with an explosive offense and a good closer in Jeff Reardon, and they could go a long way this year. I'm sure the atmosphere with the Twins is going to be a lot more comfortable and enjoyable than with the Yankees. It's not a situation where you have someone looking over your shoulder every damn minute, every game you pitch. I know you liked going to Cleveland from the Yankees.

The Twins already have made me feel more wanted than the Yankees ever did. With those 10,000 lakes to fish in up there—has anybody actually counted them or is that a round number?—maybe I'll fall in love with Minnesota. Andy MacPhail, the Twins' general manager, is the first GM I've ever played for who's younger than me; I think he's 34. He tells me knuckleball pitchers have been successful in the Metrodome. I won a lot of games in Houston's dome; of course, the Astrodome is more a pitcher's park than the Metrodome.

The Twins want me to pitch two days from now, Tuesday, in Minnesota against Kansas City. If I win, I think it might put them in a tie with the Royals for first place in the AL West. I hope I can help the Twins and show the Yankees they made a mistake. I remember you thought the Yankees would have won the pennant in 1986 if they had kept you. Maybe getting rid of another Niekro will screw them up this year, too.

What are the Yankees going to do with Salas anyway? He's not very good defensively; he'll probably end up a left-handed pinch hitter. The Yankees need pitching so they trade a starter for a backup—maybe third-string—catcher. It makes no sense.

At least no more Niekro money comes from the checkbook of George M. Steinbrenner. That should be enough to make me want to run to Minnesota.

By the way, I flew back to New York on the same plane with Billy Martin. Billy said he was upset about all the recent transactions. He said George didn't consult him on anything, so he didn't go to the ball games in Milwaukee on Saturday and Sunday.

Of course, Billy had a few cocktails on the flight and was rolling in about 20 minutes. He told me how much he loved you and me. I couldn't tell if he was bullshitting or just drunk on his ass. I hope he was telling me the truth, but to me, Billy's that certain type of guy—I never know whether or not to believe him.

Billy had a couple more drinks and tried to pick a fight with a guy on the plane. I just sat back and observed. It was truly interesting, almost amusing. It was like a reminder of the life—the struggle, the fighting—I was leaving behind going from the Yankees to the Twins.

The more I think about it, Knucks, the more I know I'm going to love Minnesota and the Twins.
—Joe

June 9. Tuesday. Anaheim, California

Dear Mr. Minnesota Twin:

Joe, as I told you on the phone, this trade will turn out to be a blessing.

I know you were getting a good feeling about being with the Yankee ball club. You were pitching better and you finally got over the frustration of my release. We both knew you could have been huge in the Big Apple, but it wasn't to be.

What are they going to do with Mark Salas? There's no comparison in terms of established talent. As hard up as the Yankees are for starters, and pitching in general, why they traded a proven starter like you I'll never understand. But, of course, I'm still wondering why the hell they dumped me. I don't think we'll ever know for sure.

Joe, forget the Yankees and get into the Twins. I'm not so sure their pennant prospects aren't brighter than New York's anyway. I picked them to win their division in 1986, and I've felt since then that the Twins are a club ready to make their move.

There's certainly no one powerhouse in the AL West. They have some players in their prime who are ready to be discovered nationally: Kirby Puckett, Gary Gaetti, Kent Hrbek, and Frank Viola. You could see their development year to year and this might be the season they put everything together. Reardon was a big addition for them, and I think you will be, too.

As far as living conditions go, I know you're going to enjoy Minnesota more than the big city; it's more outdoorsy. You can drive 45 minutes and go fishing or hunting. And you won't have to pay the toll on the George Washington Bridge going to the ballpark every day.

You're going to feel comfortable again in Minnesota, and I

think it will bring the best out in you as a pitcher, too. Who knows, you might end up being the first Niekro in a World Series.

Me and your old buddy Sutton went head-up last night and we won 2–0. I pitched 7⅔ innings and allowed just three hits. I always seem to do pretty well against the Angels and Sutton. The win made me 4–5, so .500's next.

We're still floundering, Joe. We're 16 games under .500 and 15 games out of first. The middle-infield defense, Tony Bernazard at second and Julio Franco at shortstop, is killing us. Our starters still are inconsistent, but Scott Bailes is looking good in short relief.

Did you see who Detroit picked up? They signed Bill Madlock, a four-time batting champ, after he was released by the Los Angeles Dodgers. Teams throw as many left-handers as possible at the Tigers because of left-hand hitters like Kirk Gibson, Lou Whitaker, and Darrell Evans. A right-handed hitter who makes contact like Madlock should help them.

Losing Lance Parrish as a free agent and with injuries to Gibson and Alan Trammell, nobody gave the Tigers much of a chance in April. I wouldn't be so foolish as to underestimate them now.

But, Joe, you don't have to worry about the Tigers, you're over in AL West. In fact, did you know you are the first Niekro ever to pitch for an American League West team?

Go show those Twins they made a steal.

—Phil

June 10. Wednesday. Minneapolis.

Phil:

Now I know how a man feels when he's set free from the penitentiary, Knucks.

I woke up this morning, after pitching my first game for the Twins last night, and I actually felt relaxed, happy, at peace. I feel like a boulder the size of a pickup truck has been lifted off my shoulders.

Now ask me if I can live without the Yankees.

It's a situation with the Twins where you can't wait to get to the ballpark. I'm having trouble remembering when I last felt that way. I guess it had to be when you and I were with the Yankees at the end of 1985. The feeling with the Twins reminds me of 1980, when the Astros were starting to believe they could win the pennant and everybody was so up and excited every day.

I'm 2–0 in two days with this club, Knucks. I won my first start yesterday—I'll tell you more about that later—to put us in a tie for the AL West lead, and the team won a big one 4–3 in 10 innings tonight to sweep Kansas City and knock them out of first place. This series showed the Royals—and you know how tough they are every year—that the Twins are going to be a load to contend with.

Yesterday, my first day as a Twin, was a marathon. I woke up at seven in the morning, packed my Jeep, cleaned out my condo in New York, drove to the airport, and flew to Minneapolis, where I had to get ready for my first start as a Twin that night. I thought a Niekro was quietly stepping into a new baseball environment, when I got hit by the Minnesota press as soon as we landed.

It was exciting, Knucks, to be the center of that kind of attention again. TV camera crews. Radio and newspaper reporters. Lights. People stopping and watching me as I worked my way through the airport. Everybody in Minneapolis was genuinely excited about getting me, which gave me a rush of adrenaline I hadn't felt in a while.

After I unpacked at the hotel I went straight to the Metrodome about 2:30. Several of the players were in the clubhouse and they made me feel welcome and wanted. The catcher, Tim Laudner, had never caught a knuckleball before, so Kent Hrbek, the big first baseman, put a basket in his locker with a note saying, "Good luck." It helps break the ice for a stranger to walk into a clubhouse with that kind of atmosphere.

When I walked to the left-field bullpen to warm up, the Twins' fans gave me a standing ovation. It made me feel so warm inside I was afraid I might burn a hole through my T-shirt. The fans were saying: "Glad you're with us; we're going to win the pennant." You can tell these fans are sold on this ball club, Knucks. They believe in these guys.

After a busy day of travel and transition I thought I pitched pretty respectably against the Royals: $6\frac{1}{3}$ innings, nine hits, one earned run, six strikeouts, three walks. TK, manager Tom Kelly, came out in the seventh and said, "It's been a long day for you and we appreciate your effort today, but I'm bringing in Keith Atherton now." Atherton got me out of a tough spot and saved the game.

Even before I walked off the mound the fans were standing and cheering me. It gave me goose bumps. I felt loved and strong again. I can't believe the range of emotions I've felt in such a short period of time. The day before, when I was cleaning out my locker at Yankee Stadium, I was so confused, so uncertain. When I went to pack my bags, nobody was there except Nick Priore, the clubhouse man. Nick was one of the guys who missed you so much, Knucks. He's been working the Yankees' clubhouse for over 20 years, starting as Pete Sheehy's assistant. He gave me a hug and said it wasn't fair to have to say good-bye to two Niekros.

I was cleaning out my locker when I noticed something in the back. It was the big magnum of champagne Steinbrenner had sent down after you won 530. He was supposed to have sent you one at Cleveland Stadium; I don't know if you ever got it or not. I looked at the big bottle and thought about it for quite a while. It was the last thing in my locker, and I finally decided I couldn't accept it. Not from that man.

I taped a note to the bottle, nothing nasty. It just said, "No thanks." I'm sure George got the message. It wasn't only for me but for the both of us, after the way we were run out of the organization.

I appreciated George signing me to a three-year, guaranteed contract, and I think if they would have left me alone for three years and then looked for results, they would have been pleased. But they'd been screwing with me from the day I arrived until the day I left. I just can't understand why—at a time when they need pitching—they trade me when I've been pitching good.

I do know that the Twins want me, which is like getting a hug and kiss from Mom after getting gassed by George.

I did find time Monday night to watch Toronto play the Yankees on national television; the Blue Jays dropped an 11–0 bomb on the Boss's team. I'll have to admit it, Phil, I got a kick out of it. It's not that I'm rooting for or against anybody, but there was a satisfying feeling watching George's team, when it's hurting for pitching, get its ass kicked like that after trading me.

As it turned out, Guidry made his first start for the Yankees last night, too—the same night I made my first start with the Twins. I don't think Gator did as well as I did; he went four innings and gave up four runs in a 7–2 loss to Toronto. But I'm sure the Yankees are happier with Gator in their rotation than with me.
—Joe

June 18. Thursday. Minneapolis.

Phil:

What's with me, Knucks? Is this going to be one of those years when everything happens to Joe Niekro? Who'd I piss off?

Just when things were starting to look up for your little brother, more shit hits the fan. I'm afraid to think what might happen to me next month.

I win my first two starts for the Twins, my record's up to 5–4, and the team's sending out strong signals that the American League West is ours. I've bounced back mentally from the trade and I haven't had any trouble with my arm and back at all. And just when the season looked like it might have a happy ending after all, I go get hurt in a fight.

You probably saw me in the highlights, Knucks. Afterward, I thought, "What the hell is this 42-year-old dummy doing?" But, as you know, when you're part of a team, you're part of the team. When there's a brawl on the field, you brawl. It's usually a bunch of silly pushing, cussing, and farting, anyway.

The rest of the league might be having trouble with Milwaukee, but we've been kicking the Brewers' butts. We swept them three in the Dome; they lost the last game 13–1. And yesterday we were working on completing a three-game sweep at County Stadium when Milwaukee reliever Mark Clear knocked down Steve Lombardozzi. No words were exchanged, just icy glares.

Then there was a close play at second, and Lombardozzi went in hard with his spikes up. The players came up swinging, both benches emptied, and I just ran out to see if I could help. The first guy I saw was Rob Deer. Now that I know him better, I'd say Rob could play linebacker in the NFL.

Deer is about the size of a five-point buck: 26 years old, 6'3", 210 pounds, big shoulders, strong upper body. Just the guy I want to go one-on-one with in a fight, right? All I did was grab Rob from behind to settle him down, just trying to break things up.

Deer grabbed me and threw me down to the ground, something of a body slam—and I'll be damned if I didn't separate my shoulder. Today's an off day and I'm getting it treated. It hurts more than I'm trying to let on. I'll probably miss at least one start.

That's baseball, I guess. I couldn't just watch the guys run out on the field to defend Lombardozzi, especially when I'm the new guy trying to be accepted. It's amazing, though, how all the principals in a fight never get hurt, only the guys trying to break it up.

Isn't that something, Knucks? I thought I was stepping out of the Yankees' caldron of controversy and into the tranquility of Twinkieland. Some of it must have rubbed off on me; I'll have to scrub harder in the shower next time.

It's funny, the Twins changed their uniforms this year to pinstripes, like the Yankees, at home and on the road. Claire Smith called me the other night and I told her I don't feel the "electrodes" running through the Minnesota pinstripes that I did in the Yankee pinstripes: it always seemed like every time they thought you did something wrong over there, you got a shock wave sent up through those pinstripes.

It's nothing like that over here; it's really a relaxed atmosphere. I just hope this shoulder doesn't cost me more than one start. Damn, what a time for a stupid injury like this.

Lots of news lately, Knucksie. Our buddy Bullet Bob Shirley

signed on with the Royals. They need help in the bullpen, so maybe this is the break Bobby needs. Joaquin Andujar went back on the disabled list, this time with a pulled hamstring. If Oakland is going to beat us, I've got to think they need Andujar to do it.

The Twins signed David Letterman's "Tub of Goo," Terry Forster, to a Triple A contract. We're hurting for left-handed relievers, so if Terry can look good at Portland, he might get a shot here. I don't care what the reports are, I can't imagine him weighing less than 240 after being inactive.

Take care of yourself.

—Joe

June 21. Sunday. Cleveland.

Joe:

After I mail this I'm going to call Dad for Father's Day; I'm sure you'll be doing the same. It would be nice to get down to Lansing, but this is our getaway day. As you know, Joe, we're coming up to Minnesota for three games. I hope we get to do some fishing.

We're playing fairly well right now, but we're still 17 games out. I'm back under .500, 5–6. Mark Langston of Seattle beat me the last time; nobody knows that guy, but he's as tough a left-hander as there is, especially in the Kingdome. We can't put a win streak together—two games is about it for us.

Rumors are swirling all around Corrales, as you can imagine. He's been through it before, fired from both Philadelphia and Texas. And unless we get moving, I can see him getting it again.

If the Indians ever contend to the final week, they'll break attendance records in that big old coliseum by Lake Erie. The way people up here are starved for a winner, if the Indians can ever contend for a pennant into September, they'll draw three million. But the way we're going—and Indian fans are used to it, I'm afraid—we might not draw one million.

Went to my favorite neighborhood tavern, the Brook State Inn, last night and polka-ed until I nearly dropped. When I'm away from Cleveland I really miss the Brook State and all the good people there. Chicago is about the only other place I can find a good tavern with polka music.

When I was with the Yankees, Righetti and Shirley would ride me about my Polish music. Shirley always carried a tape player with him. Before the games I'd start we had a little ritual: Shirley would play a polka tape, and for about 30 seconds the guys would clap and jump and stomp and hoot. It was great.

I don't think I ever told you how I found the Brook State Inn, Joe. It was on my first trip into Cleveland with the Yankees in 1984. I was homesick for some polka music so I just picked up the Cleveland phone book and started looking for anything that said "Polish." I found a Polish-American Club and called and they said if I wanted to kick up my heels and have a ball, on Friday and Saturday nights the place is the Brook State Inn.

Of course, last night everybody at the Brook State wanted to know about my fighting little brother, Palooka Joe Niekro. What's going on here? I thought you were like me, Joe, you'd rather fish or make love than fight.

I'm proud of you for defending your teammates, but can't you stay away from the hulks the size of Rob Deer? You should have been looking for one of those senior citizen ushers or a ballboy.

One of the unwritten rules when you turn 40 is, if a fight breaks out and the guy next to you is the biggest guy on the other team, you're allowed to pretend you don't see him.

I've talked to Commissioner Ueberroth about on-field fights; some are absolutely uncalled for. They could put a stop to them if they wanted to. Most times it's a pitcher and a batter, a runner sliding into second or home; always two guys get it started.

I see no reason why 40 guys have to rush in from the dugout and the bullpen; usually a peacemaker like you is accidentally injured. If every fielder held his position, the bullpens and dugouts froze, in a matter of 10 to 15 seconds the umpires could break it up and restrain two brawlers.

We should make it like hockey: when the fight breaks out, any player leaving his position is fined, ejected, and suspended. If the batter charges the mound, the catcher can't try to make a tackle, the benches can't empty. Make the penalties tough enough so that every player knows the risk he takes if he fights.

Make it so that anyone participating in a fight between two ballplayers is suspended. If five players become involved defending a teammate, those five are suspended immediately. Your team has to play with 19. There's no reason a big bruiser like Rob Deer should get into someone else's fight and possibly injure another player.

I'm trying to convince umpires and coaches that fights can be stopped in a matter of seconds if they follow a plan and have rules to enforce it. I don't buy free-for-alls and sucker punches.

I just hope your shoulder doesn't keep you out for a while. Whenever anybody asks me about the fight, I just tell them you got run over by a Deer.

Rest and then go get 'em.

—Phil

June 27. Saturday. Arlington, Texas

Phil:

I pitched on 13 days rest tonight. I probably should have made it 14. My shoulder still felt a little sore, but I told them it was fine because I didn't want to miss another start.

I didn't lose, but Texas knocked me around pretty good. The way the Rangers hammer you, Phil, they must have thought it was you, not me, out on the mound tonight.

Sorry we had to put that three-game sweep on you guys. You can tell from that series how well we play at the Metrodome. But all I can think about is Joe Carter. I sure hope he's all right after getting hit in the face by Keith Atherton; it was a fastball with some pop, too. You knew when it happened that Joe's nose was busted. He's just coming into his own, and what a class guy, too. Sure hope an experience like that doesn't damage his career.

This was our second loss in two nights to Texas; Bobby Witt one-hit us for eight innings Friday night. We're still playing well, though, and it looks like the Twins will be leading the AL West at the All-Star break. I wonder how many people predicted that? The Twin Cities will be going crazy for the second half.

We've got a big four-game series at Kansas City coming up before the All-Star break. And you know I'm looking forward to this one: the Twins are at Yankee Stadium for three games before the break, and the way the rotation is going it looks like I'll get one of the starts against the Yankees. That will be a game I'll want very badly. But I'll have one more start at Kansas City before that, so I can't afford to look ahead.

Right now, only three weeks after the trade, I feel like New York has been in my rearview mirror for months. I've become comfortable with the Twins that quickly. There probably will be some lingering bitterness for a while, but the anger is completely gone. I almost feel grateful to George for sparing me from any more agony over there.

Every player probably should have the experience of playing for the Yankees once. There's always great talent there, so you're playing with some of the best players in the game; that, in itself, is special. It's an organization with great tradition; to wear pinstripes and be in Yankee Stadium, pitching in front of the monuments—Ruth, Gehrig, Mantle—is like nowhere else. And the fans might get a little crazy, but only because they love their Yankees so much and anyone wearing the uniform is their idol. Being a Yankee in New York is not like being a player for any other city.

My biggest disappointment with the Yankees, more than my trade, was your release. After you won 32 games in two season, George kicked the classiest man in baseball out into the street on the seat of his pants. Right then I learned that no matter how good you are—you can be a Hall of Famer—no matter how well you conduct yourself or how strong the quality of your character, if the owner one day feels like it, he can show you the door.

The way I reacted to your release—and in some ways I flat-out rebelled—was the start of my downfall with the Yankees. I said some things, but they were all true. If there are Yankee people who are holding grudges, and they think I spoke out of turn, they're wrong.

I confronted Woody Woodward: "How can you release a 16-game winner? If it's the money, take it out of my salary."

Woody said that with your release, a lot of things were taken into consideration and that I should calm down. I flat told Woody: "I'm not staying; it stinks in here."

Ever since I blew up that time and made that statement, it was like they couldn't wait to run the second Niekro out of town. Maybe I was wrong, maybe even paranoid, but that's how they made me feel. You know how warm Yankee management is, don't you, Phil?

There were things I just never could understand: crazy personnel moves, not pitching for two weeks without really getting a reason why, being put on the disabled list with no injury.

In the middle of the 1986 season I had to leave a game because of that fingernail that got pulled back. I went into Monahan and he fixed it up. Piniella told me I'd miss my next start, but that I'd pitch in Texas. Would I be ready? I said I would.

The next day I walked into the clubhouse and I was on the 15-day disabled list. The doctor's report said I had "lifted [the fingernail] ¼-inch off the finger." The nail was just loose. I didn't need to go on DL, but they were trying to take Rod Scurry off the DL and needed help in the bullpen, so I was the convenient player to put on the list. I'd heard how the Yankees manipulate the DL, but this was my first up-close experience.

I'd spent 10 great years at Houston, but I was so happy when I was traded to the Yankees because you were there. I got to see your 300th victory as your teammate—what a privilege that was. I probably wouldn't have accepted a trade from the Astros if you weren't with the Yankees. All I could think of was going to the World Series with my brother, and we had a pretty good chance of making it in 1985, until the Blue Jays put us away.

But when you got released, Knucks, the whole pot when sour. The Yankees have had their yo-yo spinning again. Charlie

Hudson got sent to Columbus and Bob Tewksbury was called back up. Charlie had been struggling after his great 6–0 start, but the man is 7–2, for God's sake. How can you demote a starter who's five games over .500?

It's great to be out of that mess in New York.

—Joe

June 30. Tuesday. Cleveland.

Dear Joe:

Love them Angels, Joe. I don't know what it is about them, or what it is about me, but my luck is either good or great with them right now. They're too good a hitting team for me to keep this up against them. We won 2–1 and I went 8⅔ innings. My record's back to one game under .500, 6–7. I wish I could figure out how to deal with Detroit and Texas.

I'm on a little roll right now. You saw my start before this one; I lost 4–3 to Bert Blyleven in the Metrodome and I went eight pretty good innings in that one, too.

Pitching in the Metrodome is no stroll through the park, but every ballpark can be tough for one reason or another. The best game I remember pitching in the Metrodome was in 1986; the Twins got two runs in the first inning and then I retired 24 of the next 25 batters. When it was over I had no idea how or why I was able to do that well in that Dome.

With you being in Minnesota, and the way it looks like the Twins are headed for the playoffs, if the Indians ever trade me to a contender I'd like to be with you guys. I think you and I could help get them to the playoffs and the World Series. I know that's dreaming, Joe, but there's no crime in that. Dreaming's about all we can do on the Cleveland ball club.

The way you guys play the Metrodome, with four games of the playoffs at home and four games of the World Series at the American League city, the Twins can be world champions. I'm sure you guys already have this mapped out. Who wouldn't want to be part of something like that? Can you imagine Joe and Phil Niekro going to the World Series on the same team?

In my game against you guys, did you see Gaetti hit that line drive back between my legs? I tried to fool him with a slider outside, but he got the bat head out and just hit it. I'm telling you, I broke out in a cold sweat when the ball zipped through my legs and almost hit me in the groin. I don't remember seeing the ball at all, but I felt something tick my cup and go through. When I got back to the dugout I was still shaking. I could be singing soprano in the church choir if it got me where it could have. Nancy and I aren't planning any more children, but I still want all my body parts to function for a few more years.

Joe Carter came back last night. Thank God he's all right after getting busted in the nose like that. What a stud. He ended up missing only five games, but we can't afford to be without Joe for one minute. He's a potential league MVP.

To me, Joe came out of nowhere last year. I've always heard more about Mel Hall than Joe, going back to when they were with the Cubs. Everything finally fell into place for Joe; he played first and all three outfield positions, hit .302 with 29 home runs, and led the major leagues with 121 RBI. He was ninth in the MVP voting, and I thought he could have won it.

You sure were right about that Mark McGwire from Oakland. He hit five home runs in two games against us, which tied a major league record. Where are the A's getting these Incredible Hulks from? Jose Canseco was Rookie of the Year in 1986, and it looks like the A's have another one in McGwire.

Lance is growing so fast, Joe, like your John did. It looks like the Niekros have another ballplayer coming up through the ranks. Lance looked good shagging balls, and he swings the bat good, too. He looks like he could be in the big leagues some day, maybe for the Twins? How about the Yankees? Would you ever let Lance play for George?

I got a feeling that baseball will not have seen the end of the Niekros once we retire. I wonder if our sons' big-league victories can be added to our total? It's all in the family, isn't it?

Philip might be the agent in my family, but John and Michael could be ballplayers, and it looks like Lance could, too. I'll never worry about Philip, he's matured a lot. John and Michael still want to fish and play ball, anything but study.

Went to the Brook State Inn again last night and polka-ed my ass off. I probably stay out there too late sometimes, but they make me feel like one of the gang and I forget about having to go home. Can't wait to take you back there.

I'm going to have some chocolate-chip cookies and cold milk and hit the rack.

See ya.

—Phil

July: "Truth and the Consequences"

July 2. Thursday. Cleveland.

Joe:

The Indians pulled an old Yankees' end-around lateral: they fired the pitching coach, Jack Aker.

That's actually a Steinbrenner-type quick-fix solution: when the team's struggling and you don't know what to do, roll the pitching coach's head out on the table for everybody to see. That way a panic trade isn't made, you don't have to do anything as drastic as firing the manager, and maybe you'll get the players' attention.

Rarely does it work, or even save the manager, but firing the pitching coach is an old front-office tactic. I can't think of any reason the Indians would want to fire Aker, except that our pitching staff's been horseshit. I've yet to see Jack throw one pitch.

I guess for appearance' sake, something has to be done to make it look like the front-office is trying to shake up a last-place ball club. Steve Comer, a Double A pitching coach at Kingston who PT played for, was called up. I didn't know much about him except I remember him with Texas. I looked up his career stats and he was 44–37 in seven seasons with the Rangers and Philadelphia before finishing up with the Indians in 1984. That means he's been coaching about two years and now he's a major-league pitching coach. That's unusual.

Comer really was nice the first time we talked. He came right over and said, "Listen, Knucks, I'm going to need help from you." Right away he wanted the old-timer on his side, and I appreciated that.

I guess the moves will happen one at a time; usually the pitching coach is the leadoff hitter for things to come. They've put Greg Swindell, our good left-handed starter, on the 15-day disabled list with elbow problems, and I think they're a little more worried than they're letting on. If Swindell was lost for any length of time, it would be a big setback for the organization. They're counting on Swindell for the rotation for quite a while.

Sammy Stewart, the former Baltimore reliever, got called up and will be given the chance to fill Camacho's old closing role. Sammy used to slam the door for the Orioles. We'll see what he's got left.

If you've been reading the newspapers, you know we've got one foot in the grave. We beat Chicago 2–1 in 11 innings today, but we're still 21 games out and the local media have declared open season on Corrales. It looks bad for him unless we rip off about 10 straight wins. I always thought Pat would be with the Indians forever; they call him "Perpetual Pat" for the perpetually renewable contract he signed that got all the publicity.

Maybe Pat will dodge another bullet and another coach will get the ax. Maybe they ought to face up to the truth: the Indians are not a good ball club, and part of the disappointment is because magazines like *Sports Illustrated* pumped everybody up thinking we were going to be a miracle team.

I don't think I've ever seen a team set up for a bigger fall than we were. It was obvious we didn't have enough pitching. Our defense couldn't turn the double play for the longest time. We don't get our uniforms dirty. Balls get through the infield because nobody dives for them.

We're too offensive minded. We think we can score six and

seven runs a day, and we can't. The good teams in the American League East are not great in all phases of the game, but they are better than average in all phases. We're not even close to that. We give too many games away.

I know what I'd do if I was running the Indians: I'd go with defense. I'd get these guys out there and see how dirty they could get their uniforms. I'd get the infielders to practice diving for balls and jumping up to make the play, like Willie Randolph does. Cut off those bleeders through the infield. The pitchers give up enough legitimate base hits, they need the cheapies turned into outs.

I'd make sure the outfielders worked on hitting the cutoff man every day. Not once or twice a week—every day. It should be a throw you can almost make with your eyes closed. The old pros could do that. We're not making the fundamental plays consistently.

It's not Pat's fault. It's just the way this organization is flowing. "Let's get a bunch of runs and win the pennant" should be the team slogan. You know that doesn't work. In Atlanta we were first or second in home runs every year and always in fourth or fifth place because the defense wasn't any good and the pitching wasn't much better.

If we don't put something together soon, the second half of the season is going to be a disaster. The dog days usually start the middle of August. For us, those puppies are going to be barking before the end of July.

I don't think firing the pitching coach is the way to get us going, but we'll see.

How about Darrell Evans? Our old buddy did something he should be proud of: he became only the second player ever to hit 100 home runs for three teams—Atlanta, San Francisco, and Detroit. When people talk about the Tigers they think of Sparky, Kirk Gibson, Alan Trammell, Jack Morris, Lou Whitaker, but I think Darrell is the unsung hero with his bat and his leadership.

I need a fix—a fix of polka music to get me in good spirits. I might make the three-hour drive to Seven Springs, over by Pittsburgh. They're having a polka festival and Jimmy Sturr's playing. I'd sure like to surprise him, plus I wouldn't mind some of the kielbasa and sauerkraut.

Hope you get some good Polish food once in a while to keep your blood red.

—Phil

July 8. Wednesday. New York.

Phil:

You know how much I wanted this game, big brother. Returning to Yankee Stadium as a first-place Minnesota Twin, I was pumped.

This game probably meant too much to me. My last two starts weren't good—both $3\frac{2}{3}$-inning jobs—and I felt like I needed a strong game going to the All-Star break to keep the Twins from considering outside options.

I had no idea how I would feel inside Yankee Stadium again. It felt strange coming out of the third-base visitors' dugout instead of the Yankees' dugout. I heard a couple of people yell my name. I exchanged a couple of handshakes, winks, and thumbs up with some old teammates: Winfield, Randolph, Henderson, Mattingly, Righetti, Rhoden. It's always great to see those guys.

But once I started pitching, the Yankees might as well have been the Blue Jays. I was into the game, but as a Minnesota Twin trying to win a pennant, not as a bitter Joe Niekro trying to settle an old score. I was happy I ended up feeling that way; it might have been the reason I felt loose and was coasting with a 7–0 lead.

I got in trouble in the seventh and Tom Kelly came and got me with one out. I went back to the clubhouse to shower, feeling good about my performance—$6\frac{1}{3}$ innings, five hits, one run—and especially happy it came against the team that couldn't find a place for me in their starting rotation. The Yankees, as it turned out, came back against our bullpen and won 12–7. I'd never seen our team lose a lead like that before.

Afterward, though, our clubhouse was no different than it was in the four previous games we'd won. I've been with the Twins a month now, Knucks, and probably what impresses me the most is how TK keeps this club on an even keel; he motivates without smothering. No one is that significant, no loss is that damaging. If we win today, let's do it again tomorrow. If we lose today, let's win tomorrow.

Teams are supposed to reflect the personalities of their managers, and that never was more true than with TK and the Twins and Piniella and the Yankees. Lou is temperamental, explosive, and shows his emotions. So do the Yankees. TK is feisty but controlled; that's the Twins. Lou's been known to kick over a few tables and throw a few things around the clubhouse. TK raises his voice, but it's usually only to pump the guys up.

A clubhouse says everything about a team's atmosphere. With the Yankees it was a pressure cooker, a time bomb constantly ticking. With the Twins it's relaxed and fun. Even in a tough pennant race—and we've lost some games that would have made Billy Martin or Lou go berserk—the Twins' clubhouse doesn't differ one day to the next, win or lose.

In the Yankee clubhouse it's win at all costs and walk the plank if you don't. It's a Russian roulette atmosphere. Everybody is on guard because you never know when somebody's going to explode.

I remember Steinbrenner and Winfield getting into it not long after I joined the Yankees in 1985. George wanted the Yankees to be leaders in the war against drugs and wanted us all to submit to voluntary drug testing. Winfield said he had no problem with testing, but not without the Players Association being involved. They got pretty loud and intense about the whole issue.

Finally George said: "I'm captain of this ship and it runs my way."

That'll end most Yankee arguments. I don't think it bothered Winny one way or the other, because nothing happened.

With TK and Andy MacPhail, the Twins' general manager, you don't expect ugly incidents like that. TK may not be loud, arrogant, or cantankerous like some managers, but he's in control in his own way. TK mixes well with the players because the nucleus of this club—Gaetti, Hrbek, Puckett, Viola, Laudner—grew up with Kelly in the minor leagues.

In my second start with the Twins I pitched six good innings and was in trouble in the seventh. TK came out and I tried to talk him into going with me a little longer. He knew what he wanted to do: he brought in Juan Bereguer and Juan threw the shit out of the ball for three innings and we won. TK doesn't give a damn about complete games, especially if his bullpen needs work. If one of our four relievers—Reardon, Bereguer, Atherton, Dan Schatzeder—hasn't been in a game for three or four days, TK is going to make certain he gets some work no matter what the score. If he sticks with that pitching plan, it should benefit the team down the line.

TK also is good at keeping players in the game, whether you're a utility man or just down on your luck. Gene Larkin, a good switch hitter, was struggling tonight. He ended up 0 for 5, leaving a couple of runners stranded. Kelly won't let a guy's confidence get down. After Larkin's fourth at-bat, Kelly told him: "Don't worry, big boy, you're playing tomorrow. You're going to have days like this. We have guys who can pick you up. Just don't take it to the field or let it carry over to tomorrow."

That little chitchat on the bench between Kelly and Larkin really impressed me. TK kids with guys, does anything not to let them feel the pressure, like we've seen on the Yankee bench, right Knucks? TK knows he's going to lose a certain number of games. He does little things to keep the team in the game, like putting on a hit-and-run play with the eighth and ninth hitters in the batting order, a steal with a guy who isn't supposed to run. He makes late-inning defensive changes and matches up well with his relievers.

If Kelly keeps this up and we win the division, he's got to be manager of the year by a landslide.

Shirley got released by Kansas City. In his first appearance as a Royal he gave up a grand slam to Dick Shofield of the Angels. I think Bobby was used twice after that. The way his arm recovered, I've got to believe he could still help somebody as a reliever.

The Yankees brought Hudson back up from Columbus, and

this time sent Rich Bordi to Columbus. At least Henry Cotto, who goes back and forth between New York and Columbus more times than a truck driver, hasn't had to travel alone lately.

Hope you got to see some fireworks on July 4th, just so they didn't go off when you were pitching, old-timer.

—Joe

July 11. Saturday. Arlington, Texas

Joe:

Well, little brother, it doesn't look like they're going to pick me for the All-Star team this year. Pat Tabler's our one All-Star; he was selected as a reserve first baseman.

Guess I'll leave after our game tomorrow and fly home to Atlanta. I'm anxious to get home.

You know I'll go fishing and barbecue some shrimp, chicken breasts, and pork ribs on the back porch. That sounds like heaven right now, even if it is only two days. We open the second half with a Thursday afternoon game in Chicago, and we've got a workout there Wednesday. So we're really only getting three-fourths of an All-Star break.

It's been anything but dull around here lately, except it's not the kind of excitement you want. What it is, is a last-place ball club crumbling into pieces. Mel Hall and Scotty Bailes got into it—nothing major, just two ballplayers venting some frustration. After getting fired as pitching coach Jack Aker was quoted in the newspaper as saying that part of our pitching problem is that Rick Dempsey calls a lousy game.

That ruffled some feathers. I don't think Aker and Dempsey got along that well. Chris Bando, not Dempsey, catches me, but Dempsey caught some great pitchers in Baltimore, and the Orioles had success when Rick was there. Shit, Dempsey was the 1963 World Series MVP.

Then there was a doozy of a fight that you probably saw on all the highlight shows. Ken Schrom hit Willie Wilson of the Royals with a pitch. Wilson was standing at first base, taking off his batting gloves, when he suddenly took off after Schrom and dropped him with a full-bore, shoulders-down tackle that looked like an instructional film for NFL kick-return teams.

Later Danny Jackson, the Royals' hard-throwing left-hander, obviously was retaliating for Wilson and threw the first pitch behind Brett Butler. The next one sailed over Butler's head and you knew it was "Everybody in the pool."

Suspensions will be coming, I'm sure, but the league ought to take into consideration that Butler only responded after getting thrown at twice by Jackson.

But the Royals better keep an eye on Al Davis; the Los Angeles Raiders' owner might try to sign Willie Wilson as the next Lawrence Taylor. I still can't get over that tackle.

When the second half of the season starts we better get it going in a hurry, or Corrales will never make it to August. The Cleveland press is all over him. Pee Wee Herman could be managing us and I don't think he could be held responsible for being 23 games out before the All-Star break.

I hope our front office guys, Danny O'Brien and Joe Klein, aren't thinking it's all the pitchers' fault because we give up a lot of runs. Our defense can be brutal; it has to share the blame.

I wish I could blame the defense for my game last night; got pounded by the Rangers again, nine hits and seven runs in five innings. We lost 10–4 to snap our four-game winning streak, our longest of the season. Damn. I wanted to keep our good roll going. I don't like ending the first half on a game like this. I'm 6–9, the team's hopelessly in last place, and you know the youth movement has to be coming at any time.

I don't know what it is about the Rangers. I still can't get Larry Parrish out; I had trouble with him in the National League, too. Pete O'Brien always hurts me, and sometimes Oddibe McDowell. I can't make pitches on those guys, and last night my knuckleball was all over the Lone Star State.

Remember Mike Duffy, Joe? He used to be a neighbor in Atlanta, we were deer-hunting buddies. Mike lives here now so I went to his place for lunch today. It was nice to get away for a couple of hours, doing something outside of baseball. I walked out in Mike's backyard and stared up at that big Texas sky, trying to figure out why the Rangers hit me so well. Is it because they see Charlie Hough's knuckleball all season? Maybe Tom Paciorek, our old teammate, knows my signs and is tipping them off?

Wish you had a tip for me. What good are you, little brother?

In my last start before this loss to the Rangers, get this, the White Sox beat us 17–0. Everything I threw up there, everything anybody threw up there, Chicago ripped. I had an exhausting three innings of punishment—seven hits, eight runs—and I just couldn't watch any more of it.

I ducked out of the stadium about the fifth inning and drove over to Seven Springs, the polka place I want to take you to over by Pittsburgh. They were having a polka festival, one of the biggest in the country.

When we ever get out of this game, Joe, we ought to consider doing this. Load up our families in a couple of motor homes and drive up to this polka festival every July. It has to be Polish heaven on earth. Everybody's got their red and white Polish eagles on their hats, their sleeves, their backs, somewhere. You can feel the Polish pride with these people. All they do, starting on Thursday, is polka for four days. You'd be a big hit up here, Joe, the way you kick up your heels.

I'll write to you after the All-Star break. Enjoy your time off and then get ready for a big second half. With me riding out this season with the Indians, you've got to be the Niekro to get into the World Series. The Twins can do it and I know you can play a big role for them. Good luck.

—Phil

July 12. Sunday. Baltimore.

Phil:

I'm sitting in the Baltimore-Washington Airport waiting to fly to Tampa. I hope to get home in Lakeland by 7:30 tonight. I know the three days will fly by before I have to get back to Minneapolis Thursday to start the second half against Toronto, a team that wears the Twins out.

It wasn't the best game for the Twins, or myself.

Dave Schmidt, a reliever the Orioles have been starting, threw a two-hit shutout at us. I gave up all five Baltimore runs in six innings, and my record dropped under .500, 5–6. They'll just have to play another All-Star game without me.

We're leading the American League West, I know, but our 49–40 record isn't impressing anybody. Most writers still think Kansas City will put on one of its second-half charges and win the division in September. The first six weeks of the second half will be crucial for us. With most of our games in September at home, if we can take a modest lead into the last month, we'll be awfully tough to catch.

All I want to do is stay out of fights, get my knuckleball over, and start winning some games for this ball club. If we get to the playoffs or the World Series, I want to have pitched well enough to start a couple of games and not be pushed aside into a long-relief role. I really want to win for this club, Knucks.

There were more than a couple of guys upset about the American League All-Star selections. Kirby Puckett and Jeff Reardon are the only Twins going to Oakland, and we're leading the AL West. That's horseshit, two guys from the division leader.

Hrbek, with 23 home runs, didn't get picked and Herbie was so upset he said he'd never go to another All-Star game. Don Mattingly was voted the starting first baseman by the fans, and then John McNamara, the All-Star manager from Boston, picked Mark McGwire and Pat Tabler as backups. You can't argue with McGwire, because he's leading the league in home runs with 33 and probably has been the hottest player in the league. Tabler's a .300 hitter, but he was on the team because you have to have a player from every team and he, apparently, was considered Cleveland's best representative.

You know first base is a deep position in the American League when Hrbek, the Angels' Wally Joyner, Pete O'Brien of Texas, and Baltimore's Eddie Murray can't make the All-Star squad.

Gaetti is another guy who deserves to go. He's going for his second Gold Glove at third base, he'll probably hit 30 home runs again, and he's a leader on our ball club. Rat has gone unnoticed because George Brett, Wade Boggs, and Paul Molitor play third base, too. But I'll bet after this season, if we get to the playoffs and the World Series, Gaetti will be discovered nationally and you'll see him in the All-Star game in 1988 at Cincinnati.

I have no trouble recalling my All-Star game performances—there was only one, in Seattle in 1979. Being my first All-Star game after 13 seasons in the majors, and a couple of trips to the minors, I was excited. With a 13–4 record at the break I thought I would start. I was well rested—it would have been my fifth day—and with a 2.00 ERA and the most wins in the league, you figure you might start.

Tommy Lasorda, the Los Angeles Dodgers' manager, started Steve Carlton instead. I didn't even get into the game, but it was great to be in a clubhouse with all those stars—Carlton, Dave Parker, Bruce Sutter, Gaylord Perry—because you never know if you'll ever be back to a game like that. It was a thriller, even though I wasn't involved; Lee Mazzilli hit a pinch-hit home run in the eighth to tie the game and then he walked with the bases loaded in the ninth for a 7–6 National League victory.

I'll always remember Lasorda, that old Astros' fan, for not getting me into that All-Star game. When we beat the Dodgers for the 1980 NL West title, I couldn't help but think it was my personal payback to Tommy.

Hope you have a restful All-Star break, and I'm going to whisper around here and see if the Twins could use another Niekro for the pennant stretch. It would be a great way for us to finish the year, wouldn't it?

—Joe

July 16. Thursday. Chicago.

Joe:

The ax dropped on Pat Corrales today. You knew it was coming, especially the last week of the first half. You knew O'Brien and Klein hated to do it because they have been solidly behind Pat, here and in Texas, too. Even Pat knew the time had come. He's probably relieved he won't have to be responsible anymore for something that's not really his fault.

Pat was notified about nine in the morning, and Doc Edwards got the job to finish the season out. Pat got caught in the middle—aside from hitting, they didn't give him a lot to work with. The pitching still needs to be improved and our defense keeps giving runs away. It's easier to fire one guy than trade three or four, even though some trades definitely need to be made.

I'm sure Pat will manage again somewhere; he's highly regarded by baseball people. I'd have liked to see Pat spend more time in the clubhouse with the players, I think a communication gap developed here for him because he didn't. I thought Pat kept to himself too much. When the players would come in from the field, Pat would be in his room with the door shut.

I don't know, the way we were going maybe Pat was just trying to keep himself from strangling one of us. You couldn't blame him for that.

That's one thing I'll do if I ever get a chance to manage: I'll stay close to my players. I don't want a separate office; I'll dress right with the players in the clubhouse. Whatever I have to say to the press can be said in front of the players, as far as I'm concerned. They'll read it in the newspapers anyway. We're all in this together, and I don't think there should be a wall between manager and team.

Doc managed pretty well in the minor leagues, and I guess the Indians are trying to be an organziation that promotes from within. Doc hasn't said much as bullpen coach over the season, so it'll be interesting to see how he runs the ball club. You know how much I want to manage, and I sure fell in love with Cleveland in a short time, but nobody asked me anything about the manager's job.

The player moves started up again yesterday. We traded Tony Bernazard, our second baseman, to Oakland; the A's just lost their second baseman Tony Phillips for six weeks with an ankle injury. We received the A's pitching prospect, Darrel Akerfelds, and top catching prospect, Brian Dorsett. I don't know anything about either of them or when they might be able to contribute.

Then we brought up Tommy Hinzo, a kid from Double A, to play second base, so we're shaking things up around here. Bernazard is probably the first of several veteran players to go.

I've had Minnesota on my mind for several days now. I keep reading the rumor that you guys might be interested in a second knuckleballer named Niekro. It's obvious the Tribe's not going anywhere; we're 23, 24 games out and just trying to save face for next season with a new manager.

If the Indians trade me for a prospect, I'd sure love to try it with you over at your place. Put a bug in somebody's ear, will ya?

I thought the All-Star game was a helluva interesting game, the National League winning 2–0. It was kind of ironic that the MVP was Tim Raines, the player no teams wanted to sign as a free agent last winter.

I see where Oakland released Ron Cey, an old National League opponent of ours when he played for the Dodgers. The Penguin. He had some great seasons and he was always a tough out for me.

Every now and then you see an old name from the early seventies pop up—somebody retiring or being released—and it makes you realize how many guys we've outlasted. We've both been fortunate.

I need a few extra dollars so I'm going fishing with Dempsey tomorrow; I'll probably get five dollars from him for the first fish and ten dollars for the largest fish.

One time in Cleveland Dempsey and I went fishing and I caught the biggest bass that came out of the pond that day. Dempsey paid me five dollars and signed the bill. I've got it tacked up over my locker, which is next to Dempsey's. Every day Rick comes in and I always make sure he sees that five-dollar bill.

Rick keeps saying he's going to get it back, but he knows he can't outfish the Old Knuckleballer. I told Rick he'd better start fishing against you, Joe, before stepping up in class to the oldtimer. Right?
—Phil

July 22. Wednesday. Kansas City.

Joe:

I think I lost my fishing partner for a while. Dempsey broke his thumb last night and they put him on the 21-day disabled list. If you'd have seen how Rick broke it, you'd be wondering why the boy isn't in traction for the next two months.

Dempsey got hit by a truck and the license plate read "Bo."

It was about a week ago that Bo Jackson made headlines when he said he was thinking of taking up professional football as a hobby. Bo's been playing left field for Kansas City and having a good rookie season, but when he made his surprise announcement he started taking shit from all sides. His teammates were down on him because of his timing—they're trying to win a pennant. The football players were taking shots at Bo in interviews because he treated the NFL like it was something he could do in his spare time.

Joe, believe me, Bo Jackson could walk into almost any NFL camp today and probably become the starting tailback. The speed he has for being 6'1", 222 pounds, is incredible. The only athlete I can think of like Bo is Jim Brown, the Cleveland Browns' great fullback, and I'm not sure he had Bo's world-class sprinter's speed.

You can imagine the collision if Bo ran head-on into a hulk like New York Giants' linebacker Harry Carson. So what about this 24-year-old stud in peak physical condition hitting a 37-year-old, 184-pound catcher?

Bo was trying to score and he turned third base going full blast, no intention of stopping. The throw got to Dempsey in plenty of time, and being the veteran catcher he is, Rick squared around to the third-base line to block the front corner of the plate.

At top speed, Bo bent slightly at the waist and ran over poor Rick. I told him I thought he had more sense than to stand in front of a charging rhino like that without a rifle.

It was like a cement mixer hitting a Yugo, but Dempsey took the hit like a helluva man and held the ball for the out.

Mentally, Bo had the football in his hands and home plate was the goal line. Dempsey made a damn strong goal-line stand, but let there be no doubt, Bo Jackson could play football anytime, anywhere, any league. Bo may become a superstar baseball player, but he looks born to be a superstar in football.

First Camacho, now Dempsey. I can't keep a fishing partner. I told Dempsey I'll get him a cane pole, a bobber, and a few worms and he can try to catch some bluegill—and then I'll use them for bait.

My record is a boring 7–9; I'm still trying to get up over .500. I've got to go 4–2 to equal my 1986 record.

I did join some select company in a game against the Royals; I gave up my 5,000th career hit, to Danny Tartabull. Cy Young and Pud Galvin are the only other pitchers to give up 5,000 hits.

It's not like beating the Perrys' record, but it is a longevity record. I had to be good enough to pitch in all those games to give up that many hits—at least that's my rationale.

Keep in touch; let me know if there's any talk with the Twins. If they've got a suggestion box, drop in a slip of paper that says "Phil Niekro."

—Phil

July 29. Wednesday. Seattle.

Phil:

Since I joined the Twins almost two months ago, I've been telling you , Knucks, that this ball club doesn't know how good it can be. It does now.

I lost last night to the Mariners 6–1, but the last two weeks our club has been playing like a team that will not be denied. We've been in first place for 45 straight days, and the Royals and A's have not made runs at us like I thought they might.

Toronto had beaten Minnesota nine straight games going back to 1986 before Viola, Berenguer, and Reardon teamed up to beat the Blue Jays 3–2 July 17. If splitting a four-game series at the Metrodome against the Blue Jays boosted our confidence, an unbelievable 4–3 win against the Mariners last night strengthened our character.

We were down 3–0 going into the ninth inning against Mark Langston; as you know, Knucks, he's probably the toughest left-hander in the league. You would think that's a Seattle victory 99 times out of 100. But Steve Lombardozzi hit a three-run home run to tie, and Gaetti hit his 20th home run of the season to win it.

It was the kind of game the Twins were only supposed to win at home. Coming from behind against Langston, on the road, it was like we cleared another hurdle, we proved ourselves again, passed another test.

If people would look closely at the Twins, they'd stop underrating us. We're a well-balanced club. With Gaetti, Puckett, and Tom Brunansky, we have as much right-handed power as any team in the league. We're not that strong from the left side except for Hrbek, and he has tremendous power, especially at the Metrodome. A left-handed hitter I think is going to come through is Randy Bush; he's got a great swing.

Our defense gets no credit and it's probably the secret to the Twins' success. Gaetti is a Gold Glover at third with a great arm. Greg Gagne was a total surprise to me. He's one of the better shortstops in the league, a dependable everyday player. Lombardozzi, at second, is steady and can turn the double play.

Hrbek is amazing; he takes shit for weighing 230 or so, but the big boy can play some outstanding first base. He's surprisingly agile and at 6′4″, his stretch makes the difference on close plays.

Puckett brings back more home runs over the fence than any centerfielder around. I can't believe the things Puck can do with that 5′8″, 220-pound body; he's built like a bullet.

It's been a rough year offensively for Timmy Laudner, but he is solid defensively behind the plate, and Sal Butera is a good backup.

Our pitching staff gets no respect, as far as I'm concerned. Frankie Viola has won more games than any left-hander in baseball the last four years, and nobody knows it because they think he's pitching up in Iceland. Bert Blyleven still has a great curveball and he's a great competitor. Les Straker is a longtime minor leaguer who's had some good starts. And I keep hoping, if my shoulder stops bothering me, that my best games of the season are still ahead. To me, our rotation is strong enough to win this division.

Besides our right-handed power, our strength is the bullpen. Keith Atherton and Juan Berenguer are power pitchers from the right side for the middle innings; Dan Schatzeder filled our need for a left-handed reliever. Then there's Jeff Reardon to close games out. Knucks, Jeff throws a lot harder than I thought. His fastball rises. I like the way Jeff battles, sometimes with the fastball, sometimes with the change-up, but always aggressive and in command.

California signed Bill Buckner, your old nemesis, to play first base while Wally Joyner is injured. Buck can be a good left-handed DH too. There are reports the Angels might bring back Don Baylor out of Boston; that would worry me. Baylor's the type of experienced hitter and leader who would be great for our club.

The Angels are loading up for the stretch run, trying again to get Gene Mauch in a World Series. But it looks like they'll have to finish without their ace reliever, Donnie Moore; he's on the 21-day disabled list because of his shoulder.

Knucks, *you* ask *me* for tips on the Rangers, Parrish and O'Brien? All I can think is, "My idol is asking me?" They've whipped on me, too, remember? I'm struggling myself; I haven't won since June 14, my second start with the Twins. I'm trying not to let my shoulder bother me, but my control is not what it usually is—my knuckleball is all over the place.

I need something to get me going; I don't know what it is. Help, big brother.

—Joe

July 31. Friday. Toronto.

Joe:

My heart broke today, Joe. With you guys getting Steve Carlton from us, that about kills my chances of joining you in Minnesota.

This is the time contenders are making pitching moves, and I'd been hearing for three weeks how it looked like I was headed to the Twins. I was trying to play it down and not get my hopes too high, but I'd reached the point where I actually was counting on it. You and me, our third reunion, in the year of 530. It just seemed like a storybook ending to the season, maybe my career.

I'm happy for Carlton; Lefty will help you. I know you guys needed left-handers, and he's been throwing good.

Hey, little brother, I never give up hope. You tell Kelly if they still need another arm, you know there's one back in Cleveland ready to join you. I'm trying to pick myself up right now because finding out I'm not the guy going to Minnesota has made it a downer day for me. Does this mean my 24-year career is going to end with double-figure losses for a last-place ball club?

I don't know if the Indians can do anything with me or not; maybe there isn't a contender out there who thinks I can win anymore. If I'm not going to Minnesota, I guess I'd just as soon finish the year out in Cleveland with a good bunch of people, unless I could find a way to go out with the Atlanta Braves.

I pitched a good game against Toronto tonight, and we still lost 8–3. I went six innings and had a good knuckleball; I gave up three hits and one earned run. I've pitched pretty well up here since 1985, I don't know why. The start before was against Texas, and guess what happened? No thanks to you and your lack of advice, Joe, they kicked my ass again, 7–3.

I'm 7–10 already. If I'm not careful I could end up with 20 losses, and that hasn't happened since I went 21–20 with the Braves in 1979.

It's not easy, though, being a .500 pitcher on a team playing barely .350. Our home runs keep coming—Joe Carter, Cory Snyder, and Brook Jacoby have more than 20 home runs apiece. But our defense is getting no better; Jacoby's had a rough season at third and our middle infield has been a weakness from the start. We make bad pitches at the wrong time.

We've been a bad baseball team, that's the hard truth. I just want you to get going, Joe. You've got a pennant race to get wrapped up in, and the Twins need you to win some games.

I looked it up: we don't play Minnesota again until you guys come to Cleveland September 11, a Friday; Saturday night I want to take you to the Brook State Inn for polka dancing.

I think we both could use some dancing and a couple of moon shooters, what do you think?

—Phil

August: "Momma Raised No Cheaters"

Phil:

Where do I begin, big brother? My mind is mush right now after what I went through last night. Un-friggin-believable.

You've probably seen it on ESPN. They rerun the tape every 10 minutes. It's the "Scuff Scandals," a made-for-TV hardball soap opera.

This is embarrassing, Phil, but your baby brother was accused of cheating, of scuffing baseballs in front of 30,000 people, a TV audience, God, and everybody. I emphasize the word "accused" because I was not caught doing anything illegal. I was thrown out of our game against California last night because I had an emery board in my back pocket; you know, the kind I've been carrying back there for the last 16 years.

I don't want to get too far ahead of myself, Knucks, so let's start over. Better grab a beer for this letter, Phil; this is like nothing I've ever been through.

It was just another ball game, Knucks. I haven't won since June 14 and I was pumped up to have a good game. I tried to remember those pointers you gave me on pitching to DeCinces. I was psyched up to the level I like before I take the mound, and I retired the side 1–2–3 in the first.

I struggled the next two innings, but we tied the score and it was 2–2 going into the bottom of the fourth. Dick Schofield led off with a ground ball to Greg Gagne at shortstop. I had a 2-and-0 count on Brian Downing, and Sal Butera, my personal knuckleball catcher, called for a slider. I threw it on the outside corner for a strike.

Home-plate umpire Tim Tschida tore off his mask and called for the baseball. I flipped it to him and Tschida dropped it. He picked it up and looked at the ball closely, turning it and scrutinizing it suspiciously. It was as if he was searching for a secret message hidden in the stitching. He dropped the ball back into his game-ball bag like he would any other he was putting back in play.

Then Tschida walked to the mound and said, "I've got to see your glove."

That quick, Knucks, I was surrounded by the other three umpires, Dave Phillips, Dan Morrison, and Steve Palermo. I couldn't believe how fast all four umpires were all over me.

Knucks, this was the first time in my career I'd ever been checked for anything. I knew the emery board and a piece of sandpaper were in my back pockets. As a knuckleball pitcher, you know as well as I do that the fingernails of your first and second fingers are most important. You have to keep them neat and rounded to be able to get a good, secure grip to stop the spin on the knuckleball.

I've always carried an emery board in case I have to file off a hangnail or touch the nail up during a game. I've done it on the bench between innings, and in the bullpen, but I've never pulled it out while on the mound and filed my nails like a secretary on her coffee break, let alone work over the ball in full view. The sandpaper is a backup, that's all, and I rarely use it.

I've carried them for 16 years because nobody ever told me I couldn't.

I said to Tschida, "If there's something wrong with that ball, show me the ball." He said, "No." I asked, "What the hell's going on here?" and then it turned into an all-out search party.

You know what it was like, Knucks? You've seen professional

wrestling when a four-man tag team gangs up on one guy in the corner? That's how I felt on the mound, hemmed in on all sides by baseball cops.

One umpire wanted to see my glove, another wanted to check the waistband of my pants, the third wanted to look at my hand.

"Time out," I said. "What's going on? If there's something wrong with that damn ball, show it to me."

Tschida refused.

Damn it, Knucks, if I'm the home-plate umpire and I suspect the pitcher of illegally doctoring the baseball, then I'm going to show him the ball—face the evidence, buster. If there were marks on the ball, I would show the baseball to you to prove I have sufficient grounds to search you.

I never was told anything like that. I've yet to see the ball I'm supposed to have scuffed.

During the $3\frac{1}{3}$ innings I pitched, there was not one request from California manager Gene Mauch to have the baseballs checked. Not one of the Angels' players complained.

Tom Kelly wanted to know what was going on, but he and I knew what was happening. It was obvious the umpires were out to search me. Why, I don't know. What I did to make those guys take a contract out on me, I'll never know.

There was nothing wrong with the last baseball I threw to Downing, otherwise Tschida would not have put it back in his game-ball bag. If you're going to take a ball out of the game as evidence in a scuff case against a pitcher, you don't put it back in your game-ball bag, do you?

They were on me like I was giving a million dollars away to each of them.

Phillips says, "Empty your pockets."

I'm still in shock: "What the hell's going on here?"

Not once in 21 years of professional baseball had I ever been accused of cheating. I never read anybody in the newspapers ever hint I scuff baseballs, not like I've read people accuse Tommy John, Mike Scott, Don Sutton, Rick Rhoden. There was a book once that listed 20 pitchers who throw spitballs and my name was in there. But I'm telling you the truth, brother, I've never thrown a spitball and don't really know how or would want to know. It would probably pop out of my paw like a watermelon seed.

It happened so fast, and since I've never been searched before, I emptied my pockets. Later I found out I could have refused. I wonder what they would have done, ejected me for suspicion of hidden foreign objects? I'm not the Iron Sheik, for chrissakes.

I think people doubted me when I said this after the game, but it's the truth: when it's hot like it was in Anaheim, your perspiration makes the emery board sticky. When damp, the rough, sandy side becomes almost adhesive.

Anyway, as all the world knows now, I reached into my back pocket to pull the emery board out and it stuck between my fingers. I felt it stick so I tried to give it a little flip to get it off my fingers. Maybe it looked worse on television, like I was a high school kid trying to ditch a cigarette. But let's be serious: where am I going to flip it, out of the stadium? I knew the emery board was coming out. I was making no attempt to fake anybody out or try to get away with anything. If I knew I had something to hide, I wouldn't have pulled the emery board out. I reacted innocently and honestly by freely emptying my pockets, like a falsely accused pickpocket.

I had no idea that carrying an emery board might be an offense punishable by ejection.

Phillips picked up the emery board and said, "You're gone." Why?

"Because you've got this in your pockets," Phillips said.

The umpires picked up the sandpaper, and Tschida said they had baseballs that were marked and scuffed.

"Where are they?" I kept asking. "I haven't seen a scuffed baseball."

Tschida said, "Oh, we have them."

End of argument. I walked back to the clubhouse in a daze; it was the first ejection of my career. Ejected for cheating? I couldn't believe what had just happened to me.

Knucks, you remember when you're young and your ass is in a

jam, about the first thing you think of is, "What are Mom and Dad gonna say?"

For a second right then, the thought did hit me: "I hope Mom and Dad won't think I really was cheating."

I sat on my stool in the clubhouse, and the more I thought about what had just happened the angrier I got, thinking how unsubstantiated and undeserving the ejection was. I wondered if the umpires were sitting back in their room putting another notch in their belts.

Never before have I seen the home-plate umpire walk to the mound, and almost at the same moment have the other three umpires surround the pitcher like the guy just spit in their daughters' faces.

It was like the umpires had said: "OK, if he throws anything but a knuckleball, we're going to get him."

I was attacked on the mound, big brother. That's the simplest way for me to describe it. It was premeditated. I received no warning. I was shown no evidence of scuffed baseballs. I heard after the game that you're supposed to receive a warning that is made official with an announcement over the public-address system. They didn't follow proper procedure, and I feel like screaming, "False arrest, false arrest!"

Anybody can cut a ball during a game. A third baseman can do it just before he throws the ball back to the pitcher. Catchers have been cutting balls on shin guards and spikes for years.

They didn't catch me in the act of doing anything. If umpires had treated Gaylord Perry like this, giving him the thumb when he was suspected of throwing a spitter and not having to show him the evidence, he wouldn't have been in enough games to win 300.

When the reporters asked me if I scuffed, I told them, "I take the Fifth Amendment." You know, Knucks, there are scuffed baseballs in every game—that doesn't mean the pitcher put them there. I wasn't thrown out for scuffed baseballs; I was thrown out for having an emery board in my back pocket.

I heard that Palermo said you can have a chain saw in your back pocket as long as you don't use it to scuff baseballs. I say,

"Where is your proof that I used the emery board to scuff base-balls?" They don't have any.

I told Andy MacPhail I wanted to appeal. At the very least I want to be confronted with the evidence. I guess tomorrow we'll talk to Dr. Bobby Brown, the president of the American League, about it.

I can't believe the commotion I've stirred up with this, though. Already today I've heard from David Letterman's people. They want me. I guess that means I'm officially a hot item.

I keep thinking about our 530; we didn't get nearly the attention or publicity I'm getting for this fiasco. There's a statement there about what the media think is news, I'd say.

They can hide baseballs all they want, or make an issue out of something I've carried in my back pocket for 16 years. The bottom line, big brother, is those four umpires accused a Niekro of cheating. They've put a black mark on the Niekro name, which is a shame and an insult to hard-working, God-fearing people like Mom and Dad. Momma raised no cheaters.

I'll let you know how the meeting with Dr. Brown goes. Some guys think I'll get suspended. What a time for this to happen, with only 55 games left in a pennant race. This better not screw us up down the stretch or make me ineligible for the postseason roster.

Keep your fingers crossed for me, buddy. I don't think this mess is going to go away for a while.

—Joe

August 6. Thursday. Cleveland.

Dear Mr. Emery Board:

Everybody's talking about you, Joe, and nobody can understand what happened.

I must have watched the replay 50 times. You flipping the emery board, the umpire picking it up and giving you the thumb. That film clip will make the Bloopers Hall of Fame.

The Yankees beat me 5-2 yesterday. Now I'm saying I'm having a "convenience-store season": my record's 7-11.

Anyway, about the third or fourth inning I accidentally dropped the ball. The home-plate umpire—must be getting old, I can't remember who it was—came out right away and checked the ball.

I'd never been checked before, Joe. I looked at him like, "Is this open season on Niekros or what?" The ump couldn't keep from smiling and tossed the ball back to me.

This scuff stuff is the hottest topic in baseball, a full-blown controversy, and my little brother's in the middle of it. Never a dull moment.

When I went to the bullpen to warm up, there was an emery board waiting for me. Two or three emery boards were put in my locker. I'm calling it "Scuffmania." You've got to take advantage of this craze, Joe: market some T-shirts, "Scuffing in the USA," "Scuff is not enough," "Scuff Animal." How about "Joe Niekro" brand emery boards, "Joe Niekro" power-sanders from Black & Decker.

You've got to strike when you're hot, little brother. You'll be great on Letterman. Don't show Dave up though, Joe; you might be funnier than he is.

I can't believe I'm laughing about this after the way the news hit me late Monday night. Stump Merrill, the Yankees' coach, and I were having last call in the downstairs bar at the Bond Court Hotel. We're the only two guys in the place and about ready to leave when Claire Smith and Tommy Pedulla walk in and Claire asks me if I'd heard what's happened to you in California.

From the look on Claire's face I thought something serious had happened: a heart attack, you got hit in the face with a line drive, you were in a car accident, a plane crash, you pitched a no-hitter. I got chills all over.

Then Claire tells me you were thrown out of a game for "defacing" a baseball. She might as well have said you got thrown out for not shaving. It was the weirdest reason for getting thrown out of a game I'd ever heard.

Claire didn't know the details, so Stumpy and I sit there trying to figure out what the hell you did.

I told Stump that as far as I knew, you never cheated, and that's not just one brother standing up for another. I never knew you to do anything like that, though I'm sure you've played around with a greaseball or Vaseline ball, like we all have a time or two.

Claire did say something about an emery board, and finally we caught ESPN on the TV at the bar. I didn't see Gene Mauch raising a stink; I saw nobody calling for baseballs.

The umpires ask for your glove and you give it to them. They look at it. Then you empty your pockets and you flick away the emery board. I don't think it was you flicking away the emery board that amused people so. It was your little shrug of "Oh, what have we here?" that tore everybody up.

It looked like they caught you by surprise, Joe—kind of like the mouse with the cheese in his mouth. I know you've carried emery boards for years, but I never dreamed you could get ejected for carrying one.

I pitched an entire game with a hand-warmer in my pocket one time in New York. I kept my right hand in my back pocket all the time, keeping my fingers warm. The umpires knew what I was doing back there.

I've carried an emery board before, a metal one even, and I certainly didn't feel like I was carrying a concealed weapon. What I'm trying to figure out is how you could scuff a ball on the mound with an emery board and not have anybody see you do it.

With all the pitchers who actually do scuff, I can't understand why they picked on you. You've been in the major leagues since 1967 and never been suspected once before. I've never seen four umpires close in on a pitcher like that.

If you did do something to the ball, you were awful slick about it because nobody caught you. Gaylord Perry was the slickest of all time; everyone knew he was doing something, but nobody could ever catch him. Gaylord would go through his routine—touching the bill of his cap, tugging his ear lobe, wiping his brow, rubbing his fingertips across his chest—on every pitch, so you never knew when he was actually greasing up. He'd only go to it when he needed a double-play ball or a strikeout.

I've watched you pitch for years and know you never needed to resort to anything like that; knuckballs move better than scuffballs anyway. Hey, if the ball comes back and there's a cut on it, any pitcher might use it to improve his grip, but that doesn't mean he's out there playing Crocodile Dundee with a blade.

The umpires had to be sitting on you, little brother; that's all I can figure. It's like they had the whole thing set up, like a Smokey waiting behind a bridge to catch that jacked-up 4-by-4 doing 80 on the highway. You were dead meat, it looks to me.

The more I think about it, Joe, the more pissed I get. It's a slap in your face and a slap at the Niekros. They are accusing a Niekro of cheating. You could get a 10- to 15-day suspension, and I'd fight that sucker. If they're accusing you of cheating, tell them to prove it or you're taking them to a court of law for defamation of character.

The untold story is why there were no scuffed balls presented as evidence against you. Something stinks.

I'm going to watch these other pitchers closely and see how they get away with it. If they want to catch the violators, they could make a rule that when the umpire is suspicious, he may say at any time he's going to check the pitcher and the pitcher must freeze. Everybody, players and umpires, must stay at their positions. If the pitcher makes any kind of move, tries to take off his glove or brush something behind his head, he's gone.

The umpire calls both managers out and checks whatever he wants. I guarantee you, Joe, there would be guys who would have to retire if they went by that rule, and you're not one of them.

When I got beat by New York last night somebody told me Pat Gillick, the Toronto general manager, was sitting up in the stands. Other than Mike Pagliarulo hitting a home run off me, I pitched seven decent innings. Somebody said Gillick was there looking at me; I don't know why he'd be here otherwise.

Never know, Joe, I might end up in Canada. The Blue Jays have a helluva chance for the playoffs, maybe against you guys. Can you imagine: we started the year thinking we might be on teams dueling for the AL East title, New York and Cleveland, and we might end up on teams going head-to-head for the American League pennant, Minnesota and Toronto.

A lot's got to happen right for me to get in that situation, though. Let me know if they throw you behind bars, OK?

Meanwhile, I'd be talking to Black & Decker, if I were you.
—Phil

August 8. Saturday. Minneapolis.

Phil:

Today is the first day of my sentence, big brother. I feel like I ought to be wearing black-and-white convict stripes—sounds like my old Yankee uniform. I'm in exile until August 18th for the scuff stuff.

After what turned out to be a joke of an appeal process, the American League suspended me for 10 days. The letter from Dr. Brown to the Twins didn't say the suspension was for scuffing, so I assume it was for carrying and concealing that lethal emery board.

I wanted to make a strong appeal, but I didn't know how to go about it. After going over the evidence, Dr. Brown set up a conference telephone call with me, Andy MacPhail, Tom Kelly, and pitching coach Dick Such. I was pleased the ball club supported me the way it did.

After I told Dr. Brown my side of the story, I thought that was the appeal process. I told him: "If I'm going to be suspended for having an emery board and sandpaper in my back pocket, I've been wrong for 16 years and should have been suspended 16 years ago. Why didn't anyone tell me?"

Andy read a couple of rules, one saying a pitcher shall be warned if there are suspicious balls in the game. I never got any kind of warning like that. I thought it was a legitimate beef.

As far as I was concerned the umpires ignored the rule book and took baseball law into their own hands. They decided they were going to do something under any circumstances, and they did it.

I thought we presented a good case, and since this was my first offense and there was no evidence that I knew of, I thought I might get a fine instead of a lengthy suspension that might hurt a team in a pennant race.

Dr. Brown called back four hours later and said the suspension was upheld.

Evidently, simply presenting my story was not an official appeal. After the suspension was upheld I was told the only way to make an official appeal was to go through the Players Association. Baseball has enough red tape to wrap every Christmas present in the country.

I had a tough decision to make, Knucks. Do I stand up for my personal and family honor and drag this appeal process out, possibly risking being ineligible September 1 for the postseason rosters? Or do I get the suspension over with right away and get back to pitching as soon as possible?

I know you wanted me to fight harder, Phil, but after all I've been through this year, I didn't want to do anything to possibly jeopardize going to the playoffs, and maybe the World Series, with the Twins.

I know how angry you are about it, mostly because of the way it was handled. I was a victim that night, pure and simple, and I just want to put it behind me and try to salvage this season. Overall it's been a nightmare for me.

The first two days after "The Night of Scuff" were wild. I had stacks of telephone messages two inches high on my stool when I came in. By then I was talked out, sick of the subject. The only people I wanted to talk to were you, Mom, and Dad.

After batting practice our traveling secretary, Laurel Prieb, brought a gift out to me. Laurel said he was told it was from you, Phil. I unwrapped it and inside the box was a power sander with 50 feet of extension cord. You know me, I thought it was a great joke so I played along.

"All right, you guys, if you want to learn the proper way to scuff, listen to the master," I said. I hooked up the sander in the dugout and stretched the cord out to the mound and stood out there working over the ball. "To do a professional scuff job, you need professional tools." I thought, "Look out, Ed McMahon."

I'm trying to make an embarrassing subject humorous at this point. What's the old saying? "I've got to laugh because I don't want to cry."

You're right, Knucks, I'd be a helluva advertisement for Black & Decker. Aside from talking to an emery board company that wants to give me a lifetime supply, I haven't heard anything from anybody. I guess me and my emery board were just another fad.

My start against Oakland last night was my last before taking my 10-day vacation. I really wanted to look good, to leave a positive impression with the Twins so I don't find things different when I return to the rotation. I didn't want them to forget that I can win for them down the stretch.

It was my best game in almost two months: eight innings, five hits, two earned runs. My record is now 6–8.

Knucks, do you have any idea what I had in my back pockets during that game? You guessed it: an emery board in one pocket and a piece of sandpaper in the other, just like every other start for the last 16 years. Nobody checked me, nobody even asked me about it. Not an umpire, not anybody.

Actually, I felt a little let down. Did everybody forget what went on four days earlier?

Did you see where Bob Shirley went back to the Yankees? He accepted a Triple A contract and reported to Columbus. I don't know which it is: the Yankees can't get along without Shirley or Bobby can't get along without the Yankees. I'm glad Bobby's got a job again. With extra time on my hands I plan to drop Shirley a note.

—Joe

August 10. Monday. Boston.

Joe:

I'm not talking to you as a Cleveland Indian anymore, little brother. As you know, I got traded, but not to the Twins like I hoped. I'm now a member of the Toronto Blue Jays and I really don't know how I feel about it. I will say I'm not doing cartwheels, but then I've never been able to do cartwheels.

Even though I knew it was a possibility last week, it still came as a surprise. The Indians got outfield prospect Darryl Landrum for me. I really thought it had gotten to the point where I'd be playing out the string with the Indians.

I was sitting in the U.S.S. Thunder whirlpool in the trainer's room about the eighth inning, my normal routine when I'm pitching the next day. Danny O'Brien, the club vice president, walks in. He never walks into the trainer's room. Danny's just standing there with a little grin on his face. "We made a deal," he says.

I'm wondering, "Who? Carlton just left." O'Brien keeps looking at me with that grin, and I thought, son of a gun, it's me.

Honest, Joe, the first place I thought of was Minnesota because of the speculation. I was ready to bail out of the tub with one big joyous jump. Thank you, Lord, thank you. Brothers back together again and in a pennant race.

Then O'Brien said, "You're going to the guys we're playing today, Toronto."

I had no reaction, Joe. It was like I'd been shot with a stun gun. I kind of blanked out.

I just sat naked in the tub after O'Brien walked out, sort of dumbfounded. Toronto seemed pretty set in their rotation, with Jimmy Key, Jim Clancy, Dave Stieb, and John Cerutti. I thought they might be interested in Ken Schrom from our club. I never thought seriously about playing for the Blue Jays.

I showered, dressed, and didn't tell anybody. It was emotional leaving the Indians. In less than two years I'd grown attached to the players, coaches, organization, and especially the city. Not getting to go to the Brook State Inn regularly on Saturday nights at home was one of the first things that came to mind when I thought of moving to Toronto.

Shit, I wonder if there's any Polish music in Toronto, Joe. I'll have to carry my cassette tapes again.

The guys started coming into the clubhouse after losing 5–1 to the Blue Jays. Word got around quickly and we said our good-byes with handshakes and hugs, the usual stuff when someone leaves the ball club. I never cleaned out a locker in the middle of a season to go somewhere else. It was all new to this old-timer.

I waited for the ball club to pack up—it was getaway day for Baltimore—before calling Nancy. She was positive about the trade from the start and excited that I was going to a pennant contender.

I guess, ultimately, what made me take off the Indians' uniform, fly to Boston this morning, and put on a Blue Jay uniform this afternoon was that Toronto may be the best team in baseball, and maybe this 48-year-old man will get to a World Series after all.

It was tough walking out of that Indians' clubhouse. Jimmy Warfield, the trainer I spent so much time with getting treatment or playing cards, was speechless. He wanted to say something, but he was too choked up to get out the words. I signed a bunch of stuff for the young guys in the clubhouse. I had accumulated so much stuff in Cleveland, I told Cy Buynak, the equipment man, to pack up the bicycle you sent me for my birthday, fishing rods, and a few boxes, and I would get it all along with my car after the season.

On the flight to Boston this morning I leaned against the window and looked out, lost in a cloud of thoughts: pitching all those years in Atlanta and still wanting to somehow end my career as a Brave; Warfield, Johnny Goryl, Cy, Joe Carter, all the great people in the Cleveland organization; being from Ohio, playing just three hours from Mom and Dad; dancing on Saturday night at the Brook State.

It seems a little late to be starting over in Canada. It's going to take a while before I feel comfortable wearing this new cap and uniform. Tell you the truth, brother, I still feel out of place with the Blue Jays—a bird of another feather, you might say.

When I walked into the visitors' clubhouse at Fenway Park today, the first person I saw was John Sullivan, the Blue Jays' bullpen coach who used to coach for the Braves. Cito Gaston and Billy Smith, two other coaches, had been in the Braves' organization, so that helped getting settled in.

Jimy Williams, the manager, called me in and said he was going to pitch me the first game back in Toronto, this coming Thursday; that will give me eight days between starts, so I'll have to throw in the bullpen. I hope I latch on to this Blue Jay uniform and have it feel like the Atlanta and Cleveland uniforms did.

I had to laugh. You saw what the Yankees did with the guy they got for you from Minnesota, Mark Salas. They put him on the La Guardia–Columbus shuttle. It turns out to be a worthless trade for them, and I feel sorry for Salas because he didn't ask for any of this, I'm sure.

I'll admit I felt old when I saw that Dale Murphy got his 1,500th career hit. It wasn't that long ago that Murf was behind the plate trying to catch my knuckleball. Indirectly, I can take partial credit for making Murf a two-time National League MVP. He tore up his knee trying to catch my knuckleball in 1978, and after surgery the Braves moved him to first base. After that didn't work, Bobby Cox moved Murf to the outfield, eventually to center field, and the rest is history.

Just relax, Joe. Get your daily running and work in and have some fun during the suspension. I know you'll take it like a man. Then get the baseball and do something with it. You're going to help the Twins down the stretch.

You've done it before and you'll do it again.

—Phil

August 15. Saturday. Minneapolis.

Phil:

Knucks, need your shoes shined? I can get you a good price. I hear the guy who does it used to throw a pretty decent knuckleball, too.

That's my specialty now, big brother: shining baseball spikes. This is the seventh day of my 10-day suspension and I'm probably close to driving the Twins' clubhouse man, Jim Wiesner, berserk, I'm hanging around so much. I do my daily workout—running, stretching, throwing lightly—then go shower, sit around, bullshit, and go home.

During games, I've been trying to get Wiesner to let me shine the spikes. You know what polish I use, don't you? "Scuff Magic," of course. The guys get a kick out of me using that brand of shoe polish.

You regain perspective about what kind of life playing baseball really is when you spend some time picking up dirty underwear, hanging up jocks, taking laundry out of the dryer. You remember quickly what a privileged existence baseball players lead. Is it any wonder nobody wants to retire?

The guys haven't missed me much; we're 5–2 since my suspension started. We're 10 games over .500 and our four-game lead over Oakland is the biggest margin any first-place team has in the four divisions.

The Twin Cities have gone bananas over this team. Against the Angels we had our 11th straight crowd of at least 30,000. I remember a few years back when there was talk the Twins might have to move because Calvin Griffith, the former team owner, didn't have the money to compete and the fans were no longer supportive. That's all changed. Carl Pohlad, who bought the franchise from Griffith, has the resources to pay top dollar for his best players, and a winning team with young stars has brought the people back out.

Houston was in love with the Astros when we went to the playoffs in 1980, but I've never been in an area so excited, so charged up, about its team as Minnesota is about the Twins. From what you've told me, Phil, this is probably what Cleveland would be like if the Indians ever were in a pennant race.

My next start, my first since the suspension, will be next Thursday at Detroit; it will be 12 days since my last start. I sure hope it happens so I can stop all the questions about the scuff incident—they're starting to get to me a little.

After coming out of the shower yesterday I stood in front of the mirror and got hit in the face with a frightening fact about myself, big brother: I keep losing hair. I've been fighting this battle of the bald for almost 10 years, and bald is winning. I do my best to brush what I have in the right places and use hair spray to keep it there, covering the most head possible. Trouble is, I'm finding fewer and fewer blond strands to work with.

Knucks, I wouldn't bring this up around any other living soul, because I know you're sensitive about it and I'd never want to embarrass you. But, between brothers, should I consider getting a hairpiece? You must like yours, you've had it now for years.

I'm torn. I know yours takes a lot of work, and I don't know how self-conscious I'd be about wearing one. I never asked you about what made you decide to get a toupee, but if you've got some extra time, I'd like to know what you think on this one, Phil.

Should I keep brushing what I've got left and live with it? Should I look into a hairpiece? Should I try one of those hair-growth products? Should I just get my head shaved and go Kojak? They could call me "Marvelous" Joe Niekro.

It's not easy finding someone to talk to about your hair, so I hope you don't mind me dropping this on you.

Say, Detroit made a smart pickup, Doyle Alexander from Atlanta. Doyle's a quality pitcher, and with Jack Morris, the Tigers have a tough one-two punch.

Nobody's paid Detroit much attention, because of a bad start, but they're about ready to run down Toronto for first place in the East. And now the Tigers have Alexander, and he's been a great September pitcher over the years.

It sounds like the Yankees are on the verge of self-destructing again. Steinbrenner, as he always does, came out of nowhere and ripped Piniella, who evidently wants to get rid of Rickey Henderson. Of course, the New York press had to get a statement from Billy Martin, who said he's not after Lou's job.

You can almost count on the Yankees being their own worst enemies at this time of year. Steinbrenner's timing stinks when it comes to ripping the ball club. It always takes a couple of weeks for all the bullshit to die down and the team to get back on track. George never learns, it seems.

Mark McGwire hit his 39th home run yesterday; it gave the Oakland redhead the all-time home-run record for rookies, breaking Frank Robinson's and Wally Berger's record. The kid is a one-man gang. Now he's getting hit with all this 60 home runs and Roger Maris stuff. I hope the press doesn't strangle him with the pressure they put on Maris in 1961, when he broke Babe Ruth's record. I read McGwire is almost blind—he couldn't see a lick without contacts. You'd never guess it the way he reacts to pitches.

OK, Knucksie, you wanted a joke. A guy goes into a drug store to buy some condoms. The clerk tells him that will be "$4.50 plus tax." The guy says, "Plus tacks? I thought they stayed up by themselves!"

How about this one? How does Gary Hart talk to his wife after sex? By telephone. You hear some beauties when you hang around the clubhouse as much as I've been lately.

I'm just counting the days—and the number of jock straps I hang up—until I'm back on the mound.

See you in the playoffs, Blue Jay.

—Joe

August 18. Tuesday. Oakland.

Joe:

Just call me "The Eight-Day Man," little brother. It seems like that's my rotation—pitching on eight days rest—which is anything but an ideal situation, as you know.

The Blue Jays checked the statistics and found out I have good success against California; for some reason they have trouble with knuckleballers in general, not just me. I know you one-hit them once and also won number 529 against them.

Jimy Williams backed me up three days so I catch the Angels in Anaheim instead of pitching at Oakland. I realize you can't knock them for playing the percentages like that, it's just that eight days is too much time between starts for any pitcher.

Joe, after 23 years in the big leagues, I can't remember being more nervous for a ball game than I was for my first start with the Blue Jays last Friday. The buildup was incredible. The headlines were "Niekro starts tonight." With the team coming home with a half-game lead in the East, I really felt on the spot.

The game was a sellout of more than 45,000. I heard scalpers were getting $150 for two $13 tickets to see a 48-year-old man throw knuckleballs. Walking out to the mound for the first inning, I received the biggest ovation of my career to start a game. To be pretty much a stranger and walk out to that kind of welcome gave me chills.

People were yelling: "We're getting a Niekro in the World Series"; "We're going to win the World Series and you're coming with us." They really made an old-timer feel young and appreciated.

I don't know if they were looking for me to be a magician or a savior or what. I just wanted five or six strong innings, like Jimy Williams asked for, and then watch the Blue Jays' bullpen do its thing.

That's basically what happened. The White Sox put me through the ringer. I allowed five hits and three runs in 5⅔ innings and took the loss in a 10–3 butt kicking. I held them in check pretty good, except I made a bad pitch to Donnie Hill and he hit it for a two-run homer that knocked me out of the game. I had struck Hill out the time before on a high fastball, and he was up there looking for it. He got it all.

I don't know why I forgot what a deep and talented bullpen the Blue Jays have, with left-hander Jeff Musselman and right-hander Mark Eichhorn setting up for Tom Henke, who's an overpowering closer. If I'd have thought about the firepower Williams had to call on, I wouldn't have thrown that fastball to Hill. I'd have thrown another knuckleball and taken my chances with a walk.

I guess with the big crowd and wanting to make the Blue Jays look like they made a good move in getting me, I fired up trying for the strikeout and got burned. I had two outs, too. Damn.

As it turned out, Musselman and Henke both got lit up and the White Sox blew us away. That might be Henke's first bad outing since May; I can see why they call him "The Terminator," as fast as he gets that fastball of his to home plate. Henke's a horse and a big reason a lot of people think the Blue Jays will end up winning the AL East.

I'm still trying to get comfortable wearing this uniform and spending Canada's colored money. The guys have been great to me. Garth Iorg and Henke told me the fishing's great up here; I can't wait to get my gear up here from Cleveland. If I can't listen to polka music in Toronto, at least I can fish.

Nancy brought John and Michael to Toronto for a visit last weekend. John had a great baseball season at Shiloh High School; he was 6–0 pitching and they won the state championship. John's looking at some small colleges in Georgia. We think we're going to put Mike in Woodward Academy; it's highly regarded in our area. Phil's enjoying the University of Georgia.

The AL East is looking like a head-to-head fight between Detroit and us. Our All-Star shortstop, Tony Fernandez, is having trouble with his knee, and we can't afford to lose him in a tight race.

The Yankees and Milwaukee keep hanging around and still have a chance. Sounds like the Yankees have all three rings of their circus in action again. With Rickey Henderson hurt, that kills them. Willie Randolph's been out, too. If Steinbrenner would leave Piniella on his own, to do what he wants, I think Lou could do a great job. Nobody can manage with George's constant interference.

The last 10 games of the season, we play Detroit seven times. That looks like when the division will be decided.

Joe, if you guys played all your games at home, you'd never

lose. We're getting ready to play Kansas City and Oakland, so maybe we can do some damage for you. You guys help us out when you play Detroit and Milwaukee.

Almost forgot: I wish I could take credit for it, but I have to tell the truth to my little brother. I wasn't the one who sent you the power sander. It may have had my name on it, but it wasn't my doing. It was somebody else's scheme.

Just thought I'd let you know.

—Phil

August 20. Thursday. Detroit.

Phil:

That well-known outlaw Joe Niekro made his return to the mound tonight, big brother, and I guess I should have pulled the emery board out of my back pocket and scuffed up the baseball.

Of course I didn't, and I got my butt kicked 8–0 by Detroit and Doyle Alexander. You were moaning about eight days between starts, Phil; this was on 13 days rest for me, and the Tigers chewed me up pretty good: seven hits and six runs in 3⅓ innings.

When you asked me about tips on how to pitch the Tigers, I told you I didn't know any more than you did. This game proved that.

The Tigers are rolling right now, big brother; the Blue Jays better kick it in gear. Detroit actually came to the Metrodome and swept us three games, the first time that's happened all year to the Twins. It wasn't exactly a classic series, either; the Tigers outscored us 26–3. If we see the Tigers in the playoffs, we're going to have our work cut out, with Detroit able to throw quality right-handers like Alexander, Jack Morris, and Walt Terrell against our right-handed lineup.

I guess when you're going horseshit, like I was against the Tigers, nobody cares if you're scuffing the ball with an emery board or a chain saw. Nobody said beans to me about the emery board—my first game back from suspension—and it was right back in my pocket as always.

I'm scheduled to be a guest on Dave Letterman's show tomorrow night. I'm flying in on Friday morning to tape the show in the afternoon and out Friday night to join the Twins in Boston, if everything works smoothly. I wasn't going to do it, but the more I thought about Letterman's show being fun, the more I figured I might as well get into the spirit.

Juan Berenguer came off the disabled list today. So with me back in the rotation, and Juan back throwing 95 miles an hour out of the bullpen, we're pretty healthy heading into September. Many people thought California would be better that its AL West championship team of 1986, and I was one. But the Angels can't get over .500, and Kirk McCaskill, who pitched so well for them last year, continues to struggle. I think we're sitting pretty cozy with a four-game lead and 38 games to play.

I talked to Nancy and we're trying to look ahead for the playoffs; we'll take Natalie and Lance out of school at least a couple of days so they can make it up to Minneapolis. It's tough planning over the telephone, as you probably know, Knucks. Nancy and I end up disagreeing, getting frustrated, and we both get a helpless feeling because we're separated by so many miles.

These are the toughest times in a baseball marriage. She's carrying the load at home, being both mother and father. She asks for your input, but she doesn't agree with it. I'm trying the best I can to be involved as much as I can, considering the circumstances. I realize she's the one who has to do it all, so why should she give up doing it her way? It's a vise that seems to be squeezing us sometimes.

Anyway, I'm trying to keep my mind on pitching because the Twins need some good starts out of me, and I need some good starts if I'm going to feel involved during the most important part of the season.

Hope you can get a win for the Blue Jays, big brother.

—Joe

August 24. Monday. Seattle.

Joe:

I don't like the looks of things, Joe. Already they've skipped me in the rotation.

I'm not pitching until Saturday against Oakland; it will be my fourth straight start on eight days rest. How can anyone find a groove with that schedule? Jimy Williams told me last week the reason he held me back to face California was so I'd also catch them on my fifth day during our next homestand. Now I'll miss the Angels for the second straight series.

I don't know what all this means, but 20-some years tell me it's not good.

I'm 0–2 already with Toronto. When a team's in a pennant race you wonder how many times they'll let you out there when you're losing. I just hope Jimy and the players don't give up on me. I really don't know what they think of what they've seen of me. Nobody's said anything.

The newspaper articles on me have been favorable, and Jimy's telling me I'm doing fine. But what else are they going to say? You're not going to tell somebody he's going like shit and wreck what confidence he has left—unless you're the Yankees.

Everybody hopes to pump you up a little bit, but I can't seem to get in sync right now. I'm still uncomfortable wearing the Toronto uniform. I can't get in my normal frame of mind and I don't know what the hell's wrong with me. I keep telling myself: "Niekro, pick yourself up and get going. You're on a pennant-contending ball club and they are counting on you, the old-timer, the old master of the knuckleball, to win some games."

Joe, I'm not doing it the way I want to, and I'm sure it's not the way they want it, either. I'm close, but not good enough to win. A few more runs wouldn't hurt, but I'm the one giving up the home runs, walks, and runs. I just have to give up fewer runs, that's the only way I can look at it.

On eight days rest again, I lost 3–1 to the Angels in my last start; my record dropped to 7–13. Pretty poor.

I'm keeping us in the game, but I can't lock up the victory. I've got to get in gear. I just can't hook on these eight days between starts; I don't know what to do with myself on those days in between. I don't know whether to throw BP twice—you know I don't normally throw that much on the side.

I'm used to pitching every five days. Usually I throw BP two days before every start—that's all—and then go get 'em. That way I'm not too strong, just right. With eight days rest I go out there strong as a bull and I feel like I'm going to throw the knuckleball through the backstop.

Charlie Moore's been catching me and doing a good job. He doesn't know how I like to pitch a game, but he's hung in against the knuckleball real well. We've faced two left-handers when I've pitched, so I haven't worked yet with Ernie Whitt, the other catcher and a dangerous left-handed hitter.

I just can't get that Cleveland Indians, Atlanta Braves feeling in me with this ball club. Physically, I feel as strong for this time of the season as I have in several years. Mentally, I've got to get a better attitude. I can't understand why I'm having trouble getting up mentally. I don't know if it's the new ball club, new environment, the excitement, or what.

I'm not thinking on the mound the way I have for almost 30 years. For the first time I've felt lackadaisical, and I really can't believe I'm saying that about myself. I've never known myself, two times in a row, to be a little out of control of myself, not pitching like I'm capable.

I realize I'm going to have to accept this unusual rotation for myself. I just know how crucial my next start against Oakland is— I can't lose again.

If I'm not winning, I hope it's not contagious for the rest of the staff. Henke is outstanding; he's struck out the side something like 28 or 29 times. They ought to call him "Hurricane Henke" the way he blows people away. I was working with Eichhorn on a quicker release for his pickoff move. He's got a pretty decent knuckleball, too. With his hesitation from his sidearm delivery, if Eichhorn ever uses the knuckleball occasionally, he'll be almost unhittable.

Henke and Eichhorn have to be the best one-two relief punch in baseball. The ideal contrast: first Eichhorn goes through the order once with his tantalizing off-speed pitches, and then Henke comes on like a steamroller with his high, hard fastball for the final three outs.

Jim Clancy and Dave Stieb, two established starters, have been up and down, but Jimmy Key is having a Cy Young–caliber season.

To this point, George Bell has to be the league MVP. He has carried the Blue Jays offensively all season, and in a short period of time I can tell how much this club depends on him. Probably the first thing I learned about George is that when he wants to be left alone, you leave him alone. It's not like George isn't talkative; he knows how to be heard when he wants to be.

George will piss off other teams because he does have a tendency of showing people up, and that's what gets guys down on him. On the Blue Jays, though, George is well liked and a leader, probably because of his physical presence.

About the only thing I haven't liked about Toronto is going through customs. I know I probably should keep that to myself because when Doyle Alexander was with the Blue Jays, he complained about going through customs and it turned into a mini international incident.

I thought that being with the Toronto ball club, customs might make it easier for the players by passing them through without their luggage. No way. We have to lug our bags along and go through security just like you foreigners, Joe. Those people should realize that when a team's coming or going on a two-week road trip, those bags get heavy.

I'd give somebody $20 just to carry my bags through customs. I know that probably sounds trivial to the general public, but when you're 48 and you just joined your fourth team in four years, lugging baggage through customs is a hassle you'd like to do without.

Wish me luck for my next start, little brother. It's a big one for me.

—Phil

August 28. Friday. Milwaukee.

Phil:

The sound you just heard, brother, was the Twins falling out of first place. For the first time since June 10 we no longer are leading the AL West.

A Milwaukee rookie, big right-hander Chris Bosio, threw a two-hit shutout at us tonight; it was our ninth loss in our last 10 games. We're only four games over .500 now and we're a hair out of first, one percentage point, .516 to .515.

Oakland, a team that never does as well as it looks on paper, moved into first after beating you guys 3–2. Dave Stewart, probably the favorite to win the Cy Young at this point, won his 18th game, and Carney Lansford hit his third home run in three games. With the power of Mark McGwire and Jose Canseco and a good manager in Tony LaRussa, the A's can't be underestimated.

I'd say we're a little tight right now, but Tom Kelly has not changed at all. Our manager is showing no more concern now than he did when we got up to 12 games over .500 just before this slump. A team not used to pennant-race pressure, like the Twins, might panic at a time like this. But we're not panicking, because we don't see TK panicking. The guys really look to Kelly to set our tone.

Things just aren't going our way right now; heck, even our Gold Glover Gary Gaetti made an error, stopping his club record for third basemen at 47 consecutive errorless games. Kirby Puckett isn't hitting—Puck hasn't hit a home run in 18 games.

During this losing streak, Detroit beat up on us five out of six games. Kent Hrbek had to pull a game out in the ninth against Willie Hernandez for us to take one.

Boston swept us in a three-game series at Fenway Park. Roger Clemens beat Frank Viola in one game and Don Baylor hit a grand slam off Steve Carlton to win the third.

There's no getting around it, we are a much better team at home than on the road. That's why, even though we look vulnerable right now, I still feel we're in good position with 18 of our 27 games in September at the Metrodome.

I was rooting for Paul Molitor; his hitting streak was stopped at 39 games by Cleveland rookie John Farrell. Did you see how it ended, Knucks? Molitor was in the on-deck circle when Rich Manning won the game in the bottom of the 10th, 1–0. After going 0 for 4 against Farrell, Molitor's fifth at-bat would have been against a different pitcher, Doug Jones. You never know what might have happened if he got that one last at-bat.

If any player today besides Wade Boggs can challenge Joe DiMaggio's 56-game hitting streak, it's Molitor with his great swing, speed, and athletic ability. I think he has Hall of Fame talent, but his many injuries have cost him so many games he'll probably not have the lifetime totals to get elected.

I know you saw me on "Late Night with David Letterman" August 21. You've been on with Letterman before and you were right, he's a pisser.

I flew from Minneapolis to La Guardia Airport and was picked up in a limousine; they treated me first class. I had decided, what's the use of going on David Letterman if you're not going to have fun with him? That's why I brought the workman's utility belt with a sander, shoe polish, jar of vaseline, wire brush, and, of course, emery boards.

Dave saw my outfit before the show started and he thought it was great. He tried to pin me down on whether I doctored the ball and I told him, "Do I look like a doctor?"

On the same show, Dave was doing "Stupid Pet Tricks," and when I first walked in, there were dogs barking and jumping everywhere; I thought I'd made a wrong turn somewhere and ended up in the NBC kennel. As soon as people recognized me, though, they wanted me to pose for a picture with their dogs— Missy, Charley, Champ.

All I could think of was that I'd come all that way, hadn't even been on the show yet, and I was going to the dogs. Suddenly, network television didn't seem that glamorous anymore.

Well, the end of August approaches, Knucks, and I'm praying you're safe with the Blue Jays. As you know, there's usually a shuffling of bodies by contending teams when it comes down to the 31st, the deadline for postseason rosters.

I'm not exactly a lock for the Twins' postseason roster, either. Here's hoping the Niekros are not in for two more big surprises this season. We've had our share this season, haven't we?

—Joe

September: "No Time to Send Out Laundry"

Joe:

I'm out of a job, little brother. I got laid off. The Blue Jays gave me my pink slip and now I'm trying to figure out what the hell a 48-year-old unemployed ballplayer is going to do.

Jimy Williams called me into his office after we lost 7–6 in 10 innings to California; it was about 11:30. Jimy told me they had made a deal and were getting Mike Flanagan from Baltimore and that they were releasing me. The silence in Jimy's room was uncomfortable for both of us.

Jimy looked me in the eye and said, "Releasing a Hall of Famer like you is the hardest thing I've ever had to do." From the look on his face, I believed him.

Your heart jumps a little when something like this happens, but I guess I shouldn't have been that surprised. I don't know what they expected from me. I started three games, all on eight days rest, and I went 5⅔ innings in the first two.

Then last Saturday against Oakland, I knew when I walked off the mound after not being able to get out of the first inning that this could be my last stand, my final flight as a Blue Jay. It was an ugly outing. I was lucky to get anybody out.

144

Nobody said much to me the next day, Sunday, but I did hear we were trying to get Flanagan, a former Cy Young winner who had been pitching better lately for the Orioles. I thought they might send Jose Nuñez down to Triple A—that was the clubhouse talk. I never heard my name mentioned, but I guess you never do before the old trapdoor opens under your feet.

When I showed up at the ballpark today they wanted to know if I could relieve. I said, "Sure," as if I could say anything else after Saturday's disaster. I didn't get into the game, but they did warm me up late, maybe just to make me feel like I was still included.

I hung around the clubhouse after they told me and drank a couple of beers. Word got around in a hurry and I said my good-byes and wished the guys luck down the stretch. It was only a few weeks ago that I did this in Cleveland. I signed a few baseballs for the clubhouse guys.

I drove around downtown Toronto a while, trying to figure out what I was going to do, so I'd have something to tell Nancy when I called her. My Toronto baseball career lasted 21 days. Right now I definitely feel like a foreigner lost in a strange land.

My car's still in Cleveland. So I guess I'll fly from Toronto tomorrow, pick up the car, and drive to Lansing to Mom and Dad's.

Wait a minute, I can't leave first thing in the morning, because I have to pick up my laundry and dry cleaning. Can you believe this, Joe? You always hear about never sending out your laundry the day before August 31st because of exactly what happened to me. Your dummy brother sent his clothes out yesterday, and I don't think they'll be ready for a couple of days. I'm going to have to make arrangements to have my laundry shipped to Atlanta before I can leave tomorrow. Shit.

I guess that's the least of my worries right now. I'm unemployed. I guess I'm done for the year, and it looks like I'm going to have to admit I'm done for a career. There's no place to go; today's the last day to make a trade to be eligible for the playoffs. I'm out of that picture for sure. Maybe somebody will want me for just a couple of starts before the regular season ends, maybe to fill in for an injury.

Shit, who am I kidding? That's doubtful.

I guess it's time to admit I've had enough, time to say "Uncle," time to turn the game over to the younger guys. I had one more shot with the Blue Jays and I couldn't do it. They treated me well, gave me three starts. I just couldn't get in the flow of things in Toronto.

There's just one thing: after 24 years, 318 victories, more than 850 games, and almost 5,500 innings, my last pitch thrown as a player in a major-league ballpark would have to be in the bullpen warming up as a middle reliever for the Toronto Blue Jays.

Damn, Joe, I wanted my last pitch to be from the mound. As far as I'm concerned, I really haven't walked off the field, officially, for the last time yet.

At least if I had finished out the season with the Indians, I could have prepared for this moment a little better. Being in the last year of a two-year contract with the Indians, I knew I probably wasn't going to get invited back to spring training; I could tell from the way they talked to me they weren't going to re-sign me.

I never had any hope of Toronto inviting me back. How could they after what they saw of me in three starts—plus they've got so many good young pitchers coming up.

It's a funny feeling knowing baseball is going on and I'm driving home in a few days without a job. No season ever has ended this way for me. I'll get another paycheck without working, which also will feel strange.

The more I think about my new situation, the bigger the rock in my throat feels, little brother. I can't believe I'm no longer a ballplayer.

I would like to have made it up to 320 wins, a nice round number, instead of 318; 320 sounds like a number to shoot for, 318 sounds like a number that fell short.

I do have one possibility left, and it would be the storybook ending I've always dreamed about, Joe: returning to Atlanta and walking off the field for the last time tipping a Braves' cap. I don't think it's a secret that's how I've envisioned my retirement since the Braves released me in 1983.

The Braves' season has been over for quite a while. Maybe I could go back to Atlanta and hook up for one last game. Who knows?

So, it looks like you're on your own, buddy, as far as getting the Niekros into the World Series. You guys have a helluva shot, and I can see you having a big game in the playoffs or World Series. It would be justice for all the shit you've been through this season.

After I get my car in Cleveland I'll probably drive over to the stadium to talk to Danny O'Brien and Joe Klein, see if they have a place for me. When I get back to Atlanta I'll call Bobby Cox with the Braves and throw out my idea about pitching one last game for them.

As of today you're on your own, little brother. Go for it and make me proud. Carry the load for me.

I meant to tell you how great you came off on Letterman wearing the utility belt—that's solid comedy, as Dave would say.

It's been three years since Letterman had me on when I was with the Yankees in 1984. Dave wanted to catch my knuckleball. We were only about 40 feet apart and my arm wasn't loose, so I didn't have much movement on the ball and Dave was making it look like anybody could catch it. Just when I was ready to throw him a decent knuckleball, he quit and went to a commercial.

When I settle back at home, I'll get back to you. Right now I just don't feel like talking to people for a couple of days. The drive from Cleveland to Atlanta will do me good.

—Phil

September 2. Wednesday. Minneapolis.

Phil:

I just wish they'd have left you in Cleveland, Knucks.

When I heard Toronto released you, I immediately became a Detroit Tigers' fan for the rest of the season. I just don't know how teams can throw players away, especially someone as classy as you.

At the time you were traded to the Blue Jays I thought it was great because all that was in my mind was the two of us in the playoffs, which would guarantee a Niekro finally getting to the World Series. I never even considered a down side to it all, the possibility of you getting released in Canada. That's no way for you to go out.

I thought your first two starts for Toronto were good; you kept them in the ball game through five innings. They told you that's what they wanted out of you. If it was the Blue Jays' intention to give you a couple of starts and release you if they didn't like how you pitched, I wish they'd have left you alone so you could finish out with the Indians, more on your terms.

I think Toronto did you an injustice, Knucks, and now it's happened for the third time. First the Braves, then the Yankees, and now the Blue Jays sent the classiest man in baseball out into the streets like a journeyman nobody. It just ain't right.

Don't forget that Ted Turner's always left the door open for you in Atlanta; as a Brave, that's how you should walk off the field for the final time, Phil.

We'll probably never know—and, believe me, I really don't want to know—how close we came to having two Niekros shocked on the same day. I was put on the Twins' postseason roster by the September 1 deadline; I'm sure there was considerable discussion and I doubt seriously that the vote to include me was unanimous.

Steve Carlton and Mike Smithson, who's been with the Twins since 1984, didn't make the roster. They optioned Carlton to Portland for one day and then recalled both Carlton and Smithson for additional pitching depth this month.

I'm still struggling, big brother. I haven't said anything to anybody, but my shoulder still bothers me. I can pitch with it, and I did last night; the Red Sox beat me up pretty good in four innings of a 9–0 loss. But I don't feel the freedom of motion I usually do, and there's uncertainty in my mind. My 6–11 record says I'm a lot uncertain.

Nobody said anything to me afterward, but I wouldn't be surprised if I get passed over for my next start. I guess I should feel fortunate I'm on the postseason roster; I don't feel very wanted around here right now.

Big deal: We got Don Baylor from Boston, and after playing with Donnie briefly in New York, I know what a positive influence he's going to have on our clubhouse. Besides that, we can use some additional punch from our designated hitter, and in Baylor we're talking about a proven, clutch RBI man. I know the Angels were thinking about going for Baylor, too, so I'm sure Gene Mauch doesn't like us getting him for the pennant stretch.

Apparently Andy MacPhail had been talking to Lou Gorman of the Red Sox about Baylor for weeks. I don't know what the holdup was, but I heard the trade was made not long before the midnight deadline. If Baylor plays a major role in the playoffs or the World Series, those will be some of the most precious moments of the season.

I talked to my buddy Dave Bergman of the Tigers and he had an interesting story for me. He said he talked to Dan Morrison, one of the umpires in my scuff game, and the incident came up in conversation. Morrison said they had seven baseballs as evidence, "because we took one ball out after each inning." Bergman asked him why there were seven balls, when I only finished three innings. That's suspicious, if you ask me.

We've been leading the AL West for all but one day since June 10th, I think, and I still get the impression people think we're going to blow the division title. It might take until the seventh game of the World Series before the Twins are given credit for being a helluva good ball club.

—Joe

September 4. Friday. Lansing, Ohio.

Joe:

I'm back where it all started, Joe. Back in the old hometown, and you know what, little brother? There is a sense of accomplishment, of completing what you started, when you return like this to the place where you grew up.

I left town at 19, after accepting a $500 signing bonus, to pitch at Wellsville, N.Y., for the Milwaukee Braves' organization. I return

28 years later with 318 career victories, an all-time brothers record for wins, and, I'm told, a chance to go to the Hall of Fame.

I've been a God-blessed man, Joe. You, too.

Right this minute I'm sitting in the old bed we used to share as boys in Mom and Dad's upstairs bedroom. How many times did I wake up in this bed?

The three-hour drive from Cleveland to Lansing did me good, like I figured. Quiet thought while driving has snapped me out of the doldrums before. I can't blame the Blue Jays; they play Detroit six times late in the season, and as much trouble as the Tigers give me, and with as many left-handed hitters as they have, a trade for a veteran left-hander like Flanagan makes good sense. I can see that move.

I drove up and Mom and Dad were not surprised to see me. They'd heard the news of my release. I still feel strange not playing ball. I look at the clock at different times and think, "I should be heading to the ballpark now . . . I'm supposed to throw in the bullpen in 10 minutes."

Wonder how long the withdrawal will linger? Probably until the season's over.

I really couldn't pick up on how Mom and Dad felt about me being out of baseball—unemployed. Dad, of course, doesn't say a lot anyway. They gave me the Mom-Pop stuff: "Nice going. Hang in there."

Mom was a little ticked off at Toronto, but I guess that's a mother's normal reaction when she sees anything go against her child. She just couldn't see them releasing me after only three starts. Try to explain to a mom how baseball organizations make moves when they feel they have to.

Mom's feeling is that we both started going down hill after the Yankees released me and traded you. I guess if you look back, you could get that impression. We really haven't done that well since 1985.

Took Dad fishing at the private lake at the country club in St. Clairesville. Mom and I wheeled him down by the lake in his wheelchair as best we could. I got some stones and logs to secure the wheels and I fixed Dad up with a spinning rod and a can of worms. We must have sat there fishing and talking for two hours. I was razzing Dad about missing more fish than he was catching.

We did bring back 30 bluegill. I know how you would have loved to be in on that, Joe. I'm just glad Mom and I could get Dad out fishing again because the weather will turn cold soon and this might be his last time for a while.

The entire day was like turning back the clock and I didn't want to go back to the present. I wanted to bring our present back to the past.

When I was in Cleveland I went up to Danny O'Brien and Joe Klein. I wanted to thank them for treating me as well as they did. It was a friendly conversation. I told them I wasn't looking for a job now, but when the season's over to keep me in mind if they make any big changes.

I did say I'm going to manage someday—whether it's next year, the year after, or whenever. That's my goal, as you know Joe, to manage in the big leagues, preferably in Atlanta. But the way I feel about the Indians now, I'd come back up to Cleveland to manage in a second.

Klein told me I'd "no doubt" make a good manager. O'Brien asked me if I didn't think I should "pay some dues" managing in the minor leagues. As I said, I would accept a managing job in the minor leagues, but I don't think you have to manage in the minors to be able to manage in the major leagues. Lou Piniella learned the game well when he played and he's done a good job with the Yankees, even with Steinbrenner's interference.

Danny and Joe did offer me a job in the instructional league. Go down to Florida for a couple of weeks, no pay, just hotel and living expenses, and work with the kids. I appreciate the offer—it's just that I hope the Braves might have something more for me.

I'd like to spend more time with Mom and Dad, but I need to get back home to Nancy and go talk to the Braves. Nancy's alone, with the boys away at school. John's at Oklahoma State, Phil's at the University of Georgia, and Michael's away during the week at Woodward Academy.

I was thinking about it on the drive here: this will be the first time Nancy and I have been alone at home since we had our first home built in Atlanta in 1967. We're both looking forward to it.

Being at home will be nice. I'll catch up on the yard work, reseed the grass, and get all that household shit taken care of so when hunting and fishing seasons roll around, I'll have time to take off. Believe me, I can't wait for our fishing trip to the Everglades down at your condo in Chokoloskee in November. It can't get here fast enough.

You, keep your head up; you're carrying the ball for both of us now. Mom thought with both of us playing for contenders, the odds were pretty good of a Niekro getting into the playoffs and World Series.

Now it's up to you, Joe, and I really like the Twins' chances of going all the way. The whole family's pulling for you. Just be ready when they need you, that's all you can do.

Remember, I'll be after you for some World Series tickets.
—Phil

September 9. Wednesday. Minneapolis.

Phil:

Just call me "No Go Joe," big brother. I've been passed up in the rotation for the second straight time.

Mike Smithson has taken my spot; he pitched well against Milwaukee and gets my start again Friday at Cleveland. It's already been eight days since I last pitched. Sounds like your rotation in Toronto, Knucks.

I'm trying hard not to get down. The team's going well and I certainly don't want to disrupt anything. I expect to get back in the rotation; I just hope I can start pitching better.

Puck's hitting again—he's had three home runs since the start of September. That's a good sign for us. Bruno, Tom Brunansky, beat Milwaukee with a ninth-inning home run. The defense has been outstanding; we've made one error in the last nine games.

Viola and Blyleven are in grooves, both going eight or nine

innings almost every time out. I don't think we have one ace of the rotation—we open with a pair of aces. Neither of them has to feel the pressure of having to carry a pitching staff.

Reardon's amazing to watch, a real professional. Berenguer is throwing well again after coming off the disabled list.

This is amazing: We just finished this homestand 6–3 against Boston, Milwaukee, and Chicago to make us 49–23 at home. That's 26 games over .500. That's almost unheard of.

But for some reason we're one of the Jekyll-Hyde teams of all time. Going into Cleveland, we're 26–43—damn near the opposite—on the road. It's been a big story about the ball club since I got here, especially recently.

Nobody has any answers. I do think that because we like to play here with the enthusiastic fan support, and knowing other teams don't like to play in the Metrodome, it kicks our game up a level. The team has built up a confidence at home that we are unbeatable in the Dome.

A three-game lead, like we have, in the West, is not bad. Since Kansas City switched managers—firing Billy Gardner and hiring John Wathan—I've been watching to see if they're ready to make their charge, but they're still a game under .500 and Saberhagen is still struggling. Oakland would be nowhere without Dave Stewart; he's 19–9 and has to be the Cy Young favorite at this point.

How fleeting is fame, big brother? Since about a week after the blowup about the emery board I haven't heard anything about it. I haven't heard back from the emery board company that offered me a lifetime supply about doing any advertising. As big and controversial and publicized as all that emery board stuff was, it's as dead now as an old carp.

I was sitting on the bench one game last week when I remembered I haven't seen you since June. I miss talking to you, Knucks; I miss having a few beers and your famous moon shooter with you. I was thinking about the best nights out we've ever had together. Maybe because it's still pretty fresh in my mind, the surprise party we had for your 300th victory in 1985 stands out.

After you won number 300 in Toronto we had to wait until we

got back with the Yankees to New York. We went back to our place at Loew's Glen Point and, I remember, we were cooking up some shrimp when somebody knocked at the door.

You answered the door, Knucks, and there was Jimmy Sturr and his polka band, and they all started playing and singing the "Hey Niekro Polka." What a riot.

We loaded everybody up in the band's bus and went down to the E Street. We cleared the floor, set up the band, and danced to polka music until four o'clock in the morning.

I miss our times together like that, Knucks. Maybe that's why we're both looking forward to fishing in the Everglades in November.

Before that, though, I'd like us to have a small private party in my hotel suite when the Twins get to the World Series. More and more I feel like we're going to do it, with or without me in the rotation.

I'm going to keep listening for a news story out of Atlanta, big brother. Follow your dream.

—Joe

September 12. Saturday. Atlanta.

Joe:

Haven't been home a week, Joe, and holy hell has broken loose around here.

Not long after I got home, Dave Kindred of the *Atlanta Constitution* wrote an article asking, "Wouldn't it be nice to have Phil Niekro pitch one more game for the Braves before the season ended."

It was spooky, like Kindred had been monitoring my dreams. Honest, Joe, I did not speak to him.

His article talked about what a tough year it's been for the Braves and how my bringing back some old memories might get the fans back to the ballpark. The article really lit up my eyes; I hoped a seed had been planted.

A couple of days later Bobby Cox called. We chatted and I told him I was coming down to the stadium to see a San Diego game. Bobby asked me if I would stop by to talk to him. Guess what my answer was, little brother.

When I met with Bobby he wanted to know what I thought about Kindred's article. I told him I liked it. So did Bobby. We started discussing the possibility of me coming back to pitch one last game for the Braves. Nothing official, but the last home game of the season, September 27 against San Francisco, was the date mentioned.

I came home and started to get excited, even if Nancy wasn't. She thought it was time for me to hang it up; turns out she wasn't alone.

Word spreads fast around Atlanta, and it wasn't long before my phone was ringing off the hook with newspaper and radio reporters asking if I wanted to pitch for the Braves again. I'd say, "Yes, as long as it doesn't bother anybody," and pretty much leave it at that.

The thought of putting on the Braves' uniform again kept me up nights. My dream to retire as an Atlanta Brave was going to come true, or so it seemed.

Then someone named Mark Bradley, a sportswriter from the *Constitution* I don't know, wrote an article basically knocking the idea Kindred had brought up. Bradley said that me returning to the Braves would be a "circus," just an effort to get more people into the ballpark. He said if I get a start it takes one away from one of the young pitchers. Basically it was, "How could the Braves do such a thing? The old man's done, enough is enough," on and on.

I read the article, slumped back in my chair, and thought, "Wow, what a hatchet job."

The same night, Jeff Hollinger, a sports announcer for an Atlanta TV station, either had the same idea as Bradley or read his article in the morning. This guy took the knife to me, too: why doesn't the old man quit, it's over, say good-bye.

Two blasts in one day. I was stunned. I'm thinking: "Is this what it's going to become?"

Who do Bradley and Hollinger think they are, anyway? Here are a couple of local sports guys who are kicking the Braves while they're down, cutting down the idea before we've even decided whether we'll do it or not. I started thinking that maybe it wasn't such a good idea after all.

If my return to Atlanta is going to bring about negative publicity for the Braves, maybe I should forget it. I always thought sports announcers, especially from the hometown, should help build up a team when it's going badly instead of tearing it down. I know that's old-fashioned thinking.

I'm really undecided—I feel like I'm sitting on pins and needles trying to make up my mind. I really want to put that Braves' uniform on again so badly, Joe. I'm going to retire, I know this is it. I don't have to have somebody in the newspaper tell me it's over. I don't care what they say about me—I've heard it all and more before. They can cut me up as much as they want and they won't break through this old-timer's leather skin. But they don't have to keep kicking the Braves' organization when it's down.

There's even talk that Cincinnati and Houston, since the NL West isn't over yet, might not like me pitching against the Giants. It's obvious to me, though, that San Francisco is going to win it.

Something that looked so perfect and special has turned into a complete mess. Right now I can't tell you what will happen, but I'll let you know.

—Phil

September 15. Tuesday. Chicago.

Phil:

Not much to say, Knucks, except I finally got to pitch tonight and lost 6–2 to the White Sox. I can't believe I'm 6–12. I haven't had a record above .500 since 1984, and it doesn't look like I will this year either.

It was my first start in 14 days. Considering that, I didn't think I pitched that poorly. I went six innings and gave up four runs on six hits. I struck out three and didn't walk anybody. I was encouraged, I know that much. Now if they can give me another start in five days—that would be at home against Texas—maybe I can put something together.

Tom Kelly's got this team running so smoothly, it's like we're on automatic pilot. People know their roles; it's a different guy winning the game each night.

We've been going from a one- to 3½-game lead for the last two weeks. It looks like California ran up the white flag; they traded John Candelaria to the New York Mets. If you think you can successfully defend your division title, you don't trade a left-handed starting pitcher the quality of Candelaria, even if it does seem like he's hurt all the time.

A writer talked to me today about a story he's working on: Were the baseballs livelier, juiced up, this year? I told him about the first game of the season, when I was with the Yankees, and how I saw Larry Herndon hit one about 500 feet to straightaway center field in Tiger Stadium. Since then I've seen balls rocket off bats like never before.

As a joke, I said I even saw balls that I *didn't* throw jump off bats like never before. I hope he got it. I'm not sure, though, because he didn't laugh. He just kept writing on his notepad.

I know *USA Today* did research into the baseballs, and it came out they are not any livelier. But you can't help but think that when you see even the little guys hitting long home runs. It's like the balls explode off the wood.

Another thing that might contribute to all the home runs is the umpires' smaller strike zone. I know I've seen more pitchers behind in the count. When you have to pitch from behind to hitters with the power of George Bell, Mark McGwire, Kent Hrbek, or Don Mattingly, they are going to consistently drive the ball somewhere, and many times it's beyond the fence.

I keep watching the newspapers to see if you're going to pitch for the Braves or not. That's kind of dragging, isn't it? Hey, do what you want and to hell with everybody else.

Send me some old Knucksie luck for my next start, will you?
—Joe

September 19. Saturday. Atlanta.

Joe:

I don't even know if I want to bore you with this, little brother. You've got a pennant to win. But I feel like I'm being tied to a tree and the rope just keeps going around and around, tighter and tighter, and I can't get away.

This has been a week of total confusion and chaos. You'd think my name was Joe Niekro.

After the Bradley article, and the negative reaction I got, I became convinced I didn't want to go through with pitching for the Braves again. I told Bobby Cox I appreciated the opportunity, but that I wasn't going to do it.

Bobby said, "Are you sure?" I told him I was.

I met with Stan Kasten, the Braves' president, and told him I was set to do it until all the negative stuff started and that it changed my entire frame of mind.

So what happens? Dave Kindred writes another story, this one a write-in poll: "Should Niekro pitch or not?"

In four or five days Kindred comes out with the results of his poll: 98 percent of the people who wrote in want me to pitch.

Ted Turner was somewhere in Europe and he heard about the results of the poll. He called me long-distance: "Phil, why don't you want to do it?"

I told him about the negative articles and Ted said: "Boy, if I let reporters and newspaper articles decide what I did with my life and my career, I wouldn't be where I am today. It's your choice, do what you want. If you do it, I want to be there. If you don't, I understand. But don't let people like that keep you from doing something you've dreamed about."

Everywhere I went I kept hearing, "Do it, do it, do it." "Don't let a couple of guys keep you from doing it." I just don't know. I'm in such a tug-of-war with myself, I'm stumped.

I've already told Bobby Cox I wouldn't do it, but now there seems to be more positives coming out of it than when I first made my decision. It's been cleared with Commissioner Uebberoth and

National League president Bartlett Giamatti. The Cincinnati Reds don't seem to mind anymore, and Houston is almost out of the race.

Joe, you know me: when I've made up my mind I stick by it. Nancy liked the idea of me not going back out there; she thinks I'm going to make a fool of myself.

Even though it looks like a lot of people want me to do it, I don't think I'm going to reverse my decision. I can't believe the Braves already have publicized that I'm pitching September 27. I'm not even under contract yet. I haven't decided. As a matter of fact, as of this moment I'm not going to pitch, because that's what I told Bobby.

Turner wants me to do it, but he wants me to do it September 24, which is a Thursday. He's coming in for a day game Thursday against Houston. He wants me to pitch that game and then he's having a dinner for the ball club at the Stadium Club.

Now, if I do pitch, I have to do it on the 24th, or at least that's what Ted wants. Now there are two dates involved. One's Thursday at 5 o'clock and the other is Sunday the 27th, which they've already publicized.

I never dreamed this old man's little wish for one game back home would turn into such a controversy. I've got people calling me from all over the country. Reporters and TV people coming to my house, not even calling first; they're driving up just to ask, "Why aren't you doing it? Will you change your mind?"

Why does it have to be this tough?

Four years ago, when I was released by the Braves, I told myself that someday, someway I was going to return to Atlanta and put that uniform on again, even if it was just for one pitch. The day I would retire from baseball, it would be as an Atlanta Brave.

If I do it, I've got to change my mind at this point, and I don't like doing that. There are only a couple of weeks left in the season and I haven't thrown a ball in three weeks.

I wish you could help me, Joe. Mom, Dad, Phyllis, and the kids want me to do it; Nancy doesn't. Bobby Cox says the opportunity is still there. I already told him I wasn't going to do it. I told the press, I told everybody. There were big headlines: NIEKRO SAYS NO.

I feel trapped. If I do change my mind, it's a major change of mind. I'm just trying to figure this shit out the best for everybody, and I still can't come up with the answer.

Do I sound confused, little brother?

—Phil

September 22. Tuesday. Atlanta.

Joe:

It's about 10:30 at night, Joe, and I just got off the phone with Bobby Cox. I'm going to do it.

I had to change my mind, and it was difficult, but I'm pitching Sunday for the Atlanta Braves against the San Francisco Giants. I can't pitch Thursday, when Ted Turner wants me to; that's only two days away and since I haven't thrown in three weeks I can't possibly get ready in time.

To have this decision over with is such a relief; I feel 200 pounds lighter. Nancy still doesn't like the idea, but I guess everybody's entitled to their opinion. I talked to Dad and he was happy about it.

Somehow I always knew I'd wear the Braves' uniform again. Now I've got to get ready in five days to pitch against a team that may go to the World Series. I told Bobby I wanted to throw batting practice tomorrow and again Friday before pitching Sunday. That's the plan of attack for now.

The nice feeling is knowing that after Sunday, that's it; I'm going to officially retire as a player. But before I do, I get to wear that Braves' uniform again. The Braves got new uniforms before this season, and I can't wait to put number 35 on. They've got the big tomahawk across the chest like back in the Milwaukee days when I came up. They're the best-looking uniforms in baseball, I think.

I always wanted to play for Chuck Tanner, so this is my chance. It's still a little hard to believe I was willing to change my mind to do it, but I just said to hell with Bradley and people like that. I don't want to say that publicly, even if I might feel it inside.

I was not going to let a couple of guys stop me from doing what I've dreamed about for four years. I know this is what you wanted me to do, Joe.

Shit. I was bitching about pitching for Toronto on eight days rest, and here it's going to be four weeks by the time I start Sunday. I dread how my arm is going to feel after I get it rubbed down, put some hot stuff on it, and sit in the whirlpool. But it's all for one last trip to the mound. I'll handle the pain.

It won't be long now before the Twins wrap up the AL West. You guys clearly have been the best team in that division all year. I know you're probably making plans for the playoffs, so your Nancy and the kids can see the games in Minneapolis.

Tell Nancy I said hello; I hope everything's going all right with you guys, Joe.

The best to you and your family.

—Phil

September 25. Friday. Minneapolis.

Phil:

Go get 'em, Knucks. Cut those Giants down to size. I'm so happy you followed your dream and didn't let a couple of opinions deny you your chance to say good-bye the way you wanted.

I know you haven't pitched in a long time, but as pumped up as you will be when you put that Braves' uniform back on, I'm sure you'll have the knuckleball dancing again in no time.

Your little brother finally won a game—my first win in over a month and only my second since June 14. I only went $5\frac{1}{3}$ innings, but we beat Texas 6–4 Tuesday to reduce our magic number to 7 for winning the division.

It sure felt good to contribute—it's been a while. I just hope maybe this will get me into a groove heading into the playoffs. I know I've got to finish strong to get a start in the playoffs; it's going to be me or Les Straker for the number three spot in the rotation.

We're starting a big series at home against Kansas City tonight. We've got a six-game lead with nine games left, so the Royals almost have to sweep us to have a chance. No way will they sweep us in front of our home crowd.

Knucks, did you hear about Tony Fernandez? I saw the replay on ESPN late last night. In the first game of Detroit and Toronto's showdown series for first place in the AL East, Bill Madlock, Mad Dog, took Fernandez out with an old-fashioned, aggressive, National League cross-body slide. Fernandez went down on his elbow and hit the edge of the artificial turf, breaking his elbow.

Some people thought Madlock went out of his way to dump Fernandez, but I thought it was just a good, hard-nosed slide that has to be made in the heat of a pennant race. If that would have happened in the National League, I don't think anybody would have said a thing.

The Blue Jays still won 4–3, but they really have to be down about losing their All-Star shortstop, who's probably the best in the business next to Ozzie Smith. I don't know any team that could lose an important player like Fernandez and not be affected.

You're always supposed to tell the media you don't care who you play in the playoffs, and that's no trouble for me this time. I can't really say who we match up better with, Detroit or Toronto. The Blue Jays always give us a tough time, but now they're without Fernandez. The Tigers have those powerful left-handed hitters—Kirk Gibson, Darrell Evans, Lou Whitaker, Matt Nokes.

The Tigers and Blue Jays both beat us four out of six at the Metrodome this season, so it wouldn't appear our home-field advantage affects either of them. A good team, though, doesn't care where it plays. You know that, Knucks.

We're down to the nitty-gritty. I'm uncertain when I'll start again, but since I'm coming off a victory against the Rangers, I could see it being Texas when we go there after this Kansas City series.

I'll be watching the scoreboard Sunday to see how my big brother's doing. It will be great to see that "35" for Atlanta up there again. No matter what happens, you deserve to walk off tipping that Braves' cap. I wish I could be there standing and cheering with everybody else.

Phil, I can't ever say this enough: you've made me a proud brother. Give 'em hell.

—Joe

September 27. Sunday. Atlanta.

Joe:

This is going to be a very different day, Joe, so I'm going to tell you about it in a different way.

I'm sitting on my back porch. I just finished drinking my coffee and reading the newspaper. The birds are chirping and the squirrels are scampering up the trunk and across the branches of my Georgia pine trees. It's seven o'clock in the morning, and with you not able to be here, I was thinking about how I wanted you to know about this special day for me, start to finish.

So, I'm going to write to you now and then again late tonight, after I've pitched my final game for the Atlanta Braves. I've seen Nancy write letters in stages, start it now and finish later, so I guess this will be one of those.

We got up this morning and there was a television crew from WTBS sitting on the lawn waiting for us. I agreed to let them follow me around today, so I guess I'll have sort of a boxing-style entourage with me for my final day as a player in the major leagues.

I'm leaving in 45 minutes. I feel great, I had no trouble sleeping. But I do feel the anticipation bubbling inside me. I don't think Nancy slept very well; she's still apprehensive about this farewell game. I can't tell if she's overexcited or underexcited, but she still thinks I'm going to go out and get my butt beat. She's afraid I'm going to go out looking bad.

That's happened to me more than once, I keep telling her. I really don't know what kind of feeling I have right now—it's like nothing I've had before. Going to the ballpark for the last time as a player. What a thought. I'll never have a morning like this again. I felt the adrenaline kick in when I rolled out of bed at 6:30.

Not having pitched for almost four weeks, I have no idea what I'm going to be like when I stand on that mound today. I hope I throw strikes, and when the Giants hit it, I hope they hit it at somebody instead of over them. Maybe I can set a record for most triple-play ground balls in a nine-inning game. Maybe we'll get 10 runs in the first and I'll be able to coast.

Of course, the Giants are going to be trying to hand this old man's ass to him. They can clinch NL West with a win today. They're going to want to jump on me early and put the game away as fast as they can. Jeff Leonard, Will Clark, Chili Davis—they've got some dangerous bats.

I remember when the Giants came to Atlanta in late September 1978 and Jim Bouton made his comeback start. He tricked them with his knuckleball and won his first game in eight years. The Giants couldn't believe what happened to them that day. Bill Madlock, especially, was embarrassed; he said his little boy could hit Bouton. It sounded pretty flimsy right after Bouton had beaten them.

Maybe one more old knuckleballer can put the whammy on the Giants.

John's here from Oklahoma State for the game and he's riding to the stadium with me. Phil's got some college buddies going with him. Mike's all charged up. I figure even Nancy will get with it once she gets to the game. All the neighbors are going—kind of like the old days with the Braves.

It sure will be a warm, homecoming kind of feeling when I drive into the tunnel of Atlanta–Fulton County Stadium again. I just hope I feel that warm on the mound. My arm felt like it weighed 250 pounds after I threw batting practice yesterday. I sat in the hot tub on the back porch and put some lemon on my arm last night.

I know you're pitching again soon; you guys are about ready to clinch your division. Maybe you'll be on the mound when you do. I wish you the best luck I could ever give anyone.

I'll get back to you after the game. I'm starting to get a little nervous-excited, if you know what I mean.

I'm back home, Joe. It's all over.

I've taken my spikes, tied the laces in knots, and officially hung them up. I put up a sign, "Gone fishing." Never will I throw another pitch in the major leagues, or at least I don't think I will.

You know me, Joe. If somebody thinks I can do it and gives me the chance, I'd make more comebacks than Muhammad Ali. I'll probably think I can get people out with the knuckleball until they cover me with six feet of dirt.

Actually, my farewell game went better than I thought it would. I didn't get my butt kicked like Nancy feared, but we did lose pretty badly, 15–6, and the Giants won the division title. Even though my line is going to look brutal, I'm anxious to see my name in a Braves' box score again tomorrow morning.

When I got to the stadium this morning it was like the Braves had made the playoffs. People were everywhere; they were backed up getting into the parking lot and there were lines at the ticket windows. And that was three hours before the game. I even heard there was some ticket scalping. We did have a crowd of 35,000, which was about 25,000 more than the Braves had been drawing the last month.

The Braves were giving away Phil Niekro posters, so I stood outside and must have signed 200. Then, in the clubhouse, it was like everybody who came in brought a baseball for me to sign. I must have signed as many balls as I did posters before I finally got dressed. I was afraid my right hand would be too weak to grip my knuckleball.

Just about the time I started feeling a little irritated signing so many things, I thought, "How many more times are you going to be in demand like this?"

I signed everything I could.

The team seemed pretty fired up for the ball game—this was more commotion before a game than the Braves had been involved with for a while. Players passed by and wished me luck, mostly the guys from the old days—Dale Murphy, Bruce Benedict, Glenn Hubbard, Rick Mahler, Raffy Ramirez. I missed seeing Gene Garber, he's been traded to Kansas City.

We didn't take batting practice, so I went down to the batting cage to take a few swings. Shit. I'd been in the American League for four seasons and hadn't batted. I've got to be honest, though, I was smoking those balls, brother. I couldn't wait to get my first at-bat, because I felt so good swinging the bat I really thought I might have a home run in me, at least hit the ball hard somewhere.

The Giants were starting Atlee Hammaker, a left-hander, so I thought maybe the stage was set for something memorable. Damn, I was geared up. I was as charged up about getting to bat as I was about getting to pitch.

I went out to the field about 25 minutes early because Skip Caray wanted to do an interview for WTBS. I stepped out into the dugout and you'd have thought the World Series or the All-Star game had come to Atlanta.

The dugout was full of people. There were media people all over the field, TV cameras lined up by the dugout. It made me realize that maybe this was an important day for more people than just myself and my family. It made me feel good to have so many people show that much interest in me and my baseball career.

It was at that moment, after 27 years in professional baseball, that I realized I was about to warm up to pitch a game for the last time. You can't imagine the feeling that runs through you when your mind and body comprehend once and for all what's taking place.

I walked down to the right-field bullpen, and in the picnic area there was Big John's polka band playing and people dancing. Big John told me they were going to play the "Clarinet Polka," one of my favorites, when I got up to bat the first time. I don't know if they did or not—I was so excited when I got into the batter's box I couldn't hear anything clearly.

Felt great warming up; it probably was as high mentally as I've ever been going into a game. A young kid, Terry Bell, started warming me up; I think he thought I was going to throw pitches he couldn't catch, but he didn't miss one knuckleball. Benedict came down to finish up, and then I walked back to the dugout and the fans were on their feet going crazy. They sounded like 70,000 to me.

I told Chuck Tanner before we went out to treat this like any other game. The first objective is for the Braves to win. If I'm having trouble, get me out of there. If I'm getting them out and we're ahead, stick with me. Managing a game is difficult enough; I didn't want to make it any more complicated.

Even if I threw only one pitch or got only one out, my mission had been accomplished: to return to Atlanta and walk off the field a Brave for the final time.

I got the first two Giants—Eddie Milner and Kevin Mitchell—out on screwballs and sinking fastballs. I knew they were looking for knuckleballs, so I tried to cross them up the first time around. Then I walked a couple and ended up with the bases loaded, two outs, and I got behind Bob Brenly.

I threw Brenly a slow-breaking curveball and he hit a hard line drive. Ken Oberkfell, our third baseman, made a Brooks Robinson diving catch to end the inning. The Atlanta fans went bananas; me, I just felt pretty lucky to get out of the inning alive.

I plopped down in the dugout and thought, "Oh, shit, it's going to be one of those games. I'm going to walk 12 guys, always in a jam, and I'm going to have to pray for double plays."

Second inning, somehow I got out of another bases-loaded situation. In our half of the inning Gary Roenicke hit a three-run home run off Hammaker, and after the third inning we were actually leading 5–0.

I was beginning to think this could be a blowout—like when I beat Toronto 9–0 for my 300th win in 1985—and all I had to do was throw the ball over the plate, let them hit it and let somebody catch it. Only two more innings and I could win my last game in the major leagues. I was psyched.

Then my bubble burst, Joe. I couldn't get an out in the fourth inning. Before I knew it the score was 5–2, bases loaded, and here comes Tanner out to the mound. Chuck said, "That's it, I'm bringing in Chuck Cary." Chuck wanted a left-hander to pitch to Mike Aldrete, a left-handed hitter.

I told him, "Do what you think is best," but inside I was a little pissed because even if I give up a grand slam, we're only down by one run. I wanted this to be my game to win or lose, but I had to listen to the manager. I was ready to walk off the mound and Chuck says, "You're not supposed to leave right now."

I thought, "Oh, shit, what's going to happen now?" I told him that as soon as Cary got to the mound, I was leaving. Tanner said, "No, you're going to stay right here with me."

Cary finally got to the mound, ready to take his warm-up pitches. I was anxious to get to the dugout, and Tanner wouldn't let me. Finally I said, "To hell with this," and I took off. Tanner was right after me.

The fans were giving me the ovation every player dreams about. We almost got to the dugout and Tanner turned me around and walked me back to the first-base coaching box. "Look at the scoreboard," Tanner said, and then he walked away. He left me standing there alone.

They showed a videotape of my career highlights on the Matrix scoreboard screen. The memories went straight to my throat. I was shaking so, I thought I had swallowed one of the liveliest knuckleballs.

When it was over, my feet felt frozen to the turf. I didn't know which way to turn or what to do. All I could think of was that I didn't want to stand out there too long, because Cary, being a young kid, was nervous enough in that situation without the extra hoopla. He's trying to get himself up for a bases-loaded situation, and the stadium is swept up in nostalgia.

I wanted the reality of the moment to return, so I walked swiftly back to the dugout. The people kept standing and cheering, calling me back out for one of those curtain calls I really don't think are necessary. I just wanted the commotion to die down so Cary could concentrate on the batter.

The Giants' manager, Roger Craig, played lefty-righty and pinch hit Candy Maldonado, a right-handed hitter. Cary got behind in the count and, wouldn't you know, Maldonado hit a grand slam to put the Giants ahead 6-5. We never scored again.

I finished the game in the clubhouse, talking with Bruce Sutter and Ted Simmons, two of the greatest players I'd ever gone against. We just kind of reeled in the years, as this old fisherman calls it, until the game was over.

Bill Acree and Dave Pursley, two great old friends with the Braves, both looked at me, and all three of us swallowed hard; we've been through many times together and this moment was special. I know this is a cliché, little brother, but it's the truth: there are no words to describe it.

So many guys are released or forced. I'm fortunate to be able to say good-bye to the game I love the way I wanted to—on my terms. It's very satisfying, very gratifying.

Like you'd expect after a loss, there were long faces in our clubhouse; I know the guys wanted to win this one for the old-timer, but it wasn't to be. Cary came over to me and said he was sorry. I told him, "It won't be the last home run you give up, so don't let it bother you." I felt bad for Chuck because his concentration had to be frazzled with all the commotion made over me.

Tanner called me into his office and said, "I took you out because, before the game started, I decided if you were in the position to be the losing pitcher in your last game, I was going to take you out."

It was a tough spot for Chuck because we were still leading 5–2 when he gave me the hook. Some people were booing, others were cheering. It was a no-win situation for him with the fans. Hey, they gave me my shot and I couldn't come through—that's all there was to it.

After the game the Braves organized a big press conference. I wasn't going until Nancy and the boys came down to the clubhouse, as they usually do. Nancy was ecstatic about the way everything turned out. Phil ducked out early. I guess some of his friends were anxious to get back to Athens, and since I was out of the game and we were behind 10 runs, they decided to get going. I couldn't blame them.

I told Bob DiBiasio, the Braves' public relations director, I was not going to the press conference unless the family could go with me. Bob said it was no problem. I just couldn't see going in to meet the press by myself, with everybody wanting to talk about my career.

I didn't want one person to get the impression I had done it all by myself. I hadn't.

As you know, Joe, our wives are the most important factor in our careers. That's certainly true in my case with Nancy. She was a flight attendant for United Airlines and I was engaged to be married when I first met her on a Milwaukee Braves' charter flight from Chicago in 1965. She got called in to help, but they didn't need her so she was just sitting by herself. We started talking and ended up playing gin rummy; one of us won $2 million, but we don't know who it was.

I remember getting off the plane and telling Gene Oliver, "That's the girl I'm going to marry." It was a strange thing to be saying because I was engaged, but that's how sure I was about Nancy Lee Farrand of Santa Monica, California. Soon after, I broke my engagement, but, of course, I forgot to ask for Nancy's telephone number or address and didn't know how to get in touch with her. Luckily, Nancy must have felt the same way I did because she wrote me a letter and sent it to the Braves.

We were married August 6, 1966, in Richmond, Virginia. As it turned out, the Catholic priest who married us left off a portion of the vows and we had to do the ceremony over again in our sister Phyllis's living room. Nancy wore slacks and I was in shorts and sneakers. But we got it done officially the second time.

Nancy's pulled me through it all. I've cried on her shoulder, she's kicked me in the butt. She's fed me well and been the best possible mother a baseball player could ever want for his kids.

Nancy has been everything, and more, any man could ask for. If it wasn't for her I'm sure I couldn't have gotten through my toughest years, when I was thinking about giving it up three or four years ago. She never stopped believing in me. She kept telling me, "You can still pitch, you can still pitch."

Wives are right most of the time anyway; I hope you know that by now, Joe. Nancy gave me the strength and the support every ballplayer hopes he can get from his wife. I know I was blessed to have found Nancy, and I'm very grateful.

It's all over now. Sitting here at home tonight, the feeling I have is not of sadness, because I'm not sad I'm retiring. I know I don't have to get up in the morning, go to the ballpark, jump in the whirlpool, and try to get those tired, sore muscles worked on again.

Knowing I don't have to throw on the side with a half-sore arm two days from now, like it often is after a start. Knowing I can start living at my own pace and not be revving myself up, trying to get a 28-year-old's performance out of a 48-year-old's body.

When the game was over today I took the biggest, deepest breath of air I could and then just blew it all out. What a total sense of relief. It was a feeling of: "There it is, Niekro, it's all over. You don't have to go through the injuries, the nagging pain, the sleepless nights, the long road trips, airports, hotels, bus rides, the five- and six-game losing streaks, fourth, fifth, sixth, and seventh-place finishes."

Just knowing I'm going to be home in Atlanta, or close to it, no matter what I do means so much to me now. When Hal McRae said one of the reasons he turned down the Kansas City manager's job was because he finally wanted to be home, I really understood what he meant.

Timingwise, this couldn't be better. We're about ready to build our new house at Lake Lanier, so I can be involved with it. Nancy's been home alone most of the time, with all the boys away at school. Now she can have me under foot.

Sportswriters like to ask, "What were you thinking when you . . ." At the time, I'd tell them I really don't recall, that the full impact of, say, my 300th victory will not hit me for months, maybe years. Now is when I'm going to start remembering those special moments.

I still look back to 1958, when Milwaukee scout Bill Maughn came to our house in Lansing, walked into our kitchen, and I signed a piece of paper that said I was going to be paid to play baseball. It was the highlight of my life at the time and still is number one. I know you feel the same way, Joe, about signing your first contract.

Out of all the young men who dream of playing professional baseball, I wonder what the odds are of two coming from under the same roof.

I've been the luckiest, God-blessed person in the world to be able to play for 28 years. I haven't had any serious physical problems. I've taken my shots of cortisone in the arm and, Lord knows, I've had more than my share of aches and pains. I feel it's remarkable to have played so long and only been on the disabled list once; that's when Rich Mahler hit me in the ribs with a line drive four days before the 1982 season opener. Having such a poor personal record in openers, I swore my being on the DL was why the Braves got off to their record 13–0 start.

I've been in two playoff series, both with the Braves; we lost the National League pennant to the New York Mets in 1969 and to the St. Louis Cardinals in 1982. I've never been in a World Series, as has been duly noted, but neither was Ernie Banks, and players don't come more deserving than Ernie.

I pitched a no-hitter against San Diego in 1973, won 20 games twice, won five Gold Gloves, and was selected to five All-Star teams. I led the National League in sacrifice bunts one season with 18. I always strived to distinguish myself as a complete player, not just a knuckleball pitcher.

I've led the league in most every pitching department, good and bad. I had the lowest ERA, 1.87, in 1967, and the most strikeouts in 1977. I had the most losses and gave up the most hits, most runs, and most walks three times each.

I don't know what else I could have asked for in a career, except to get into a World Series. But I still feel I'll get to a World Series wearing a uniform some day. I don't know how I'm going to do it, but my goal from now on is getting the Atlanta Braves to the World Series.

I'd like to do it as manager, certainly, but being a member of the coaching staff or front office would be fine, too.

My family and the Braves have been the most important things in my life. I look back and I see how much growing up in a small

Ohio town, our family, our friends and neighbors meant to our development. Grade school, high school, fishing and hunting together.

Everything was related. We were in the middle of a tightly wound niche of life and we couldn't have gotten out if we had wanted to. All the pieces of our life, little brother, made us whole.

That's what kept me going. I wanted to win a game for Dad, then I wanted to win one more for Mom. I wanted to win one for Nancy, Phil, John, and Michael. I wanted to win for your family, Joe, to make them proud of our family name and heritage.

I wanted Lansing, Ohio, to know, "Hey, Niekro won another ball game." I wanted Bridgeport High School to know, the Sportsman's Club to know, all of the Ohio valley to know that there's a kid out there from little Lansing, one of about 3,000 people, who won another game in the big leagues.

That's what made me feel like a success. Even as the years went by, and the games seemed to fade into each other, I would get my biggest kick from everyone else enjoying the wins more than I did. I knew Dad's coffee was going to taste better in the morning; I knew Mom was lit up like a Christmas tree.

I can honestly say not too many pitchers have been as happy and fulfilled throughout their baseball careers as I've been. Moving to Atlanta in 1966 made my life and established the foundation for my family. Nancy and I bought our first house, started our family, and I pitched 18 years for the Braves.

Besides Lansing, there is no better place to raise children than Atlanta. I know how you love Lakeland, how much it's meant to your life—your Nancy's from there—but I don't think any family could get attached to a town, a ballpark, and an organization the way the Niekros have to Atlanta and the Braves.

Coming back to the Braves like this, even for one day, has been like running into Mom's arms. When Ted Turner bought the Braves, it was a gift from God for him to come into our lives. He's taken good care of the Niekros; he made me a million-dollar player. I never dreamed I would make that much money doing the only thing I ever wanted to do.

To some extent, maybe I was worth his investment; only Ted

can say for sure. I pitched many games, won many, and put some people in the stands for him. I don't think the player ever really knows what his true value is; it's entirely what the owner judges it to be. And that's why the owners only had themselves to blame when players' salaries started doubling, tripling, and quadrupling until three or four years ago.

The Niekros owe Ted Turner, and I hope I can someday repay him by helping put the Braves in the World Series. I know that would be the ultimate for Ted.

I have this vision of a World Series flag flying over Atlanta–Fulton County Stadium. I won't feel my job is done until I see that. I'm supposed to talk to Bobby Cox about what I'll be doing for the organization, but even if I don't have a uniform on, I'll be the first to buy a ticket if the Braves ever make it to the World Series.

I'll always be a Braves' fan, Joe, just like you'll always have some Houston Astros in you.

It's just a shame Atlanta has not had any great ball clubs like other towns have had. I have no idea how long it will take, but I'm going to help bring a championship team to Atlanta. I want to help make it a proud organization again.

If I can't do it, maybe John will be pitching and winning games for the Braves someday. Give John a couple of years and he's going to be an outstanding pitcher. Michael's come up with a pretty good knuckleball for his age; he's got a good sinker, too. And it looks like he might grow to be 6′6″, like John.

If those boys have the fight and determination of their grandfather, they'll make it. I hope in some ways I can inspire my boys the way Dad inspired us. I know there were times when he was so sick he could have given up. But I think his sons, you and me, Joe, kept him from throwing in the towel.

You know how much pain Dad has endured. I know neither of us will ever forget going to the hospital and seeing a priest there to give Dad the last rites, going home in the black suits, not knowing if we'd ever talk to Dad again.

Dad has been a man among men in my book. I don't know

how you express your feelings about your father other than saying you love him. He's just the finest man I've ever met, and I know you share those feelings.

I'm only hours into retirement and already I feel contentment. I don't know what's ahead, but I do know when we get the new house built up at the lake, I'll be doing plenty of fishing and watching my boys becoming men pursuing their own dreams.

If John and Michael turn out the way I think they will, I might have to become their agent. Phil might beat me to it, though. He'll succeed in whatever he sets his mind on; I'll never worry about him.

John and Mike are so set on being major-league pitchers, I just hope they don't fall on their faces and then have nothing to land on. I know that right now they are not looking for anything else out of life but baseball, but I hope they'll be prepared with a college degree to fall back on.

If that scout hadn't signed me in 1959, I probably would have been headed for the coal mines or pipe factory. That's why I was so determined not to blow my chance at baseball, because I didn't want to work in the mines. If I couldn't have played baseball, I'd have wanted to be a game warden. But not the mines.

Don't ever feel alone, little brother, because I'm always with you. If you need help, just talk to me. I may not know how to answer you, but I'm sure you'll probably know what kind of answer I'd give. We've always felt close enough for mental telepathy, haven't we?

I know you're going to tack on more wins to our 538—I'm sorry, I've got to say it—the most victories by brothers in the history of baseball. Those words will never get old to me, Joe. That record will be our family legacy to baseball; records are made to be broken, but I think this one will stand for generations.

So put some more W's on the top. Get in the playoffs and pitch a shutout, a no-hitter. Before you throw the first pitch, nobody can tell you that can't happen. That's the attitude I took to the ballpark for every one of my starts over 27 years.

Always remember, you're a Niekro, and we fight our hardest

when it seems the odds and everybody are against us.

Let me just say this: it has been my great pleasure to play the game of baseball while you also were a player. You've kept me young and strong when the years said I shouldn't be.

I'll say thank you right now, buddy, for being the brother you have been, for sharing the love of life with me and my family. Seeing the competitiveness and the zest for life in you, Joe, revitalized me when I felt my time was running out. You made me a better ballplayer, a better man in life.

I don't know any man who could possibly love his brother more than I do you. I'm serious when I say this, you're absolutely the best brother a man could have. You're my best friend, my fishing buddy. I'll always cherish our memories together, and I hope we have many more as we grow old together.

I wish you, Nancy, Natalie, and Lance nothing but the best forever. May your days be full of sunshine and all the love you can stand.

When you get out of baseball I'll be there for your last game; I know you'd have been there for me today, but you've got a pennant and a World Series to win.

You're quite a guy, Joe, my favorite buddy. I'm thankful to the Lord for you, little brother.

God bless.

—Phil

September 29. Tuesday. Arlington, Texas.

Phil:

We did it last night, Knucks.

The Minnesota Twins won their first AL West championship since 1970, beating Texas 5–3, and I'm proud to say I had a hand in it. We have a seven-game lead over Kansas City with five to play; Oakland was eliminated Sunday, your big day in Atlanta, Knucks.

The West has been won by a team that used to be known as the Twinkies.

Yes, big brother, a Niekro will be going to the playoffs; it's the second time for me and fourth time for our family. I don't know what my role will be yet, but at least I felt part of our celebration last night.

I was supposed to start the Sunday game against Kansas City—I still don't know what happened. I came in Saturday and my hip was bothering me, so I told our trainer, Dick Martin. At first he thought it was a hip pointer, but it turned out to be a pinched nerve.

One of the team doctors said they could give me a shot of Xylocaine and that the hip would feel better by Sunday. All I wanted to know was if I could pitch one day after getting the shot. I was told I could, so even though it was against my better judgment, I went ahead and took the needle.

My hip started feeling better in a matter of hours. After Saturday's game Tom Kelly called me into his office and asked me how I was feeling. I said I was fine. Then TK tells me he's starting Bert Blyleven Sunday instead of me. Naturally I wanted to know why.

Kelly said, "We can't send out a guy who took a shot in his hip the day before." I told him the doctor told me I could pitch one day after getting the shot.

Evidently that's not what the doctor told Kelly, and that ticked me off. All I could think was "Oh no, don't tell me the shit's going to start dropping on me again?"

Anyway, I was held back to Monday. After one inning it didn't look like this was going to be our night to clinch; I was already down 3–0.

I settled down and pitched 6⅓ innings and we were tied 3–3 when I came out. Steve Lombardozzi's RBI put us ahead 4–3 in the eighth and Juan Berenguer got the win. It really was exciting; when we got the last out we just kind of exploded. You know how I like champagne, Knucks.

Actually, the clubhouse celebration didn't last that long, because winning the division is not where we want our season to stop. We haven't reached the mountaintop yet. We've felt we could win the division for quite a while, now our sights are set on the

American League pennant and bringing the World Series to Minnesota.

Before going to Texas, the series against Kansas City was interesting and emotional. The Royals beat Dan Schatzeder and Jeff Reardon in the first two games to cut our lead to five games with seven to play. With four of those seven against us, the Royals were acting like they thought they were going to put on a miracle kick and nip us at the wire.

After the Royals beat us 7–4 Saturday night with three runs in the ninth against Reardon, they were doing some talking that woke us up for Sunday's game. Danny Tartabull, who hit his 31st home run, was heard saying, "No bubbly, no bubbly," meaning we were not going to clinch the division against them in this series.

We read more of Tartabull's crap in the newspaper Sunday morning and there were more than a few guys pissed off about it. Even some of the local Minneapolis–St. Paul writers suggested we were reverting back to the Twinkies of old; they were even using that dreaded sports term "choke."

As you can imagine, Knucks, all the knocks and nonsense fired us up to a frenzy, and our fans showed up at the Metrodome Sunday wanting us to blow the Royals away.

We came out and scored five runs in the first inning off Charlie Leibrandt, one of the Royals' best pitchers, and went on to an easy 8–1 victory that clinched us a tie for the division title. Even though we couldn't clinch it until we got to Texas Monday, our message to the Royals was that this year the division was ours.

Now we just have to find out who our opposition in the playoffs is. Kirk Gibson's timely hitting helped Detroit salvage one game out of four at Toronto, but the Tigers are only $2\frac{1}{2}$ games behind the Blue Jays going into tonight. I have to favor the Tigers at this point, with Doyle Alexander almost unhittable, Jack Morris pitching well, Alan Trammell playing like he could steal the MVP award away from George Bell, and the home-field advantage to finish the season.

I don't think it will matter who we play. With the first two playoffs games at the Metrodome, and Viola and Blyleven pitching for us, I think we've got a great chance to go up 2–0, and from there I see no reason we can't win two of the last five playoff games, if we even need that many.

Congratulations are overdue from Sunday, I know, Knucks. I saw the tape of you walking off, tipping your Braves cap, on ESPN. I know how much that moment meant to you; I'm so happy you could go out your own way.

I sure hope you can make it to the playoffs. Not only could I use some of your advice and support, but we haven't had a moon shooter yet to toast your retirement.

Take care, big brother. We'll be fishing for snook in the Everglades before we know it. I hope I'll have some World Series gossip to tell in the boat.

—Joe

October: "A Visit to the Promised Land"

Phil:

The American League Championship Series opens tomorrow, and from reading all the so-called experts, we don't have a chance in hell of beating the Detroit Tigers. I think that's a joke, Knucks.

Even though we led the AL West almost all year, people are still talking about us like we're some unknown ball club just south of the Arctic Circle. I knew we'd be the underdogs, but some of the writers are predicting the Tigers will beat us in four or five games—like it's no contest.

You should hear the theories, Phil. We won an inferior division while the Tigers won the best division in baseball. Detroit's right-handed starters—Jack Morris, Doyle Alexander, and Walt Terrell—will neutralize our right-handed power hitters. We don't have enough pitching. The Tigers are one of the few teams not affected by the Metrodome—they did win four of six games from us in the Dome.

The only reason anybody gives us a chance is because we could play four games at the Metrodome if we can force the playoffs to the seven-game limit. We ended up 56–25 at home, which is incredible. If four of the seven games were going to be

180

played at Tiger Stadium, they'd be closing the books on us already. We were an atrocious 29–52 on the road for the season.

Somehow, I think this general lack of respect is going to work to our advantage.

As far as my role in the playoffs, I may be back to shining shoes like I was during my suspension. Since our last game of the regular season Sunday, and I'll tell you more about that in a minute, nobody has said anything to me. Not Tom Kelly, not Dick Such. I guess I'm lucky our clubhouse guard, Irv, even said hello to me yesterday.

Kelly started me at Kansas City Sunday, and I'll have to admit I was horseshit. I was wild as hell. My knuckleball barely stayed in the state of Missouri. I was gone after just $1\frac{1}{3}$ innings; I gave up three hits, three walks, and six runs in a 10–1 loss to the Royals. That put me at 7–13 for the season; six games under .500 is my worst record since I was 8–18 for the Chicago Cubs and San Diego Padres in 1969.

Sunday's start may have been a trial for me to see if they want to put me in the rotation for the playoffs. Les Straker, our other starter, who finished 8-10, has had a blister on his finger, but after the way I looked Sunday I'm sure Kelly will go with Les in Game 3 at Detroit, and I guess I can't blame him.

I know Kelly and Such are down on me; I haven't pitched the way I had hoped since coming over from the Yankees. It's been a crazy year—from getting traded to the scuff stuff, and I've been slow coming around from the separated shoulder.

On the bright side, Knucks, at least I'm still in the game, and how many 42-year-olds have a chance to go to the World Series this year? I don't want to overlook my blessings just because things aren't going my way right now.

If I'm not going to start, I wish they'd tell me what my role in the bullpen will be. Probably the only way I'd get a start is if we go up 3–0, maybe 3–1, and even that's an extreme long shot. If I'd have done better in Kansas City, who knows?

Like always, I'll just try to stay ready in case my fortunes turn around and they end up needing me. I wish they were counting on me more, but all they see is a pitcher with a 7–13 record. I'm taking this better than I would have a few years ago, but I guess that's all part of growing up, right brother?

George Frazier probably won't see much more action in the playoffs than I will. We were joking around and made a bet on who gets to warm up first in the postseason. This is one wager that may end up being a wash because we both could get shut out.

Reporters keep asking us if losing the last five games to Texas and Kansas City, after we clinched the division, will mean we're flat going into the playoffs. They're always looking for reasons we can't do it, rather than the reasons we can.

We've already forgotten those last five games. Since we clinched, everybody's been excited about the playoffs and we've been resting people and setting our pitching up for the Tigers. Even though this club isn't used to postseason games we're loose and confident, and all that goes back to Kelly, who still has us living by his "one at a time, do the best you can" philosophy.

The Twin Cities are flipping out over the Twins, Knucks. The Twins are all you hear about on the radio and television. I remember how loud the Houston fans were inside the Astrodome for the 1980 playoffs against Philadelphia. But when they get over 52,000 screaming fans in the Metrodome, it's going to be deafening. At least we know what to expect—and they'll be cheering for us.

We've played so well at home, some people think we've been cheating. We're being accused of having a camera hidden in the center-field football bleachers to steal signs. Tim Laudner said it best: "If there's a camera out there, how come I'm hitting only .190?"

Nobody is asking why Detroit plays so well in Tiger Stadium; they were 51–27 at home. When we played the Tigers there it seemed like they were sitting on every pitch we threw, and we never accused them of cheating or spying. I think it's the environment and feeling comfortable playing at home. Every club should be almost unbeatable in its home ballpark.

I still have many traditional baseball values, but I like playing indoors, even in the Metrodome, which definitely is a hitter's ballpark. I've seen some little guys hit balls way back in the seats here. In the Astrodome the ball didn't seem to carry, which is why every pitcher in the league wanted to get a start in Houston.

Detroit is starting its best pitcher in Game 1 of the playoffs, and it's not Jack Morris, who's the winningest pitcher of this decade. Doyle Alexander, your old teammate from Atlanta, is unbeaten, 9–0, since coming over from the Braves. He's been untouchable. Doyle's a master out there; our hitters can't afford to get overanxious and fall under his spell.

We'll get Morris in Game 2, and you know he's going to be pumped up to be coming back to his home area. Jack's from St. Paul and he wanted to sign with the Twins as a free agent after last season, but Andy MacPhail thought his asking price (about $1.8 million a year) was too much. I don't think Jack's ever lost in the Metrodome, so we're not guaranteed anything just because the playoffs are starting at our place.

Sparky Anderson and I go way back; I remember him when he still had dark hair. We were together in San Diego when he was the third-base coach. Even then, the way he taught and coached and handled players, there was no doubt in my mind he'd become a great major-league manager. I picked up a lot from Sparky.

The only other time I've been in the American League playoffs was when I was with Detroit in 1972. We lost the series 3–2 to Oakland's powerhouse with Reggie Jackson, Rollie Fingers, Catfish Hunter, Joe Rudi. The only time I got into the playoffs was as a pinch runner in the ninth inning.

My fondest playoff memory, though, was with Houston in 1980, when I pitched 10 shutout innings against the Phillies. It was a thrilling series, but we lost and Philadelphia went on to beat Kansas City in the World Series. I'd sure like to be on the winning side of a playoff series for a change.

Ever since you pitched your farewell game I've been wondering what the Braves have planned for you, Knucks. Any indication yet? Let's hope that one day you'll be taking number 35 back out of retirement and carrying the lineup card out to home plate as the

Braves' manager. You deserve that shot, Phil, and I think it would be great for the city of Atlanta, too.

Atlanta may be ready for Phil Niekro as manager, but I don't know if the Braves' organization is. I know Chuck Tanner's in the middle of a big contract and I certainly respect him. But the Braves haven't gained any ground since he's been there, and sometimes bringing back a local legend like you will light a fire under the players and revive attendance.

I'm sure Ted Turner knows what a positive move it would be to bring you back as manager, but we'll have to see how committed they are to Tanner. If it's not your job next year, maybe a couple of years down the line. By then I might be able to be your pitching coach. Wouldn't that be something?

Nancy and I are making plans for the playoffs and the World Series, but we're still having trouble communicating. I'm so tired of trying to work things out over the telephone—it usually ends up in an argument.

Not that Nancy and I are having serious problems, Knucks. I'm sure you've been through some difficult times like this with your Nancy. What'd you do? How did you guys get back on the same wavelength? If you have any answers or advice, I'd sure like to hear it.

Anyway, tomorrow we tee it up for the playoffs. I wish I felt more involved, but you never know what might happen. I think Gary Gaetti and Jeff Reardon will be the keys to the series for us.

I know we're psyched up to put on a good show for the nation. When it's all over, guys like Gaetti, Kirby Puckett, Kent Hrbek, Frank Viola, and Greg Gagne finally will be discovered.

As you know, Knucks, you don't have to play in New York, Los Angeles, or Boston to be a good ballplayer. The Eskimos from Minnesota will prove that once and for all.

—Joe

October 9. Friday. Atlanta.

Joe:

Reserve me World Series tickets, little brother. The way you guys beat Alexander and Morris to take a 2–0 lead against Detroit, I see no way you guys can't win the pennant.

A Niekro in the World Series. I don't want to look too far ahead, but that's how it's beginning to look and I couldn't be happier for you, Joe.

Shit, you might get a playoff start after all if you guys can win tomorrow at Detroit and go up 3–0. As good as you guys looked in the first two games, and I know you're a different ball club on the road, this might be a shorter series than anyone dared dream.

Wonder what all those experts who picked the Tigers are saying now? You guys have shoved it up their—and the Tigers'—asses so far. I love it.

I've watched the playoffs at home on TV just like every other fan in America. I've really been enjoying myself, Joe—working in the yard, not keeping a strict schedule, eating a normal dinner at home with Nancy. I almost feel like a regular person.

One night I sat by the fireplace and went over all your letters from the season. Someday we'll be glad we did all this writing so we can reflect back over what turned out to be our last year as players together. I feel like I know you even better since we kept up with each other for a change this year.

I did notice I haven't responded to you on several points—one was probably intentional and the others were simply oversights and I apologize. Maybe this letter will make up for everything.

We've both seen baseballs rocket out of stadiums like golf balls this year, but I don't think they're juiced up like a lot of pitchers claim. Corked bats is another issue. There's no doubt in my mind more batters are using corked bats and getting away with it. I've seen bats that were filled with cork, but I've yet to see a baseball cut open and the core obviously tampered with.

I don't think the rule they have now works: a manager may request the umpire to check one bat a game. The umpire should be able to check a bat on his own anytime he is suspicious.

The reason I don't think the ball is any livelier than in the past goes back to the pitching. You don't find pitchers coming inside as much, which can only mean the ball is out over the plate more often, and that allows a batter to get his best swing at the ball more frequently.

Batters are digging in at the plate because they have no fear of the pitcher coming inside. If a pitch does get away and brush the batter back, he's charging the mound and there are 40 guys ready to rumble. That's horseshit, as far as I'm concerned.

In years past—especially in the National League when there were hard-ass pitchers like Bob Gibson and Don Drysdale—if there were a couple of home runs hit in an inning, you could almost bet that the next guy was going down. Today the pitchers are scared to throw inside because they're afraid they might seriously hurt someone—like Dickie Thon—or that an Andre Dawson might charge the mound.

That's why hitters are more comfortable at the plate and able to unleash their full power. The balls look like they're juiced because the batters are able to put more of their juice into a full swing on pitches out over the plate.

You had to ask about my hair, right? You know how sensitive I am about it. All I'll say is what you don't have, you can afford to buy, Joe. It's strictly a matter of taste and choice; that's all I feel like saying on the subject. Somehow, though, I can't picture you looking like Kojak. I'd say keep combing as long as you can, little brother.

As far as me and my Nancy goes, sure we have had our problems. Show me a marriage that hasn't been through tough times and I'll show you a couple of liars. That's the point, Joe; you and Nancy aren't experiencing anything every other marriage hasn't. We've been through the arguments, fights, and near walk-outs, and probably will again.

Baseball marriages are difficult because of the separation and putting the burden of running a family on the wife. You've provided a good life, and Nancy has to remember you could be away in the armed forces or making $80 a day in a factory or away for months working on the Alaskan pipeline. Both of you have done well for each other, Joe.

Just remember that no problem is too big it can't be solved by sitting down and talking. Nancy and I have enough faith and love in each other that we know somehow, some way we'll work anything out.

I don't have all the answers, Joe, I just know how Nancy and I do things. I can only hope our experience helps you and your Nancy. Keep working together, brother. Don't give up.

Before we go fishing in the Everglades in November I'm going to get down to West Palm Beach, Florida, to work with the Braves' young pitchers in the Instructional League. It might not be all kids, either. I'm told Rick Mahler, who's had a tough year, might be coming down to talk to me about the knuckleball. The way Rick throws his sinker, I think he could be a helluva knuckleball pitcher if he could get a good grip.

I'd love to see Rick be one to carry on the knuckleball. Besides you, Charlie Hough, and Tom Candiotti—I know Doyle Alexander throws one once in a while—it's becoming a dying art. Maybe when we're both coaching we can bring it back somehow. We might have to open a knuckleball school, like we've talked about.

Just stay ready because I have a feeling the Twins will need old Joe Niekro before it's over. Keep your head up and enjoy the one year a Niekro goes to the World Series.

I know you're going to be there, brother.

—Phil

October 13. Tuesday. Minneapolis.

Phil:

Big brother, the Niekros are finally going to the World Series.

We did it. They can't call us the Twinkies anymore. We are the American League champions, and I don't think there's a person in Detroit or anywhere else in the country who could say we don't deserve it.

Even after we won the first two playoff games, there was still some skepticism about us because we always play well at the Metrodome. We were supposed to go on the road and fall apart like rag dolls—people were predicting we'd get swept at Tiger Stadium.

As it turned out, we should have beat Detroit four straight games, and we would have if it wasn't for Pat Sheridan's game-winning, ninth-inning home run off Jeff Reardon in Game 3. In that loss, though, we came back from being down 5–0 and actually took a 6–5 lead before Sheridan's two-run home run won it for them.

But we proved to ourselves right there that we could play with the Tigers in their own ballpark and that the road hex we've been hearing about all year wasn't going to mean diddly in this series. We came back in Game 4 to beat Frank Tanana and then we bombed Doyle Alexander for the second time to end the best-of-seven playoff in five games.

Like I predicted, Gary Gaetti, the Rat, was the playoff MVP. Tom Brunansky probably could have won it, too, except Gaetti really set the tone for the entire series when he hit two home runs off Alexander in Game 1. After that we were confident, without being overconfident.

I'll always remember Gaetti's expression after he hit his first-inning home run off Alexander, who had been almost untouchable for two months. Rat came back to the dugout like nothing special had happened, like it was just another home run against the Mariners or White Sox. He didn't act like a playoff rookie—Rat was more like a foxy old veteran who knew his home run was only a small pebble in a castle we were trying to build. "This guy's human, too," Rat said, and it was like we took off from that moment.

Gaetti also called a pickoff play at third base on our buddy Darrell Evans that was the turning point in Game 4. Actually, that pickoff from Tim Laudner to Gaetti may have been the knockout blow of the series, as we look back on it. God, I felt sorry for Darrell because we caught him completely by surprise. You could almost hear how that play deflated the Tigers and their fans.

I don't know if the two tough series with Toronto took that much out of Detroit or if we just played that much better than they did. But the truth is, we flat kicked the Tigers' butts, and they knew it. Detroit gave us full credit, too—no sour grapes, no cheap excuses, just sincere congratulations and best wishes against the National League. Sparky and his guys were all class about it.

Since I didn't throw a pitch against the Tigers—I didn't even warm up—I didn't feel very involved with our second celebration. You know I'll never turn down champagne, Knucks, so I just kind of took my bottle and stepped to the back of the clubhouse and watched all the guys go nuts. For all the guys who grew up together in the Twins' organization—Puckett, Hrbek, Gaetti, Viola, Laudner—it was a special moment.

I felt bad for Gaetti because he was so charged up about celebrating, but he had to accept the MVP award and be interviewed. Fame does have its price, I guess. Rat made up for lost time when he got back to the clubhouse.

Rat, Hrbek, and Bruno—Brunansky—probably were the wildest. It was a combination of the food-fight scene and the toga party from "Animal House." It was men being boys, and it was beautiful. After the Dwight Gooden and Al Campanis stuff, the Twins were great for baseball—no controversies, no scandals, no hotdog personalities. Just a great bunch of guys living out their childhood fantasies.

Because the visitors' clubhouse at Tiger Stadium is so small and cramped, a lot of guys sat back in the trainer's room, which is off-limits to the press, enjoying the accomplishment. Because he didn't join the team until September, I think Don Baylor felt a little like I did, so he stepped to the back and just observed. It didn't hit me until we got back to the hotel, but Donnie's the only guy on the face of the earth who could say he celebrated as a member of the winning American League team two years in a row. He was with Boston when they beat California in the playoffs in 1986.

I don't need to tell you, Knucks, how long we've waited to get to the World Series. But it's tough to be as excited as you've always dreamed you'd be when you know you're not going to participate that much—if at all. I feel like I'm so far down on the bench I'm out of the Minneapolis area code.

Maybe I didn't deserve to start in the playoffs and Les Straker did. I was just disappointed I wasn't told anything. It was obvious I was dropped from the rotation, but at least they could have made me feel a part of things—since I was on the roster—and told me what my role was going to be. If Kelly said, "You're last-resort long relief," it would have been tough to take, but at least he would have let me know where I stood.

After 20 years in the major leagues, after pitching for seven organizations and trying my damndest to be involved with a championship ball club, suddenly I felt like a leper. I was taking up a uniform and they resented me for it.

I guess I'll be doing the same thing in the World Series I did during the playoffs: put in my daily work and flatten my butt on the bench. I knew if Viola, Blyleven, or Straker got in trouble early, Kelly was going to go with Keith Atherton or Dan Schatzeder. If he needed a reliever in the sixth inning, it would be Berenguer for two innings and then Reardon in the eighth and ninth innings.

With the pitchers not hitting in the American League ballpark because of the designated hitter, it's like I've been put in dry dock. It makes me wonder why the Twins even put me on the post-season roster.

You know what picked me up, though, Knucks? Just thinking how proud Dad must be to finally have a son going to the World Series.

The trip home to Minneapolis from Detroit was such a happy and fun flight I hope everybody can remember it. We were flying high. Everybody was excited about seeing what the Minnesota fans' reaction would be when we returned with the American League pennant. TK mentioned there would be a small celebration at the Metrodome; they were thinking under 10,000 because we were getting back to the Metrodome around eleven at night.

During the flight the captain announced, "We've been told there may be a crowd of 20,000 waiting for you at the Metrodome. Then just before we landed he came back on and said: "There's an update on that crowd. It may be 30,000, we're told." A huge cheer went up on the plane.

We arrived at the Minneapolis Airport and TV crews were everywhere. We moved along, some guys did quick interviews, and we got on three buses. We got to the outskirts of town and six cop cars picked us up and escorted us to the Metrodome. People lined the streets waving their homer hankies. When we could see the streets we were traveling on had been blocked off, the guys started to get the feeling that this homecoming might be a tad bigger than they anticipated.

When we pulled up at the Metrodome, there must have been 10,000 people standing outside cheering us. Players were slapping high-fives with fans. It was like we were 24 Bruce Springsteens. The guards took us in one entrance and lined us up behind the double doors in right-center field, under the huge Minneapolis sign.

The doors opened up and white light beamed out. I thought of when the aliens opened their spaceship in *Close Encounters*. We walked into a domed stadium with 65,000 people standing and screaming. The guys went crazy. Gaetti and Hrbek were crying; they'd seen the ball club and city come so far. It was an awesome feeling, Knucks—that's the only way I can describe it.

The public address announcer had a microphone and called each of us to the pitcher's mound. Guys were waving homer hankies, yelling "We're number one." I was introduced and I did a little polka in front of the mound and people went wild. I didn't plan it, but since I always carry an emery board in my back pocket, even away from the ballpark, I pulled it out and held it up to the crowd. I flipped it up in the air and they went bananas.

Every ballplayer should experience a homecoming like that, especially guys on teams that went through days when not 8,000 people would come out for a September game.

Even though I didn't participate, the playoffs were not exactly dull for me. I did have a couple of interesting moments, some fun and some not so fun.

Before Game 1, I ran into Dick Butler, who I knew from my

days with the Dallas–Fort Worth Spurs when he was general manager there, and he was with a gentleman I didn't recognize. He said, "Hi, Joe, I'm Bobby Brown." So here's the president of the American League, the guy I talked to on the telephone when I tried to appeal my suspension. I'd never met him in person.

Dr. Brown congratulated me for getting to the playoffs with the Twins, and I couldn't resist the opportunity. "I just want you to know one thing, I have one in my back pocket," and I pulled out an emery board.

"I'm glad you do. I wasn't even going to mention it," Dr. Brown said. We had a nice conversation. We talked about the Twins-Tigers matchup, but there was not a word brought up about my incident in California. If he'd had said something, I might have told him I never thought I received a true appeal, but I let it go.

Before Game 3 in Detroit I was coming out of the dugout when Sid Hartman of the *Minneapolis Star-Tribune* came up to me with his tape recorder and microphone. The first thing he said was "Are the Twins stuck with your contract?"

I gave him a silent stare like, "Nice question, Hatchet Head." I said, "Yeah, Sid, they're stuck with my contract." I emphasized the word "stuck" and walked away.

Sid knew I was supremely pissed because he ran after me right away, "Joe, I didn't mean it that way." Bull he didn't.

During Game 3 somebody told me Tony Kubek, who was broadcasting the game with Bob Costas for NBC, mentioned he was sorry I wasn't going to pitch in the playoffs, because my arm's hurting. I looked Tony up right away the next day to set him straight. I didn't want a rumor about my health to prevent me from seeing any action. I guess it probably didn't matter anyway, because Kelly had no plans to use me against Detroit.

George Frazier, another old Yankee, told me the hot rumor in New York: Billy Martin is coming back for the fifth time to manage and he's bringing his old buddies, Art Fowler as pitching coach and Clete Boyer as third-base coach. I still think Lou Piniella deserves another chance, but as we both know, Steinbrenner operates things differently over there. I know this much: Lou won't be without a job for long. George might not let him get away anyway.

Now we just wait for the National League winner to come to town. It looked like San Francisco was going to be it when they went up 3–1, but St. Louis is back home and can take it to Game 7 by winning tonight. The Giants have the power, the Cardinals have the speed—so we'll have our hands full no matter who it is.

But honestly, Knucks, I think with four games at the Metrodome, if the World Series goes the seven-game limit, everything is set up for Minnesota's first-ever World Championship.

—Joe

October 16. Friday. Minneapolis.

Phil:

These two towns, the Twin Cities, are going absolutely crazy. If we don't get this World Series started soon with tomorrow night's game, the hospitals are going to be overcrowded with people suffering from nervous exhaustion.

Everywhere you go around here it's Twins, Twins, Twins. I don't think I've ever seen a team loved more by its fans. If Kirby Puckett ran for mayor, he'd win by a landslide. If Kent Hrbek walked into any one of the local banks and asked for one million dollars, they'd give him two million.

The people around here even think I'm somebody—even though I feel like a nobody going into the series against St. Louis.

At the ballpark I'm getting my share of interviews, even though I'm about as much in Kelly's pitching plans as you are, Knucks. The writers mostly want to know how I feel about a Niekro finally getting to a World Series. I'm told that if I do get into a game, and right now that's a longshot, I'll break Walter Johnson's record of 18 years in the big leagues before he appeared in a World Series.

God, I'd like to break Johnson's record with a start, but unless we go up 3–0, I can forget about that.

With all the guys we've got on this club to be interviewed, I'm wondering why the hell so many of the writers want to talk to me. But, I guess, in a World Series everybody's a story to a certain degree, and I've been cooperating. The New York writers and my friend Kenny Hand from the *Houston Post* are just doing stories on a guy who used to pitch in their cities, I assume.

It does feel good not to be forgotten, especially when you feel that you are forgotten on your own ball club.

The Cardinals are supposed to be the veteran World Series–tested team, with Whitey Herzog managing, and with players like Ozzie Smith, Willie McGee, and Tommy Herr.

But I swear, Knucks, I can't believe how loose and relaxed our guys are. It's probably because we're opening up at home like we did in the playoffs. The fans are more uptight than the players are.

Bruno pulled a classic World Series gag yesterday. This one could go in the Jay Johnstone Hall of Fame.

The stadium crew was setting up the bleachers at the Metrodome for a University of Minnesota football game last night. We were having our workout and batting practice, and you know how many reporters were out there sniffing around for a good story.

All of a sudden there was a loud crash. Everybody looked over where some scaffolding had collapsed and Brunansky was hopping around holding his hand. Blood was gushing out all over and there was a nail sticking out of Bruno's finger.

Bruno ran from the field into the dugout to get to the trainer's room. Kelly and Gaetti acted like they were having heart attacks. There was general panic everywhere and the media people rushed up the stairs to our clubhouse, trying to find out what had happened to Bruno.

It wasn't April Fools' Day, but it might as well have been. Bruno had some fake blood and a rubber finger with a nail through it, the kind you've seen for Halloween. Kelly and all our guys were in on it and everybody had a big laugh. I watched the TV sports shows that night to see if anybody overreacted and used the story before finding out it was a gag. Fortunately for them, nobody did.

That showed how loose we were coming into the World Series. If there was any tension, Bruno's gag certainly broke it.

So, you're not going to join me for the World Series until we get back to Minneapolis for Games 6 and 7? Knucks, I can't believe you're willing to wait that long, but I'm sure you must have something going back in Atlanta to keep you busy.

You're going to be out of luck if we do to St. Louis what we did to Detroit. I doubt we can end this in five games. The Cardinals are being called the "Team of the Eighties" because this is their third World Series in this decade. They beat Milwaukee in seven games in 1982, and old Whitey Herzog is determined to turn around a seven-game loss to Kansas City in 1985.

Hey, I know you're a gambling kind of guy, so I guess you know what you're doing, I'm sure you'll be having a few brews in front of the TV.

I can't wait to see you, though, bro. If you can't be in the World Series, Knucks, you deserve to be in the clubhouse with me one time at least.

—Joe

October 19. Monday. St. Louis.

Phil:

Now my blood's starting to bubble in my veins, Knucks. I'm getting those chills and goose bumps you're supposed to feel when you're in a World Series.

I don't want you to think I haven't been excited about this World Series, especially with us beating St. Louis in the first two games at the Metrodome. But I'd be lying if I didn't admit I haven't felt the sensations my teammates have felt simply because I've been such an outsider, a noncontributor, since the regular season ended.

Today I actually feel like I'm a member of the Minnesota Twins again, and indirectly I probably have the media to thank.

Since we arrived here late last night the rumors have been flying that if we win Game 3 and go up 3-0, I might get the start in Game 4. It's the same stuff I heard when we were up 2-0 against Detroit in the playoffs, and you know what happened then.

I got out to Busch Stadium extra early today for the off day to do my normal running. One reason is because I wanted to be on and off the field before all the press arrived and started asking me about the possibilities. Evidently the press has also been pestering Kelly about whether or not I'm going to pitch. I think the media pressured TK into having to make some kind of statement about it.

Finally, after I came out of the shower today, TK told me I'd get the start in Game 4 if we win Game 3. My heart about jumped out of my chest. I know it's anything but automatic because of our road record and the fact that the Cardinals are going to be pumped up about getting back into this Series in their first game at home. But suddenly I've had more hope than I've had in what seems like months. Aside from a casual "Hi," this was the first time TK has talked to me about anything related to pitching since my start at Kansas City in the last game of the regular season.

Knucks, I'd finally accepted I was out of our rotation for the postseason. I was pretty much over that disappointment. What got me was being left in the dark for so long.

Dick Such still hasn't said a word to me. How can a pitching coach not talk to one of his nine pitchers? I still have a uniform on; anything can happen, especially during the World Series in the National League ballpark, where the DH isn't used and maybe the score will dictate using more pinch hitters and middle relievers.

I'm really going to be pulling for Les Straker tomorrow in Game 3, not that I wouldn't be anyway. It's just that I have a lot more riding on that game now.

Your telephone call yesterday really amused me, Knucks. Of course I'll get you tickets for any game you can come to, even in St. Louis. Even if I couldn't get a ticket I can't imagine you not being able to get into the ballpark. How can they keep out a Hall of Famer?

Just show up and I'm sure someone, somewhere, somehow will find you a seat.

I just hope we can keep playing as well as we did at home in Games 1 and 2. The combined score of those games was 19–5 so we really blew any and all of that underdog crap out the window.

The team was just glad to get Game 1 going; we all were tired of the hype. Everything in Game 1 was in our favor: the Cardinals had just come off a tough seven-game playoff against San Francisco, we had our ace Frank Viola well rested and going against a rookie, Joe Magrane, and the Cardinals had two of their biggest offensive weapons, Jack Clark and Terry Pendleton, out with injuries.

I think the tone of the first two games was established on Viola's second pitch in Game 1. Vince Coleman, the Cardinals' speedster, tried to lay down a bunt, and Viola made a good play to throw him out. If Coleman gets on, you never know, that might have established an entirely different pattern. You know Coleman's going to run, so Viola has to throw fastballs to Ozzie Smith, who's a dead fastball hitter, and maybe that gets them rolling before we even get our first World Series at-bat.

Getting Coleman out like that relaxed Viola and he went on to pitch a marvelous eight innings. We got all the runs Frankie needed when Kent Hrbek hit a two-run double off Magrane in the fourth. The highlight of that seven-run inning was Dan Gladden's grand slam off Bob Forsch. When Danny circled the bases I thought the noise from our fans was going to bust a hole in the Metrodome roof.

In the Game 2 blowout, the fourth was our big inning again; we scored six runs and knocked out Danny Cox, who might be the Cardinals' best big-game pitcher. Bert Blyleven pitched seven strong innings, striking out eight. Juan Berenguer struggled in the eighth, but Reardon slammed the door in the ninth.

You know what a sly fox Whitey Herzog is. He was complaining about Blyleven not stopping in his stretch. That's the same thing you've been accused of, Knucks, but the umpires didn't get sucked in.

A lot of guys get discovered in the World Series if they have one big at-bat or a couple of big games. Steve Lombardozzi hit a home run in Game 1 and Tim Laudner, who had been getting some laughs because of what he called his "Buck Ninety" batting average, has hit a home run and driven in four runs already. I love it when the "little guys" have their day in the sun.

Our sweep at home really puts us in a strong position—we might actually be the favorite now for a change. If the Cardinals win one game at the Metrodome, they are in position to possibly win the series with a three-game sweep at home. As it turns out, St. Louis must now win at least two games at home just to get the Series back to Minnesota for Game 6.

Tomorrow's a big game for the Niekros, big brother. I hope you have a reason to come see me in Game 4.

—Joe

October 23. Friday. Minneapolis.

Phil:

We've been in must-win situations at different times this season, but nothing like this. We can't lose again—it's that simple—or the St. Louis Cardinals are the World Series champs and the Minnesota Twins are the team that came up short, and we'll probably start hearing that Twinkies garbage again.

As you know, Knucks, the Cardinals swept all three games in St. Louis and now they're going into Game 6 tomorrow night with a 3–2 lead. Actually, though, I think we're still in good shape. We're back home, where we feel almost invincible; Les Straker is starting Game 6 after his great performance in Game 3, and we have Frank Viola ready if there's a climactic Game 7 Sunday.

Losing all three games at St. Louis was a disappointment, but it's a road trip that will live in my mind forever. I finally got to pitch in relief in Game 4—my first action in over two weeks—and you were there to see it, Knucks. I keep thinking there must have been some divine intervention there somehow. I sure wish we could have spent more time together afterward, but I'll cherish what we did have.

It would have been great to start Game 4—and for a while during Game 3 it looked like I might—but it just wasn't to be.

Straker pitched sensationally in Game 3: a four-hit shutout for six innings. When he came back to the dugout after the sixth, holding a 1–0 lead, my heart was racing. I knew you and Mom and

Dad were watching the game, knowing what a victory would mean for me and for our family. I spent the game in the corner of the dugout, plotting my strategy for each Cardinal hitter. I'd pitched division-clinching games for Houston in 1980 and this year for the Twins, and I was confident that if I had the opportunity to close out the World Series in Game 4, I'd pitch the game of my life.

I know all the armchair managers and second-guessers went wild when Kelly took out Straker after six innings, but TK was following the formula that had been successful for him for 169 games. Nobody expected six scoreless innings out of Les, and TK, I think, didn't want to expect too much out of a pitcher who's had some ups and downs this season.

The only thing that might get talked about and rehashed is TK's bringing in Berenguer, who struggled in one inning of Game 2, and not our left-handed reliever, Dan Schatzeder. San Francisco's left-handers had given the Cards all kinds of trouble, and turning their switch hitters around to the right side would have prevented them from getting a quick jump out of the batter's box. A left-hander also would have been able to hold base stealers like Vince Coleman and Willie McGee closer.

But that's kind of like looking up a dead horse's tail now, isn't it, Knucks? Who's to say Schatzeder wouldn't have gotten ripped? We'll never know.

I really felt bad for Juan, especially after the great year he'd had. The Cardinals lit him up for three runs and we lost 3–1. At that point I wasn't upset about losing my Game 4 start; I was more disappointed because I figured that meant you wouldn't be coming to St. Louis.

The next day, before Game 4, I was getting all the "Sorry you're not starting" from everybody, but I did feel like I had a shot to pitch in relief if our starters got in trouble the next two games. I got away from all the questions by staying out in the outfield shagging fly balls for batting practice.

When I came back in from BP, Don Baylor told me someone wanted to see me back in the clubhouse. As I walked up the runway I could see John Potter, my buddy from Indianapolis. Just when I turned the corner to ask John what he wanted was when I saw you, Knucks. My heart skipped a beat I was so surprised.

It's one thing to have your big brother fly from Atlanta to St. Louis to see his little brother start a game in the World Series. But it's special when your big brother shows up even when he knows you're not starting the game. I can't tell you how wonderful that made me feel, Knucks; I'll never forget you for doing that. You really picked my spirits up.

I felt so proud to have you in the clubhouse with me. Sitting side by side on stools made me think how incredible it would have been for us to be teammates in a World Series, like what might have happened in 1985 when we were with the Yankees.

When I went out to the dugout for the start of the game and found out it was unofficially "Polish Night," with Stan Musial and Moe Drabowsky throwing out the first balls—and with you in the stands—I had a feeling that maybe this was supposed to be the night a Niekro pitches in the World Series.

It was pretty obvious from the start that Viola didn't have his best stuff; he was pitching on three days rest. Still, the game was tied 1-1 after three innings.

Then the Cardinals put one of our fourth-inning explosions on us. Tom Lawless, who was playing third because Terry Pendleton was injured, hit a three-run home run to break the game open, and I think it even surprised the hell out of him. He'd hit only one other major-league home run in five years. Our guys didn't think a whole lot of Lawless for flipping his bat and taking a hotdog, Reggie Jackson–style trot around the bases.

Even then, I felt shocked when I was told to go warm up. I was up in the runway talking to somebody when Dick Such told me to go warm up. I don't know if I was more surprised to be getting a call to the bullpen or that Such was speaking to me.

When they brought in Schatzeder I knew I'd be pitching in the next inning. Schatzeder was due up third in the fourth and I knew unless we staged a big rally, Walter Johnson's record was going to be broken.

We didn't, and I took the mound knowing my job was not to let the Cardinals build on a 7–1 lead. I glanced into the stands, up where the wives were sitting, to see if I could spot you, but all that Cardinal red made it impossible.

My first batter, Jose Oquendo, hit a pretty good line drive to right that Tom Brunansky caught. Lawless lined out to Steve Lombardozzi at second, and I got the third out on a ground ball, so I felt pretty good about a 1–2–3 inning.

In the fifth Vince Coleman led off with a double. I loaded the bases up with a walk to Tommy Herr, and then I hit Jim Lindemann. With you in the stands, and remembering how poor my last start was, I really bore down and got out of the inning by striking out Willie McGee and getting Tony Pena on a ground ball to third.

I felt pretty good walking off—two innings, no runs. I was scheduled to lead off the seventh inning, so I knew I'd be coming out for a pinch hitter. My World Series ERA was going to be 0.00. Not too shabby, eh brother? I knew if I didn't pitch again in the Series, that ERA wouldn't look too bad in the World Series record book.

Not only was I the first Niekro in a World Series, as far as I know I also carried the first emery board into a World Series—had it in my back pocket, like always, both innings and nobody said boo. Only one of the four umpires who jumped me in Anaheim—Dave Phillips—worked the World Series.

TK didn't have to say anything to me afterward, but he congratulated me. He did say, "We made history," meaning I broke Walter Johnson's record. I didn't say anything, but I thought, What do you mean "we"? The Niekros made history, not Tom Kelly.

I appreciated TK using me, but I still think the press always asking him whether or not I was going to get into a game had something to do with it. Everybody wants to pitch, but I knew from the way our staff was set up that it wasn't mandatory that I get into a game. I didn't want a gratuitous call—like "OK, here's my chance to get Niekro into a game"—but somehow I have to think it was, partly.

But I did feel like a huge weight had been lifted off me. And because I did get them out with no runs, I thought I better stay ready in case Kelly has to use me again.

I feel very fortunate and gratified that my big brother, after all we've been through for two decades, was there to share it with me. I just wish we could have gone out and danced a couple of polkas.

You know we'll make up for that, won't we, Knucks?

Funny thing about Game 4, George Frazier and I both ended up pitching. Technically, I warmed up first, which was the basis of our postseason bet. But since George got in, too, I called the bet a rub. We don't need an excuse like that to buy each other a drink or dinner anyway.

Game 5 was crucial for the Cardinals because if we win it, we go home needing to win only one out of two to take the Series. Blyleven and Cox matched five shutout innings until the Cards got a couple of breaks in the sixth.

Coleman hit a ground ball toward Hrbek at first that hit the edge of the artificial turf for a bad-hop single. Then Bert couldn't make a play on Ozzie Smith's bunt. We had controlled the Cardinals' running game to that point, but Coleman and Smith pulled off a double steal to put runners at second and third. With one out, Blyleven walked Danny Driessen intentionally to load the bases.

Blyleven looked like he might pitch out of it when he struck out McGee on his money pitch—a huge, sweeping breaking ball. Like I've said before, Blyleven has the best curveball for a right-hander I've ever seen. Bert fell behind Curt Ford, another one of the Cardinals' speedy, slashing-type hitters, and Ford broke up the shutout with a two-run single to center. The Cards scored two more runs on an error by Gagne and Ozzie Smith's single off Reardon in the seventh, and won 4–2. Danny Cox pitched a good game in the clutch for them, and then the Cardinals' left-righty bullpen combination of Ken Dayley and Todd Worrell closed the game out. We had only six hits, and both runs came on Gaetti's triple that McGee almost caught at the wall.

Nancy's been following the Series, blowing her whistle with all the Twins' wives. She left for Lakeland today, though, because

Natalie needed to get home. Lance stayed with me; Rich Sloan came up to watch him for me.

Nancy and I are still not getting along like we should, but I appreciated you writing a little to me, Knucks, about what you thought about marital problems. I probably already knew what you told me, but somehow hearing it from your big brother doesn't make you feel so alone. Once the Series is over and I get home, Nancy and I plan to spend time together. Maybe not having baseball and talking over the telephone all the time will help us.

Anyway, I'm looking forward to our Everglades fishing trip in November. It seems like we've been planning for it our whole lives. Two more wins and you'll be sitting in the boat with a real, honest-to-goodness World Series champion.

I can't wait to talk to Dad once we win the damn thing.
—Joe

October 26. Monday. Atlanta.

Joe:

I'm proud to be your brother, Joe Niekro.

You're a world champion, which makes me feel like a world champion, which means the Niekros—after a combined 45 years in the major leagues—are world champions. I know, in our eyes, that's what Mom and Dad always have been, but now it's official.

Watched you guys win Game 7 last night. I was in a warm, comfortable atmosphere—fire in the fireplace, beer and popcorn on the coffee table, my head on a pillow in Nancy's lap—but inside I felt like there was a merry-go-round spinning.

I'll admit I was a little nervous after the Cardinals went up 2–0 in the second inning. But when you guys came right back in the bottom of the second to make it 2–1, I knew there was no way the Twins were going to lose in front of those wild, hanky-waving fans.

What a great game to win it with. If you guys would have lost by one run after Don Baylor was called out at home plate, when the

TV replay clearly showed his foot got in before the tag, I might not have slept for weeks. But you guys kept coming.

What a great eight innings Frank Viola pitched on three days rest; he deserved the MVP. Then Jeff Reardon slammed the door like he has all year, a fitting ending. I think I saw you on the field during that wild celebration, but you guys piled on top of each other and it was pretty tough picking people out. It made me think back to 1982 when I was with Atlanta and we won the NL West. There is no mistaking pure joy like that.

You guys did something few people outside the state of Minnesota thought you could do. I read in the newspaper today that the Twins were 150-to-1 to win the World Series before the season. If I could have legally bet a couple of bucks, I would have put them down because I thought the Twins had a chance in 1986, even before you got there.

When they traded for Jeff Reardon, a proven closer, I had a feeling he was the final piece of the puzzle.

It was pretty obvious in the playoffs that you weren't in Kelly's pitching plans for the postseason. Everybody back home in Lansing kept asking me when you were going to pitch, but I told them that Kelly had his rotation set and it didn't look like it included you.

I'm as happy for Mom and Dad as I was for you and me that you got to pitch those two innings of middle relief in Game 4. You don't know this, but I talked to Kelly and told him that since I made the trip from Atlanta, I was hoping he could get you into the game.

Only kidding. I'm just glad it worked out that I could be in St. Louis to see you pitch. I would have come to Minnesota, too, if I knew you were pitching. But you told me it was unlikely, so I just stayed glued to the TV for Games 6 and 7.

When I heard you were in line to start Game 4 if the Twins went up 3-0, I started making plans for St. Louis. And the way Les Straker was pitching, all I could think of was you being the winning pitcher of the game that closed out a four-game Minnesota sweep.

I'm not so sure that wouldn't have happened if Kelly had left Straker alone. Damn, the man had a four-hit shutout through six innings. One of my pet peeves is when a manager wants to change the captain of the ship in midstream when it's smooth sailing. I mean this was the World Series, not like it was a cold-weather April game, or that Straker had thrown 150 pitches.

It ticked me off. My mind starting dreaming things up like it was some sort of Kelly conspiracy to prevent you from getting a World Series start. I know that's not true, but as angry as I felt I couldn't help but think that. Then the way Berenguer got knocked around and lost the lead, I was not the biggest Tom Kelly fan in the world right then.

Even though you weren't going to get the Game 4 start, I just had a gut feeling you'd pitch, so I told Nancy I was going anyway. Thanks to our buddy John Potter, all the arrangements were made. Chuck Anderson picked me up at the airport, and since I wanted it to be a surprise, I didn't give you a call and we went to the Days Inn in St. Louis to have lunch with Pancho Carter and his boys.

We stopped at the Marriott before we walked across the street to Busch Stadium. The hotel was jammed. There were people who actually thought I was you. They kept stopping me for autographs and asking me where my emery board was.

I knew you wouldn't be expecting me, and the look of surprise on your face when you came up the runway and saw me made this old-timer feel mighty good. Kelly saw me and told me I could come into the clubhouse after batting practice. I wondered if he'd have been so nice to me if he knew what I was thinking about him less than 24 hours earlier. He didn't have to do that and I'll always be grateful to him.

This is the truth, Joe: I had chills walking through your club-house, a World Series clubhouse. It's a place I always wanted to be. I didn't make it as a player, so now I'll have to do it some other way. It was great to see a good friend like Don Baylor in there; a man of his character and a player of his quality deserves moments like that.

I've been in an All-Star game clubhouse, but I never felt the excitement that was in your clubhouse before Game 4. I guess the press calls it World Series electricity.

What a feeling you guys must have had during those seven games; you all had to be exhausted when it was over. I kept looking around your clubhouse for a uniform with "P. Niekro" on it. I was hoping Kelly might walk up to me and say he needed an extra pitcher in the bullpen.

I was dreaming with my eyes wide open.

Soon as the game started, Potter and I found our seats. The Cardinals were leading 1–0 in the third inning, and since it was so close, I got the feeling you weren't going to pitch after all.

It was cold as hell, my feet were freezing, the seat was cramped, and my ears were ringing from those wives' whistles. So I told John I was going to walk across the street to the Marriott to get a drink and warm up, and that I'd be right back. I kind of wanted to absorb some of the World Series atmosphere outside the stadium anyway, with so many people without tickets partying out there.

I walked over to the Marriott and I couldn't get into the lounge because it was so crowded with people watching the game on TV. One of the security guards recognized me and said he'd get me in. So we worked our way to the bar, and of course people started recognizing me. Suddenly I found myself surrounded by pens and paper, people wanting autographs.

Just for fun, I had an emery board in the breast pocket of my coat sticking out. "Did Joe give you that?" one guy wanted to know. Another wanted to know if I was going to run across the street and sneak it to you if you got into the game.

Joe, you've won 220 games and we've won 538 games between us for an all-time record. The Niekro name has been around for almost three decades and it used to mean "knuckleball." But because of one 10-minute incident, you are known for emery boards. It's amazing. It's not disgraceful, it's not embarrassing, but it's unusual and funny, and that's what sticks in people's minds.

So I'm standing in the bar talking, look up on the TV and somebody named Tom Lawless hits a three-run homer off Viola to put the Cardinals up 3–1. I swear to you, I've never heard of Tom Lawless before, but I understand it was the second home run of his career. He went around those bases like he just broke Hank Aaron's record. I couldn't believe it.

The Cardinals are down 2–1 in the World Series and this guy shows up the other team like that. I realize it might have happened because the guy's head was so far in the clouds he didn't know what he was doing, but he's been around long enough to know what an exhibition he put on. Shit, he flipped his bat before he took off.

That's one of the reasons I was so impressed with Mark McGwire, who's a shoo-in for rookie of the year with his 49 home runs and 118 RBI. When McGwire hits a home run he's no Reggie Jackson or Tom Lawless or Jeff Leonard, with his ridiculous "one flap down" trot. And heaven knows McGwire's home runs travel far enough to give him time to do one of those hotdog trots. McGwire gets around those bases in no more than 15 seconds and then it's back to playing ball. He's not flaunting or gloating or saying, "Look, world, watch me." The kid's all class, from what I can see.

A little bit later I look up at the TV and you and Schatzeder are warming up in the bullpen. I thought, "All right, a couple more St. Louis runs and you guys are going to get in there."

The next thing I know, Viola walks Vince Coleman and Kelly's going out to the mound. I'm in the middle of a sip and it finally hits me, "Shit, I'm sitting in here and Joe's about to pitch."

I drop a twenty-dollar bill on the bar and bolt outside like I'm about to pee in my pants. I dash across the street to the nearest gate, reach in my coat pocket for my ticket stub, and I can't find it. I run my hands in every pocket.

My ticket must have dropped out when I was running.

I walk over to nearest gate and tell the little old guard I've lost my ticket. You can almost guess what happened, can't you?

"Then you can't get in," he says.

"But sir, I've already been in; the ticket blew out of my coat and I can't find it."

About that time, I hear over the public address system, "Batting for the pitcher Schatzeder . . ."

Now I *am* about ready to piss down my leg. With Schatzeder having pitched and gone, I knew damn well you were coming in to pitch next.

You know me, Joe, I can't be one of those guys who stand tall and say, "Don't you know who I am?" I didn't want to have to say, "I'm Phil Niekro."

I tried to be patient and kept explaining I'd already been inside and just lost my stub.

"Right, we've been hearing that all night," the guard said.

I almost said to hell with it and busted through, but a couple of policemen had been watching us talk, so I figured I'd better not risk that. All I could think of was newspapers and headlines: "Niekro arrested for overpowering 80-year-old stadium guard." And also missing my brother become the first Niekro to pitch in a World Series.

I remained calm with the guy and finally put my cards on the table: "My brother's about to pitch and I've got to get in there."

He said, "Yeah, yeah, yeah," and turned away.

I pulled out my lifetime baseball gold card, my driver's license, and every other damn card I had in my wallet to prove I was Phil Niekro. I knew you guys had to be almost done batting in the fourth.

Finally the light came on; the elevator came down to the ground floor. The guard believed me and said, "Come on," and he led me through the gate and up into the stands.

Just as I sat down—and it's a good thing I didn't stop for a beer or a dog—you were toeing the rubber to pitch to your first batter, Jose Oquendo.

John Potter looked at me and he was sweating. He thought I was going to blow it. For a minute, so did I.

Good old John had a cup of beer and a box of popcorn ready for me. It had taken me so long, the beer was almost warm and the popcorn was almost cold. I didn't care. I sat up on the edge of my seat and focused on the first Niekro in a World Series.

I was riveted on you as if I was watching a John Wayne movie. What a first inning for you: 1–2–3. Perfect. I knew you could do it. The Cardinals are a fastball-hitting team; a knuckleball screws fastball hitters into the dirt. I know you couldn't see me, but I stood up and put my hands together for you when you walked back to the dugout. It was an emotional moment for me, Joe. I was walking right with you, brother. As far as I was concerned, that was the World Series appearance I'd always dreamed of—first in Lansing as a boy and then in Milwaukee, Atlanta, New York, Cleveland, and Toronto the last 23 years.

I sat back down and the Cardinals' fan sitting behind me put his hand on my shoulder and said, "Boy, I was afraid you weren't going to make it back in time. I know you'd have died if you'd have missed that inning."

He was right. Somebody's always looking out for the Niekros at special times like that, I've always believed.

From then on, every time you got an out, Joe, this guy would punch me in the shoulder and yell, "Way to go, Joe." This Cardinals' fan had become a Niekro fan, and I loved it.

I was focused so intensely on you on the mound, you looked about 20 feet tall and my eyes burned. When you had the bases loaded and Willie McGee up, somebody passed me a box of popcorn to send on down the line to another guy. I just grabbed the box, thinking John had gotten it for me, stuck my hand into it, and starting eating. My eyes never left the field. I don't remember any at-bat in my life I wasn't pitching that I was as into as you going one-on-one with Willie, who was only the National League batting champion in 1985.

When you struck out McGee on a 2-and-2 knuckleball about shoulder high for the second out, the guy behind me squeezed both of my shoulders, as if to say, "I know how much you enjoyed that one."

You left the three runners stranded when you got Tony Pena on a ground ball to third base to end the sixth. You did your job, you held them scoreless.

I felt like I was with you on every pitch; I just hoped your heart was not racing as fast as mine was. You were throwing the pitches I was calling; I wouldn't have changed a thing.

Maybe one thing.

No knock intended, little brother. But the next time Lawless came to bat, after his parade around the bases against Viola, it was against you. You had one out and nobody on in a 7–1 game. In the old days, Lawless goes down, he hits the dirt for that trot. But I realize the way the Twins have been handling you—one base-runner and you might have gotten the hook, so you really didn't have any margin for error. I'm not blaming you, because you've had enough controversy for one year, and Commissioner Uberroth and the league presidents are sitting over in their VIP box, knowing a national audience is watching on TV. That turns sensitivities up to a high level these days, I'm afraid.

Still your performance was outstanding; I know how proud Mom and Dad were at home, not to mention all of Lansing and everybody at the Sportsman's Club. Of all the World Series games I could have come to see you in, I hit the right one.

I missed the next couple of innings after you left the game. I just sat there in my seat, thinking back to 1959—my first year in professional baseball—and how many years and miles we both covered until one of us finally made it to the Big One, the World Series, the greatest sports series of all.

I had the opportunity to sit in Busch Stadium with 55,000 people, another 30 or 40 million watching on television, and my little brother was out there on the mound pitching. It made my whole season, Joe. The crowning moment, the cherry on top. I'll reflect on those two innings until I die—and maybe longer, you never know.

If you never make it to another World Series, the record book is going to show, "Joe Niekro, ERA 0.00." What pitcher wouldn't take that? I sure would. Nobody can beat it.

Nobody can take your two innings in the World Series away from you. Nobody can take away the fact that for at least once in your life you were able to say you were a member of the best baseball team in the world.

I'm sure Minneapolis and St. Paul went bananas when you

guys won Game 7 last night. You're going to get nice playoff and World Series shares—that ought to be a nice extra $100,000 for the holidays.

But more than the money, you're going to get the ring—the ring I've been after my whole career. I've already mentioned I want to wear it. How about a week? Even one hour would be fine with me. Shit, some people outside Busch Stadium thought I was Joe Niekro, so if I still look that young, I could wear it and get away with it.

My final season, my last year in baseball as a player. I could not have topped off my career much better than you winning the World Series. I'm serious when I say I feel like I won, too; I feel that good about anything that happens to you, Joe.

Hey, maybe you didn't pitch as much as you would have liked, but you were in a World Series game. It's something Mom and Dad will always get pleasure from, and you gave it to them, Joe.

I probably won't pitch against you again, which means you win our series 5-4. Maybe we'll manage against each other. Maybe I'll get a managing job somewhere and you'll be my pitching coach. Maybe together we can take a team to the World Series.

I'm so thankful I was able to play this game while you did. Just think how many brothers would give anything for that opportunity. I'm leaving this game with nothing to be ashamed of and everything to be proud of. The game's been good to the Niekros and I think we have been good to the game.

I'll always remember, Joe, that I never met a ballplayer who didn't say, "You've got one helluva brother." It's a fine compliment to me, Mom, and Dad.

You've been an inspiration to me, little brother. Just your face or your devilish smile has picked me up when I was feeling low. Even just hearing what you were up to would give me a little boost. I hope I've been the same for you.

It's your ball game now, Joe. I'm history and happy. If you're not actively playing, and I'm in a position to do something about it, pick up the telephone. I'd always want someone with your competitiveness and pride.

I don't know two guys who enjoyed this game more and

wanted to win more than the Niekro brothers. I don't think anybody has played it the way you have, little brother. Not even me.

We've wrapped the baseball season up and we'll be fishing for
snook in the Everglades in a little over a week. You know how I
love catching fish, but I won't care if we don't get a hit.

My year was made in St. Louis when I saw you pitch those
two innings in the World Series.

I love you, Joe.

—Phil

October 28. Wednesday. Lakeland, Florida

Phil:

I wonder if Ronnie missed me today.

The Twins—excuse me, the world champion Minnesota
Twins—were invited to the White House today to meet President
Reagan. Not that I'm used to standing up presidents, but if there's a
choice, there's no comparison between Ronald Reagan and Natalie
Niekro.

I think I've told you, Knucks, that Natalie is a cheerleader for
Lakeland Junior High School. I've never seen her cheer—can you
believe that? I promised her weeks ago that I would make it back
for her last football game tonight.

Lance, our friend Rich Sloan, and I left Minneapolis in my
Jeep wagon at 5:30 P.M. and drove straight through. Rich slept
when I drove and I slept when he drove. Lance just slept. We didn't
break any speed records and made it in 26 hours. It was a good,
easy trip.

The White House visit wasn't mandatory, and it didn't sound
like I was going to be the only one to miss it. It would have been an
honor to meet the president, but it was just a situation where my
daughter is more important to me than Ronnie. I couldn't let her
down; she'd been looking forward to me being there for so long. I
was sure Mr. President would understand.

We drove off the interstate and headed right to the junior high.
We made it to the field before the cheerleaders arrived. When

Natalie saw me, the sparkle in her eyes and the smile on her face made 26 hours of driving worthwhile.

It was my first taste of being a World Series winner. Being a Minnesota Twin was all of a sudden a status symbol. It was not my imagination that people were being a little nicer to me. I could see Natalie on the field pointing me out in the stands to her friends. It felt good, I'll admit.

I can't believe all that has gone on since I saw you after Game 4 in St. Louis. That's only been a week. All that's happened is that we experienced the most incredible homecoming in the history of sports; won Game 6, maybe one of the most exciting World Series games of all time; won the World Series in Game 7 and celebrated like champions should; and rode in a parade to end all parades.

Where do I start? Everybody might remember this entire World Series for Game 6. What a thriller. It was another game we had to win, and like almost every time since I joined the team, we won the game we had to win.

We weren't too concerned about being down 3–2 to the Cardinals, because we were back home in the Dome. What might have been on our minds more than anything was how the Cardinals' pitchers shut down our hitting at Busch Stadium. We had one home run, by Greg Gagne, in the three-game sweep. We had four home runs in the first two games at the Metrodome. We needed our big hitters to wake up, and did they ever.

I thought it was time for a Brunansky-type prank to break the inevitable Game 6 tension. Knucks, you know how Ozzie Smith does that gymnastics flip when he goes out for the first inning at Busch Stadium? I wanted Kent Hrbek, who gets kidded about his weight, to do a somersault when he went out to first base. It probably was better that he didn't, because he might have rolled right out of the Metrodome.

The Cardinals took a 4–2 lead against Straker after four innings. Tommy Herr had hit a home run for them and their singles hitters were starting to ping us to death. Then we brought out the heavy artillery. Don Baylor, who'd driven in some big runs for us, hit his first home run as a Twin to put us ahead 5–4 in the fifth.

In the sixth Ken Hrbek probably had the most exciting at-bat of the Series. With the Cardinals trailing only 6–4, Whitey Herzog brought in left-hander Ken Dayley, who'd been so effective in the Series, to face Herbie, a left-handed hitter, with the bases loaded. Dayley's first pitch was a waist-high fastball and Herbie turned it around 439 feet to dead center field for our second grand slam of the Series to blow the game open 10–4.

You could hear the Cardinals' back break. We ended up whipping them 11–4 to force Game 7, a one-game showdown, No. 174 of the season, for everything.

The Twin Cities partied until daybreak that night. Looking back, I think the Cities went more crazy after Game 6 than after Game 7, because once we boiled the World Series down to one game at the Metrodome, our fans believed we had it wrapped up.

We did all right, but we won Game 7 in a most uncharacteristic way—we played Cardinals' ball. Down 2–0 going into the bottom of the second, we started scrapping back. We scored single runs in four different innings, and no hit was greater than a double. Our two extra-base hits—doubles by Kirby Puckett and Dan Gladde—both scored runs.

I thought the ending was dramatic justice. Jeff Reardon, probably the player who put the Twins over the top, got Willie McGee on a ground ball to third baseman Gary Gaetti, our feisty, fierce leader. Who makes the final putout? None other than hometown hero Kent Hrbek. When Herbie squeezed the last out we all rushed out of the dugout and fell into a heap of human happiness.

Following the lead of the Super Bowl champion New York Giants, someone threw a cooler of Gatorade—I'm still partial to Dom Perignon—at the guys celebrating in the infield.

I started looking for Lance in the family section behind home plate. We caught each other's eye and waved. If Lance continues to play baseball, and it looks like he will, I hope he has a day like this. There's nothing like knowing you just won the World Series.

The clubhouse might as well have been turned upside down— it was a madhouse. There were so many people, mostly media, you could not take two steps. After pitching only two innings in the

World Series, I kind of faded to the back of the room like I did during the playoff celebration. I liked watching the young guys—Puckett, Gaetti, Lombardozzi, Hrbek, Randy Bush—celebrate how far they had come together.

We really didn't get a chance to congratulate each other, though. As soon as the game is over, the clubhouse fills up like a telephone booth with college students. They should keep the clubhouse closed a few minutes after the game, especially after Game 7 of the World Series, so the team can have some time together to enjoy each other and their accomplishment. It's perhaps a once-in-a-lifetime experience, and I know the press has a job to do, but it's difficult to celebrate when you're searching for ballplayers. There are 24 players and a coaching staff and maybe four times as many media people. Like Detroit, the players went back to the trainer's room to be together without the media. What happens then is we make the media miss their deadlines. If we could have had five minutes to get our celebrating out of the way, uninterrupted, we would have been prepared and in better position to receive the media, who would have been able to get their work done faster and more efficiently.

It can be done. The media won't miss out on anything. For the privilege of five minutes of privacy, the players would promise to spray champagne and shaving cream and act like fools for the cameras. You can't really fake a World Series celebration, even if it's been put on hold for five minutes. What happened was that we pretty much waited until everybody cleared out before we let loose.

Lance got soaking wet and he loved it. I felt like he was being baptized with championship champagne. We'll see what that does for him down the line. I got him into the clubhouse about 10 minutes after everything got wound up. What an experience for an eight-year-old boy.

Lance and I didn't leave the clubhouse until 1:30 in the morning. They were escorting groups of players outside to their cars because so many people were standing out there trying to see us. Lance just about got trampled. About 15 police officers surrounded us, and I held on to Lance's arm as hard as I've ever held anything. The people were reaching and grabbing. I understand they were celebrating, but sometimes when you are the object of their exuberance it can get a little frightening and dangerous. People don't realize that when you get several thousand acting wild like that, it becomes a helluva force to contend with. They're so excited, their enthusiasm overcomes their regard for human safety.

Generally, the people in Minneapolis were great—no burning cars like in Detroit in 1984. Just a party for millions. To have contributed to that kind of happiness for a town is very gratifying.

Lance and I sat up until 3:30 playing the new Intendo video games I bought him. He whips my butt good at everything— baseball, golf, shooting, racing, jumping. Lance pretty much collapsed in my arms before we went to bed. It was a night, Knucks, as father and son that will be in my heart forever.

I'm sure you're not surprised that we slept until Monday afternoon. We went out and bought some new videotapes for Lance and a radar detector for the drive home. The parade, thank God, was pushed back until Tuesday.

Nancy wanted me to fly home with Lance and have Rich drive the Jeep home. But we're going snook fishing in six days, and if Rich had trouble on the way and was late—well, the Jeep carries all my fishing gear and I also need it to pull my boat. You know me, Phil, I never gambled with my fishing plans, so I wanted my truck with me.

It was cold Tuesday and Lance, Rich, and I rode from Minneapolis to St. Paul—we must have covered 20 to 30 miles—in a convertible. It was the first ticker-tape parade I've ever been in, and it was awesome. It looked like everybody in the state had made it out to line the parade route. There were so many little pieces of paper flying in the air, it looked like a Minnesota blizzard.

We all rode in convertibles, and even though the police tried to hold people back, the crowd was so huge and powerful they pushed right up to the cars.

By now, Knucks, I've learned to play to the emery-board phenomenon instead of resisting it. I took out a bag of emery boards and threw them to the people. I wish I had one for everybody because they wanted them like they wanted the homer hankies.

St. Paul was absolute pandemonium—over there they didn't anticipate the crowd being as large as it turned out to be. George Frazier's and Sal Butera's cars caught on fire because confetti floated down into the manifolds. Those were anxious moments, and I had my guard up all the time with Lance there. Not that the people got that far out of hand, but I understand some legs were broken in the pushing of the mad rush. The parade backed up, and a couple times we didn't move for 10 minutes. That gave some people plenty of time and opportunity to try to get in the car with us.

A crowd like that can be so overwhelming in positive and negative senses.

We left for Florida from the Metrodome, where I first had to be measured for my World Championship ring. I'll admit I spent some time on the trip down looking at the fourth finger on my right hand, envisioning a big "M" in diamonds.

While Rich was driving and Lance was sleeping, I was thinking about the guys I'd come to know in Minnesota and how there was no such thing as identical Twins. Let me tell you about a few, Knucks.

Gary Gaetti: He's the type of player every manager and organization wants. Hard-nosed, in the game all the time. I didn't know how good he was until I watched him every day. A helluva third baseman defensively, a clutch hitter, he could hit 40 home runs in one year. If he played in New York, Rat would be approaching Brooks Robinson's status as a player and Reggie Jackson's as a personality. As it is now, he probably could walk down Fifth Avenue and hardly be noticed. That's going to change, though. I can see him managing down the line; his full concentration is on the game. He's highly competitive, a student of baseball, and a leader. He got the nickname Rat from Hrbek because he looks a little like one. Gary laughs about it; he's a fun-loving type who makes a clubhouse enjoyable. I know you'd really hit it off with him, Knucks. Rat could go 0 for 5, but if we win he'll still feel he had a good day.

Kent Hrbek: The big teddy bear. People ride Herbie about his weight. He's around 230 pounds, but I don't see the big deal. If he's 210, he's not going to run any faster and might lose some power— so what the hell. Maybe the most underrated fielder in the league; really smooth around the bag and being 6'4", a great target for the infielders. He got us a lot of outs with his stretch. Our kind of guy, Knucks. A great outdoorsman who likes duck hunting. Get this, he was out duck hunting the morning of Game 7. Really enjoys being a Twin because he grew up around Minneapolis and hearing about Harmon Killebrew, Zoilo Versalles, Rod Carew, Camilo Pasqual. It's been a dream season for him, except for the All-Star game. I hope he reconsiders and goes next year if he's voted in or picked, because Herbie deserves to play with the best in the game. What power. In St. Louis I saw him hit three balls into the upper deck in batting practice. That's halfway to Kansas. Herbie is like a kid who's doing exactly what he wanted, where he wanted to do it.

Kirby Puckett: What a dandy Puck is. Helluva player, helluva athlete, helluva person. Super centerfielder, the best who's ever played behind me, and a clutch hitter with power. We got to be good friends after they put my locker next to his. Lance fell in love with Puck. Tom Brunansky, another great guy in the prime of his playing career, and Puck call your nephew "Lance Romance." He loves it. Puck's a lifetime .300 hitter who is the best in the business at taking away home runs over the fence; it's amazing how high that chunky body can get up. Like Mattingly and Boggs, Puck is one of those guys who was born to hit. Even if he's around .270 into June, you still know he'll end up over .300. Puck has almost as much talent pound for pound, inch for inch as Dolly Parton.

Frank Viola: Bozo, another daffy left-hander like Bob Shirley and Dave Righetti. When I got to Minnesota he was 3–5, and he ended up 17–10 and a candidate for the Cy Young award. Maybe the best change-up in the league, and good location on his fastball. Hard-nosed; gets a little red-ass on the mound when things don't go his way or he gets a bad call. But you've got to like competitiveness like that. "Sweet Music" matured a lot this year. When Viola gets the ball, Tom Kelly knows he's getting six or seven quality innings. He could be an ace on anybody's staff.

Bert Blyleven: One of the closet crazies of all time. Known for sitting in birthday cakes when he pitched for the Pittsburgh Pirates' 1979 World Series championship team. A guy who genuinely has a good time playing baseball, and he's especially happy to be back in Minnesota, where he broke in. He's a clubhouse prankster, always trying to pull something. He wears a T-shirt that says "Who farted?" and it has brown holes all over it. It's so funny to watch him doing a serious TV interview wearing that shirt. You can never rest easy around Bert, but he's all business on the mound. To me he has Hall of Fame credentials, but you never hear that much talk about him. He's 36 and has won 244 games and has more than 3,200 strikeouts. Another great Minnesota curveball pitcher—first Camilo Pasqual and now Bert. His curve isn't as sharp as it was 12 years ago, but it's still a tough, tough pitch, as Willie McGee will tell you. When Bert gets the baseball, you can see the intensity in his eyes. One of the pillars of the ball club.

Jeff Reardon: Our opponent for years in the National League. Kind of quiet, not an overpowering Goose Gossage type, but gets the job done consistently. You don't save 177 games the last six years and not be consistent. He prepares well for hitters and situations. Throws a lot harder than I thought; his ball really rises. To me he was the MVP of the ball club. Without his 31 saves we don't win the division. The Twins always have had the offense, but they needed someone to protect their leads. He did a lot for the ball club psychologically. When Kelly brought Jeff in with a lead in the eighth or ninth inning, you didn't have eight guys in the field thinking, "Oh no, here we go again." Instead, the players are saying, "Here's a guy who gets the job done, I need to be on my toes." I think we still could have won if one of the big four—Gaetti, Puckett, Hrbek, or Brunansky—didn't have a good year. But I don't think the Twins would be world champions today without Reardon coming through. The team depended on him that heavily.

Don Baylor: Our old Yankee teammate. He and I related because we both felt a little like new sparkplugs on an engine that had already won the race. The press put the leader tag on him when he came to the Twins; like Baylor was going to fill a leadership void on the club. Donnie knew that wasn't true. Gaetti, Hrbek, Viola—they're all leaders in their own way. Because of the publicity, Don probably went out of his way not to seem like he was trying to take over someone else's territory. He was smart enough to know there's no reason to disturb a first-place ball club. If you sought out Don's experience and knowledge, he'd deliver, like he has anywhere he's ever played. He was brought in as an experienced RBI man and he contributed in the postseason. Just his presence on the bench—you know the opposing manager is always aware you have a Don Baylor ready to swing the bat. The Twins are nuts if they don't re-sign him as their DH for 1988.

Tom Kelly: Even though I thought our communications broke down, TK was my choice for manager of the year. In his rookie season he took a team that hadn't won a pennant in 22 years and never a World Series to the World Championship. What more can a man do? He had a plain-and-simple approach of playing one game at a time and having fun while you played. His mood didn't change if we won or lost five in a row. He'd keep a smile on his face and the confidence up. I've played for my share of managers, and he might not know the game as well as some guys who've been around, simply because this was his first full year. But as far as keeping a team on an even keel over an entire season, TK's the best. He raised his voice a couple of times after a few games we gave away and deserved to get chewed out about, but he doesn't turn over tables, kick and cuss, like some managers on a certain New York team we know. TK says we'll win some games we should lose and lose some games we should win. He keeps the guys relaxed and enjoying their work, and it's reflected in our play. I respect him. I always shook his hand after every game of the playoffs and World Series even though I felt so out of touch with him. Looking back, the only major disappointment was being frozen out during the playoffs. It was obvious I no longer was a starter, but nobody showed me enough respect to inform me of my new role. I felt I deserved that much. I guess Kelly must have thought I could read the old handwriting on the wall and that was good enough. If that's what he thought, it's odd because that attitude is not consistent with TK's personality. I don't hold it against him; I hope I'm back in his starting rotation next season proving I can win for him. As the saying goes, "Just tell me what you want."

Knucks, just think of the friendships we've made in over 20 years of baseball apiece. We'll have beers with them and tell stories and lies the rest of our lives. The guys on the Twins will be bending one another's ears about the year we won it all until we're on the way to the funeral parlor.

I know this knuckleball pitcher is glad to be home, but I can almost tell you to the minute how much longer we have until we're fishing in Alligator Creek. Going out in the boat with you and catching the elusive snook will be the peace and pleasure I need to revive me.

Don't be late.

—Joe

November: "A Winter of Wonder"

November 9. Sunday. Lakeland, Florida

Phil:

Hope you made it home to Atlanta all right, Knucks. I cleaned up my boat and condo in Chokoloskee and pulled out in my Jeep about two hours behind you and Bob Little Saturday. It's always a little sad for me to break up a fishing trip, especially down in my Everglades paradise, but this time I had a reason to get home. It was my birthday and my family had a small party planned.

Your little brother turned 43. I'm a little confused about my career and life in general, but I feel refreshed from the four days of fishing with you and our gang.

I know I'm going to enjoy the winter as one of the world champion Minnesota Twins.

Let's see, when you were 43, Phil, you went 17–4 for Atlanta in 1982 and led the National League in winning percentage, .810. I can't imagine playing at 48 like you did. At 45 and 46 you won a total of 32 games for the Yankees. How's that for keeping up with your big brother's career?

At 42 I was 7–13 with a 5.33 ERA. The shoulder I separated bothered me on and off, but that's no excuse for a bad year. Aside from breaking the Perry brothers' record and two innings in the

World Series, 1987 will not get a lot of time on my career-high-lights video. A trade, a controversy, an injury—I couldn't keep my name out of the newspapers.

What a coincidence that you were 7–13, too, Knucks. Here's one for people who love things that never happened before: Two Polish brothers in their 40s who throw the knuckleball and had identical pitching records. What are those odds?

Healthy, I still feel I'm a winning major-league pitcher, and I hope to prove that to the Twins next season. Andy MacPhail said I'm invited to spring training in Orlando. During the World Series there was talk among the reporters I might get released or returned to the Yankees. Ever heard this one, Knucks? I was told the Twins could return me to the Yankees for five dollars. I've been too embarrassed to ask Andy about it. I don't know if the Yankees wouldn't pay or the Twins weren't offering, but I seem to be in the Twins picture for now.

I have one guaranteed year left on my contract. The Twins can either pay me to pitch or pay me to fish. That's about what it's down to for me, big brother. After two straight injury-plagued seasons, if I don't bounce back strong in 1988 I may be going out something like you did this year.

Mark Salas, the catcher the Yankees got for me from Minnesota, is no longer wearing pinstripes. I should send him our congratulations. Salas went in another Yankee–White Sox deal. The Yankees got Richard Dotson, who should make the rotation stronger.

Danny Pasqua also went from the Yankees to the White Sox, and that might be the break he needs. If they don't pressure him and break his confidence, Danny can be a 40-homer guy. I swear, I still think of some of the shots he hit in Florida during spring training and can't believe a man can be that strong.

I've had to turn down this $1 million offer to do power-sander advertisements because I'm too tied up with emery-board endorsements. Right. I wish. I may be known for emery boards and "Scuffgate," but it certainly didn't turn into a commercial bonanza for me. I have absolutely not one thing going. About 12 minutes with David Letterman, a lifetime supply of emery boards, and more publicity than I've had the rest of my career is about all I've gotten out of it.

I've even had to file a grievance because I wasn't supposed to lose pay for my 10-day suspension—except that I missed five days pay from the Twins. It's a mess I can't seem to mop up.

My family's plans for the holidays are sketchy, Knucks. Nancy and I are trying to get together on it. Dad hasn't been feeling well and I may go up to Lansing for Thanksgiving to be with Mom and help her with Dad. If you're staying in Atlanta for Thanksgiving, maybe we can all get together in Lansing for Christmas. You know how much that would mean to Mom and Dad, plus you know I'd like our families to be together.

Maybe you and the family can come down to Chokoloskee. God. I'd love to move down here full time, Knucks. It's my environment, my Shangri-la. I know Lance would go for it. Nancy's cool to the idea, but maybe Lance and I can talk her into it this winter.

I hope I don't go weeks and months without hearing from you, Knucks. I've gotten used to knowing what my big brother's up to again. I know we've gabbed, gossiped, and grumbled back and fourth for nine months, like two teenagers sometimes. You might even be burnt out on communicating with your baby brother.

We probably won't see much of each other in 1988, you being a retired Southern gentleman now. So let's not forget what the U.S. mail is for, OK?

I feel closer to you, Knucks. I feel like we caught up on some years, shared some dreams, and remembered how great it was to be kids together.

Brothers always.

—Your Joe

November 27. Friday. Atlanta.

Joe:

It's made me feel better, Joe, knowing you've been up home with Mom and Dad. They needed us and you were there for them. With Dad's relapse, Mom needed the help and support you've given her.

We'll be keeping a close watch on Dad when you go home to Lakeland. Maybe this is the year the families get together in Lansing for Christmas. I don't think Nancy has our plans set beyond trimming a tree in the front room.

Sorry you missed my roast for Spina Bifida on November 16 at the Peachtree Plaza in Atlanta. It was a major bash, but I know you've been trying to keep up with a hectic schedule. It was our 10th annual roast—just doesn't seem that long ago since I became involved. I'm so proud we've been able to bring money, research, and attention to such an unknown and misunderstood birth defect.

I've been waiting to hear from the Braves about what job I was being offered for 1988. As it turns out, it was a waste of time. It's pretty obvious to me now that the loyalty I felt for the Braves' organization was not mutual.

When I made the arrangements for my farewell game with the Braves September 27, I was led to believe the door was open for me to do whatever I wanted to do. They made me feel wanted—at least initially—and that I figured in the long-range plans of the organization.

Stan Kasten, the Braves' president, told me: "What do you want? Work for me? Work for Bobby Cox? Work in public relations? Manage? What? You tell us."

The Braves knew my one and only goal is to manage in the big leagues. I certainly did not expect them to fire Chuck Tanner and move me right in. I was prepared to go to the minor leagues, and at Virginia, and Double A at Greenville, South Carolina. I'd have jumped at either one.

I started to see the handwriting on the wall when they named

Jim Beuchamp the Richmond manager after the World Series. Now I hear they waited for Russ Nixon to look around for something on the major-league level—which he didn't find—before giving him the Greenville job.

As it turned out, all I was offered was pitching coach at Durham, North Carolina—that's Class A—or roving minor-league pitching coach. The pay they offered me was $25,000. Can you believe that, Joe?

I knew coaches didn't make much, but I guess it doesn't really hit you until you go from making $500,000 as a 48-year-old pitcher to five percent of that as a minor-league coach who's supposed to turn prospects into million-dollar superstars. I've always felt that coaching salaries are the biggest injustice in the game.

In a way, I feel like I've been slapped in the face. I can't say anything to Ted Turner about it because he's always traveling around the world somewhere. I don't feel like going in to see Stan or Bobby. We really don't have anything else to talk about.

It's like they're trying to hide me or something. I don't feel I can get involved in the mainstream of the organization. They've got their chessboard players in place, and evidently they had some pawns left that kept me off the board.

I think they thought that since I felt so strongly about the Braves and returning to the organization, I'd take anything they offered me. I'm not bitter, Joe, because they don't owe me anything. I do feel disappointed, though, that they couldn't come up with a better position for me.

Once I heard about Nixon and the Greenville job, it took me about 15 seconds to switch professions. I couldn't pass up an opportunity to work with Dana Hersome, whose business in Loganville, Georgia, is developing all phases of fishing.

You know me, Joe, if there's one thing I know as well or better than baseball, it's fishing. If I had to get out of baseball, I couldn't have asked for anything better than this. I'm getting involved with Dana's business at every level—testing, marketing, public relations. I'm really excited.

With the new business, our new home being built at Lake

Lanier, and now actually some time to spend alone with Nancy while the boys are away at school, our household is moving into a new era in 1988. I thought retirement was supposed to be boring, but so far my life is as busy as it's ever been.

If I run out of things to keep me occupied, I can always get ahold of Johnny Gorvl and we can start working on our marketing concept for that low spades game. We're serious about that, Joe. We think it's a game that will catch on and maybe turn into a small gold mine for us.

Also, Joe, I want to get you involved with the video cassette I've been asked to do, teaching the knuckleball. We've talked about opening a knuckleball school, but this will be easier and probably more profitable. We can put our concepts and techniques on the screen, and bring about another generation of knuckleballers. It will be part of the Niekro legacy.

Who'd have thought that running into a dead end with the Braves actually would open up new paths in every direction. As you know, Joe, time marches on, nothing stays the same.

That's why it was a miracle year for us, brother—from breaking the Perrys' record to you pitching in a World Series to simply keeping closer contact than we had since we were teenagers sharing the same bed back home in Ohio.

It's gratifying to know we can be separated by miles and years, but you and I never will grow apart; 1987 was a year between brothers the Niekros will fondly recollect until our dying day.

God bless you, Joe, and your loving family.

Just make sure you bring your Twins' championship ring over as soon as possible. I'm anxious to see it on a Niekro finger.

Your brother always,

—Phil